The
FOREVER WAR

The FOREVER *WAR*

DEXTER FILKINS

Alfred A. Knopf   New York   2008

THIS IS A BORZOI BOOK
PUBLISHED BY ALFRED A. KNOPF

Copyright © 2008 by Dexter Filkins

Library of Congress Cataloging-in-Publication Data
Filkins, Dexter.
The forever war / Dexter Filkins.
p. cm.
ISBN 978-0-307-26639-2
1. Iraq War, 2003– I. Title.
DS79.76.F53 2008
956.7044'3—dc22   2008011761

Manufactured in the United States of America

First Edition

To Khalid Hassan and Fakher Haider,
friends and colleagues who were killed
while looking for the truth,
and
Lance Corporal William L. Miller,
who went first

He thought that in the beauty of the world were hid a secret. He thought the world's heart beat at some terrible cost and that the world's pain and its beauty moved in a relationship of diverging equity and that in this headlong deficit the blood of multitudes might ultimately be exacted for the vision of a single flower.

—Cormac McCarthy, *All the Pretty Horses*

Oh, horrible vultureism of earth! from which not the mightiest whale is free.

—Herman Melville, *Moby-Dick*

CONTENTS

The
FOREVER WAR

PROLOGUE

Hells Bells

Falluja, Iraq,
November 2004

THE MARINES were pressed flat on a rooftop when the dialogue began to unfold. It was 2 a.m. The minarets were flashing by the light of airstrikes and rockets were sailing on trails of sparks. First came the voices from the mosques, rising above the thundery guns.

"The Americans are here!" howled a voice from a loud-speaker in a minaret. "The Holy War, the Holy War! Get up and fight for the city of mosques!"

Bullets poured without direction and without end. No one lifted his head.

"This is crazy," one of the marines yelled to his buddy over the noise.

"Yeah," the buddy yelled back, "and we've only taken one house."

And then, as if from the depths, came a new sound: violent, menacing and dire. I looked back over my shoulder to where we had come from, into the vacant field at Falluja's northern edge. A group of marines were standing at the foot of a gigantic loudspeaker, the kind used at rock concerts.

It was AC/DC, the Australian heavy metal band, pouring out its unbridled sounds. I recognized the song immediately: "Hells Bells," the band's celebration of satanic power, had come to us on the battlefield. Behind the strains of its guitars, a church bell tolled thirteen times.

I'm a rolling thunder, a pouring rain
I'm comin' on like a hurricane
My lightning's flashing across the sky
You're only young but you're gonna die

The marines raised the volume on the speakers and the sound of gunfire began to recede. Airstrikes were pulverizing the houses in front of us. In a flash, a building vanished. The voices from the mosques were hysterical in their fury, and they echoed along the city's northern rim.

"*Allahu Akbar!*" cried one of the men in the mosques. "God is great! There is nothing so glorious as to die for God's path, your faith and your country!"

I won't take no prisoners, won't spare no lives
Nobody's putting up a fight
I got my bell, I'm gonna take you to hell
I'm gonna get ya, Satan get ya!

"God is Great!"

The shouting continued until the houses in front of us were obliterated and the firing and the music began to die.

For seven months Falluja had been controlled by jihadis who had held the city in a medieval thrall. And now the marines were taking it back, six thousand of them, going into the city on foot in the middle of a November night. I was traveling with a company of 150 marines called Bravo, of the First Battalion, Eighth Regiment. Ashley Gilbertson, an Australian photographer, was with me.

We stepped into the blackened streets and Bravo split into three columns, one for each platoon. We moved half a block before the mortar fire began. Big mortars, 82 millimeters, exploding in the next street over. Everyone froze but Read Omohundro, a stocky Texan and Bravo Company's commander. Omohundro was thirty-four, which was old for a marine captain. He'd enlisted out of high school, went to Texas A&M on a scholarship and became an officer later than most. But he was a better captain for it. Omohundro advanced in the darkness as if guided by some inner sonar, sensing the location of his men, confident he knew where the shells would fall.

"This way," Omohundro said, and we crept for another block in the darkness until he stopped and put up his hand.

Gunfire rang out and we scrambled for the walls on the sides of the street. The insurgents knew what they were doing; they were bracketing us with their shells, dropping them to the left and to the right. They were falling close now, exploding in titanic crashes, more closely each time. I'd seen mortars in the movies and even in Iraq but never this close and never so big. Their booms were crushing, and I imagined the shards of metal flying away from each shell. I felt sure we were going to die if we didn't move, and I felt sure we would die if we did. We tried to back up, to retrace our steps, but there were snipers behind us, too. With the mortars crashing closer, Omohundro and his radio man, Sergeant Kenneth Hudson, were the only ones still in the middle of the street. Hudson looked terribly young. Some of the marines were grimacing, preparing to be hit.

Four men stepped from the darkness. They were not part of Bravo Company; I hadn't seen them before. They wore flight suits that shimmered in the night and tennis shoes and hoods that made them look like executioners. The four men wore goggles that shrouded their eyes and gave off lime-green penumbras that lightened their faces. With the shells exploding I got off the wall and rejoined the captain in the street, shaking in the knees, and I listened to him tell the executioners the location of the snipers. Up ahead, he said. One of the four men mumbled something but I couldn't hear. I couldn't see their eyes through the green glowing but one of them was on the balls of his feet, bouncing, like a football player on the sidelines. Coach, he seemed to be saying, put me in the game.

The four men peeled off into the blackness without a sound. Moments passed and the shelling stopped. And then the sniper fire stopped. We never saw the men again. Omohundro got off his knee and looked at his men who were hugging the walls. "Get moving," he said.

The pace quickened, a movie reel in the dark. Sailing in from above came a white flare that shattered as it descended into our ranks. Someone yelled, "Phosphorous!" and one of the marines screamed and grabbed me and threw me into a mulberry bush. I was angry at him for that, running me over. Then another marine yanked off my pack and pointed to the fist-size chunks burning through my sleeping bag. "All the way to your bones," he shouted. I threw the pack on my back and ran to catch the marines, leaving behind me a trail of white feathers.

A moment of quiet gave way to dawn.

We broke into a trot, our boots thudding on the pavement like hooves, rounding a corner, to the right, to the left, up Tharthar Street, when a jeep, a blue Cherokee, entered our flowing ranks. The doors swung open. I was still running and wrenching my head to see when a bunch of men piled out with guns and rocket-propelled grenades. Suddenly I saw them: black eyes, pale skin and baggy gray suits with ammo belts. I thought they had us, they thought they had us, when the marines on the roof opened fire. I had no idea how the marines had gotten up there or when; I thought we were dead. The head of one of the jihadis burst like a tomato, the deep red of his brainy blood spattering against his clammy skin and his head disappearing. The jihadi fell back onto the street and spread his arms wide like a headless Christ. Three more jihadis died right there on Tharthar Street and two of them scampered away. A couple of the kids ran them down and shot them, and one of the wounded jihadis rolled over on the ground and pulled something on his jacket and exploded.

"Fuck!" the kids were yelling, running back. "Fuck! Fucking jihadi rag-head motherfuckers! They've rigged themselves. Fuck!"

The kids started slapping plastic explosives onto the Cherokee, taking out big cakes of it and throwing it on, and one of them said it's going to blow, and somebody yelled, "Fire in the hole!" and we got behind a wall and the earth shook and the jeep disappeared. An axle remained in the road and a piece of engine block and some smoke. The jihadis were gone. Like the moment never happened.

We gathered in an enclosed area behind a brick wall, spilling into it, the clop-clop of boots and clangs of metal and heavy breathing. There were forty of us, Bravo Company's First Platoon, and Ashley and me. More nineteen-year-olds went up to the roof with their giant guns. A road lay in front of us, a six-lane boulevard, one of Falluja's main drags called 40th Street. Just then the insurgents spotted us, and they opened up from both ends of the road. Bullets flew up the boulevard and down, thousands of bullets, multitudes of them, crisscrossing in front of us. The marines opened fire at once, screaming and shooting, everybody's guns on full auto, shouting and shooting. All the testosterone of forty young men. They clambered for space along the top of the wall where they could fire, standing on oil drums and old washing machines. I stood against the bricks, the boots of the kids level with my head, and felt strangely safe, almost serene against the roar of the guns. The one safe place. Bullet casings tumbled over my shoulders.

Captain Omohundro was on his knee, and Hudson was handing him the radio. Omohundro yelled something and in a few minutes the American artillery started coming in. One shot after another landed on the buildings from which the gunfire was coming, one of them the Mohammadiya Mosque. The artillery was too accurate to believe; American guys a mile back were dropping 155 mm shells right through the ceilings, one after the other after the other, each one coming in with the whistle of a train. It was a clear day and from my spot on the wall I followed the shells with my eyes, the streaking black lines, all the way in.

Without warning Omohundro yelled, "Go!" and pointed into the street and all the kids started running. Just like that, no discussion, with the firing carrying on in its horrendous way. It seemed lunatic, but everyone tore out from behind the brick wall and into the street and I tore out after them. Ashley was out in front of me, moving like a greyhound. I took ten strides and felt the bullets whiz past and bounce off the pavement and I knew I was going to die so I stopped cold, knowing immediately I'd done a stupid thing, running and stopping both. I turned and dashed back behind the wall. For a moment I felt like a coward behind that wall, and then I remembered it wasn't my war, not my army. I'm just a goddamn reporter, and

I'll wait the war out here. Come back and get me when it's over. A handful of marines who had stayed behind to cover the crossing of the others were climbing down, the last marines, and with the gunfire still roaring down the boulevard they ran and I forgot my thoughts and took off behind them.

The wind from the bullets brushed my neck. Marines were writhing in the street, tangles of blood and legs, while other marines were stooping and helping them and also getting shot. I kept running, pumping, flying toward the other side as fast as I could with my seventy pounds of gear when I saw a pair of marines standing in a doorway and waving to me to come on, come on. I ran straight for them and I could see by the looks on their faces they weren't sure I was going to make it. They were holding their arms out like they wanted to save me, and I reached them and they grabbed me by my pack and threw me through the door. I lay on the floor for a minute as I regained my senses and thought I was nothing so much now as a child. A child in his crib in the care of his parents, they nineteen and me forty-three.

I found Ash lying against a wall; he nodded that he was okay. Then I found Omohundro, who had planted himself on the second floor. Steady as a brick. He was standing next to a window, scanning the scene, and he raised his hand over his shoulder and asked for the radio. Snapped his fingers.

"Hudson, radio," Omohundro said.

"Hudson, give me the radio," he said again.

He turned around.

"He's been shot, sir," someone said.

Hudson was one of five guys hit crossing 40th Street; he lived. Sergeant Lonny Wells, of Vandergrift, Pennsylvania, bled to death on the spot, right in front of us. His worried eyes looking upward as his life ebbed away.

The shooting began to fade. I looked out the window with Omohundro. We were standing across the street from the Mohammadiya Mosque, badly damaged and smoking but still resplendent with its shot-up green dome. A squad of bedraggled marines were circling the mosque, moving around and peering into the windows but not venturing inside. At that moment, an amazing sight appeared, men in clean uniforms, as if transported from another world. Iraqi men, a long row of them, holding their guns with worried looks and stepping toward the mosque: The Iraqi army. One of the marines, stooped and filthy, swung open the mosque's front door. The Iraqi army marched inside.

It was 2 p.m., twelve hours since we'd climbed out of the troop carriers and walked into the city. We'd advanced about two hundred yards. Omohundro ordered some men up on the roof to stand watch. We put our backs against the wall, slid to the floor and fell asleep.

PART ONE

Kabul, Afghanistan,
September 1998

CHAPTER I

Only This

THEY LED THE MAN to a spot at the middle of the field. A soccer field, grass, with mainly dirt around the center where the players spent most of the game. There was a special section for the handicapped on the far side, a section for women. The orphans were walking up and down the bleachers on my side selling candy and cigarettes. A couple of older men carried whips. They wore grenade launchers on their backs.

The people are coming, a voice was saying into the loudspeaker, and the voice was right, the people were streaming in and taking their seats. Not with any great enthusiasm, as far as I could tell; they were kind of shuffling in. I probably had more enthusiasm than anybody. I had a special seat; they'd put me in the grass at the edge of the field. In America, I would have been on the sidelines, at the fifty yard line with the coaches. Come sit with us, they'd said; you are our honored guest.

A white Toyota Hi-Lux drove onto the field and four men wearing green hoods climbed out of the back. There was a fifth man, a prisoner, no hood, sitting in the bed of the truck. The hooded men laid their man in the grass just off midfield, flat on his back, and crouched around him. It was hard to see. The man on his back was docile; there was no struggle at all. The voice on the loudspeaker said he was a pickpocket.

"Nothing that is being done here is against God's law," the voice said.

The green hoods appeared busy, and one of them stood up. He held the man's severed right hand in the air, displaying it for the crowd. He was holding it up by its middle finger, moving in a semicircle so everyone could see. The handicapped and the women. Then he pulled his hood back, revealing his face, and he took a breath. He tossed the hand into the grass and gave a little shrug.

I couldn't tell if the pickpocket had been given any sort of anesthesia. He wasn't screaming. His eyes were open very wide, and as the men with the hoods lifted him back into the bed of the Hi-Lux, he stared at the stump of his hand. I took notes the whole time.

I looked back at the crowd, and it was remarkably calm, unfeeling almost, which wasn't really surprising, after all they'd been through. A small drama with the orphans was unfolding in the stands; they were getting crazy and one of the guards was beating them with his whip.

"Get back," he was saying, drawing the whip over his head. The orphans cowered.

I thought that was it, but as it turned out the amputation was just a warm-up. Another Toyota Hi-Lux, this one maroon, rumbled onto midfield carrying a group of long-haired men with guns. The long hair coming out of their white turbans. They had a blindfolded man with them. The Taliban were known for a lot of things and the Hi-Lux was one, jacked up and fast and menacing; they had conquered most of the country with them. You saw a Hi-Lux and you could be sure that something bad was going to happen.

"The people are coming!" the voice said again into the speaker, louder now and more excited. "The people are coming to see, with their own eyes, what sharia means."

The men with guns led the blindfolded man from the truck and walked him to midfield and sat him down in the dirt. His head and body were wrapped in a dull gray blanket, all of a piece. Seated there in the dirt at midfield at the Kabul sports stadium, he didn't look much like a man at all, more like a sack of flour. In that outfit, it was difficult even to tell which way he was facing. His name was Atiqullah, one of the Talibs said.

The man who had pulled his hood back was standing at midfield, facing the crowd. The voice on the loudspeaker introduced him as Mulvi Abdur Rahman Muzami, a judge. He was pacing back and forth, his green surgical smock still intact. The crowd was quiet.

Atiqullah had been convicted of killing another man in an irrigation dispute, the Talibs said. An argument over water. He'd beaten his victim to death with an ax, or so they said. He was eighteen.

"The Koran says the killer must be killed in order to create peace in society," the loudspeaker said, echoing inside the stadium. "If punishment is not meted out, such crimes will become common. Anarchy and chaos will return."

By this time a group had gathered behind me. It was the family of the murderer and the family of the victim. The two groups behind me were toing-and-froing as in a rugby game. One family spoke, leaning forward, then the other. The families were close enough to touch. Sharia law allows for the possibility of mercy: Atiqullah's execution could be halted if the family of the victim so willed it.

Judge Muzami hovered a few feet away, watching.

"Please spare my son," Atiqullah's father, Abdul Modin, said. He was weeping. "Please spare my son."

"I am not ready to do that," the victim's father, Ahmad Noor, said, not weeping. "I am not ready to forgive him. He killed my son. He cut his throat. I do not forgive him."

The families were wearing olive clothes that looked like old blankets and their faces were lined and dry. Everyone was crying. Everyone looked the same. I forgot who was who.

"Even if you gave me all the gold in the world," Noor said, "I would not accept it."

Then he turned to a young man next to him. My son will do it, he said.

The mood tightened. I looked back and saw the Taliban guards whipping some children who had tried to sneak into the stadium. Atiqullah was still sitting on the field, possibly oblivious. The voice crackled over the loudspeaker.

"O ye who believe!" the voice in the loudspeaker called.

"Revenge is prescribed for you in the matter of the murdered; the freeman for the freeman, and the slave for the slave, and the female for the female.

"People are entitled to revenge."

One of the green hoods handed a Kalashnikov to the murder victim's brother. The crowd fell silent.

Just then a jumbo jet appeared in the sky above, rumbling, forcing a pause in the ceremony. The brother stood holding his Kalashnikov. I looked up. I wondered how a jet airliner could happen by such a place, over a city such as this, wondered where it might be going. I considered for a second the momentary collision of the centuries.

The jumbo jet flew away and the echo died and the brother crouched and took aim, leveling his Kalashnikov at Atiqullah's head.

"In revenge there is life," the loudspeaker said.

The brother fired. Atiqullah lingered motionless for a second then collapsed in a heap under the gray blanket. I felt what I believed was a vibration from the stands. The brother stood over Atiqullah, aimed his AK-47 and fired again. The body lay still under the blanket.

"In revenge there is life," the loudspeaker said.

The brother walked around Atiqullah, as if he were looking for signs of life. Seeing one, apparently, he crouched and fired again.

Spectators rushed onto the field just like the end of a college football game. The two men, killer and avenger, were carried away in separate Hi-Luxes, one maroon, one white. The brother stood up in the bed of the white truck as it rumbled away, surrounded by his fellows. He held his arms in the air and was smiling.

I had to move fast to talk to people before they went home. Most everyone said they approved, but no one seemed to have any enthusiasm.

"In America, you have television and movies—the cinema," one of the Afghans told me. "Here, there is only this."

I left the stadium and walked in a line of people through the streets. I spotted something in the corner of my eye. It was a boy, a street boy, with bright green eyes. He was standing in an alley, watching me. The boy stood for a few more seconds, his eyes following mine. Then he turned and ran.

IN THE LATE AFTERNOONS the center of Kabul had an empty, twilight feel, a quiet that promised nothing more than another day like itself. There were hardly any cars then, just some women floating silently in their head-to-toe burqas.* Old meat hung in the stalls. Buildings listed in the ruins.

One of those afternoons, a thin little shoeshine boy walked up to me. He was smiling and running his finger across his throat.

"Mother is no more," he said, finger across the neck. "Father is finished."

His name was Nasir and he repeated the phrase in German and French, smiling as he did. *"Mutter ist nicht mehr. Vater ist fertig."* He dragged the finger across his throat again. Rockets, he said. *Racketen.* His pale green eyes were rimmed in black. He did not ask for money; he wanted to clean my boots. Then he was gone, scampering down the muddy street with his tiny wooden box.

Kabul was full of orphans like Nasir, woebegone children who peddled little labors and fantastic tales of grief. You'd see them in packs of fifty and sometimes even a hundred, skittering in mismatched shoes and muddy faces. They'd thunder up to you like a herd of wild horses; you could hear the padding of so many tiny feet. Sometimes I'd wonder where all the parents had gone, why they'd let their children run around like that, and then I'd catch myself. The orphans would get out of control sometimes, especially when they saw a foreigner, grabbing and shoving one another, until they were scattered by one of the men with whips. They'd come out of nowhere, the whip wielders, like they'd been waiting offstage. The kids would squeal and scatter, then circle back again, grinning. If I raised a hand, they'd flinch like strays.

If a war went on long enough the men always died, and someone had to take their place. Once I found seven boy sol-

*A burqa is a head-to-toe garment worn by women.

diers fighting for the Northern Alliance on a hilltop in a place called Bangi. The Taliban positions were just in view, a minefield in between. The boys were wolflike, monosyllabic with no attention spans. Eyes always darting. Laughing the whole time. Dark fuzz instead of beards. They wore oddly matched apparel like high-top tennis shoes and hammer-and-sickle belts, embroidered hajj caps and Russian rifles.

I tried to corner one of the boys on the hill. His face was half wrapped in a checkered scarf that covered his mouth. Abdul Wahdood. All I could see were his eyes. I kept asking him how old he was and he kept looking over at his brother. His father had been killed a year before, he said, but they fed him here and with the money he could take care of his whole family, $30 a month. "My mother is not weeping," Abdul said. I could see how bored he was, and his friends definitely noticed because one of them started firing his Kalashnikov over our heads. That really got them going, laughing hilariously and falling over each other. Two of them started wrestling. My photographer and I calmed them down and asked them to pose in a picture with us, and they lined up and grew very grave. After that they stood behind us in a semicircle and raised their guns, not like they were aiming at anything but more like they were saluting. Then a couple of men appeared on the hilltop bearing a kettle of rice and the boys descended on it. The Taliban came down the road a few months later. I've got the boys' picture on a bookcase in my apartment.

I DROVE IN from the east. I rode in a little taxi, on a road mostly erased, moving slowly across the craters as the Big Dipper rose over the tops of the mountains that encircled the capital on its high plateau. The cars in front of us were disappearing into the craters as we were climbing out of ours, disappearing then reappearing, swimming upward and then out, like ships riding the swells.

I passed the overturned tanks of the departed army, the red stars faded on the upside-down turrets. I passed checkpoints manned by men who searched for music. I stopped halfway and drank cherry juice from Iran and watched the river run through the walls of the Kabul gorge. There was very little electricity then, so I couldn't see much of the city coming in, neither the people nor the landscape nor the ruined architecture, nothing much but the twinkling stars. From the car, I could make out the lighter shade of the blasted buildings, lighter gray against the darkness of everything else, the scree and the wash of the boulders and bricks, a shattered window here and there. A single turbaned man on a bicycle.

One morning I was standing amid the blown-up storefronts and the broken buildings of Jadi Maiwand, the main shopping street before it became a battlefield, and I was trying to take it in when I suddenly had the sensation one sometimes feels in the tropics, believing that a rock is moving, only to discover it is a reptile perfectly camouflaged. They were crawling out to greet me: legless men, armless boys, women in tents. Children without teeth. Hair stringy and matted.

Help us, they said.

Help us. A woman appeared. I guessed it was a woman but I couldn't see her through her burqa. "Twelve years of schooling," she said, and she kept repeating the phrase like some mantra, like it would get her a job.

For the first time I was talking to a woman I couldn't see. I could trace the words as they exited the vent, watch the fabric flutter as she breathed and spoke. But no face. No mouth. "Twelve years of schooling," she said. She had a name, Shah Khukhu, fifty, a mother of five, missing a finger and a leg. She was hiking up her burqa to show me.

"For five years I have been living here," she said through the vent.

I wondered then and often afterwards how the Afghans endured the pain, there was so much of it. Five years in the rubble with nine fingers and five children and one leg and no husband: surely a pain proportional to injury would not in its mercy allow a woman like Shah Khukhu to survive. Forty thousand dead in the capital with no electricity. Two-year-old babies with artificial legs. They screamed, yes, and they groaned, groaned in particular, like the Northern Alliance soldier shot in the head and carried on a donkey for twelve hours to a hospital with no medicine. He made a low moaning sound. Sometimes I thought it was my own imagination: I couldn't comprehend the pain or the fortitude required to endure it. Other times I thought that something had broken fundamentally after so many years of war, that there had been some kind of primal dislocation between cause and effect, a numbness wholly understandable, necessary even, given the pain, but which had the effect of allowing the killing to go on and on.

One day near Kandahar I came across a minefield, which was hardly extraordinary in itself, and next to it a man named Juma Khan Gulalai. The field was bright and green. Gulalai was a butcher and he'd set up his table there, his apron and knives at the ready. Every day, Gulalai explained, a goat would wander into the green grassy field to graze for its meal and step on a land mine and blow apart. Gulalai would walk into the field and retrieve the carcass—braving the mines himself as he did—throw the old goat up on the table and carve up its meat for sale.

During the famines, you'd hear about people who sold their children to pay for food. There was the kid from Sheberghan who'd tried to run off with a girl coveted by a warlord; a horse had been tied to each of the boy's limbs and set running in different directions. There were millions of land mines like the ones in Gulalai's field, layer after layer of them, whole archaeologies of mines; Soviet, then mujahideen on top of that, then Taliban, then muj again, exploding dolls and Bouncing Bettys and plastic mines that would still be exploding a thousand years from now, because they don't, like the corpses, decompose. At one point twenty-five people each day were stepping on land mines in Kabul, and meanwhile the warlords were busy laying new fields as quickly as they could. Afghanistan was like the mouse in the laboratory, flipping the switch over and over again to shock itself. Maybe it was just despair.

"So many people died before us, we don't give a damn," Gulalai said.

Gulalai stood at his table and fingered his knives. Six months ago, he said, a close friend, Sarwar, walked into the field and exploded.

"Sometimes, I dream that I myself am blown up here."

As I stood there with my notebook and my pen talking to him I watched a group of children gather on the dirt path on the other side of the field and jump excitedly at my presence. I yelled at them not to, but they ran anyway into the minefield, cheering as they came to meet me, like kids springing across a playground. They were out of breath when they arrived.

Why did you walk through the minefield? I asked young Wali Mohammed, who was smiling and panting.

"Going around, that would take longer," he said.

People didn't believe me when I told them. Once I sat with Gulham Sakhi, a member of the country's Hazara minority, a refugee, father of five. We were in a house in Peshawar and he was telling me of a massacre at the hands of the Taliban from which he and his family had run away a couple of weeks before. I was using a translator, and Sakhi, numb and depressed, kept using the Dari words *barcha*, which meant "spear," and *tabar*, which meant "ax." I still have the words in my notebook. My translator was having trouble understanding, so I asked him to ask Sakhi to slow down and tell us what the Taliban fighters had done. And Sakhi told me, in the lifeless way that he was speaking, that the Talibs were doing with the *barcha* what anyone would do with such an instrument, they were pushing them into people's anuses and pulling them back out of their throats. He and his family had come on foot.

"We walked across deserts and mountains," he said.

THERE WERE HOSPITALS in Afghanistan filled with patients, burned and twisted; they just didn't have any medicine or any doctors. There were schools, plenty of them, at least in the cities, only they were empty. Kabul University, on the edge of town, looked like one of those old black-and-white photos of Dresden in 1945, blasted and razed and deserted. There was music, wonderful, rising stuff. You could see the music, even if you weren't allowed to listen to it, long streams of torn-up cassette tape ripped out and strung up on telephone poles, heaps of it, like the discarded guts of some animal. All the accoutrements of a functioning society had been in place once, and now they were gone.

One day I stood in the shattered window of the Pamir Supper Club on the rooftop of the Kabul InterContinental Hotel. The place had been dropped by the chain many years before.

"Ah, it was such a very good view," said Sher Ahmad, a hotel employee.

I followed Ahmad's eyes out the blown-out window. The mountains swept down and into the ruins and then up again, past a string of shot-up cars and pockmarked water tanks, to the barren ridge that encircled the city. Ahmad sported the mandatory turban and beard, and a white, drooping robe favored by the Pashtuns. His two front teeth protuded slightly over his beard.

"I'm the food and beverage manager," Ahmad said, pausing for effect. "No food, no beverage!"

He laughed, but only for a second. Ahmad stepped back from the window and walked through the broken glass and overturned chairs of the club.

"This place was not always like this," he said. I wasn't sure if he was referring to his hotel or his country.

In the late 1960s, Ahmad said, the capital's social scene revolved around the Kabul InterContinental, playing host to foreign leaders like "Indira Gandhi, Mr. Bhutto, and all kinds of Saudi princes." Women walked around in miniskirts, he said; gin and vodka flowed from the hotel's many bars. Foie gras and champagne were flown in from France, cooks from Germany and Switzerland.

"There were no beards then, no turbans," Ahmad said, stepping amid the rubble. "Nothing like this. It was very beautiful then. We had everything: music all the time, cigarettes, people smoking. We did not fear that we would ever be short of anything. Our only concern was that our guests were happy."

Then things started to slip, Ahmad said, and his nostalgic air departed. The coups and reprisals, the Soviet invasion and its retreat. Then the mujahideen, who had beaten the Soviets, turned on one another. By 1992, Ahmad said, the foreign staff of the hotel had fled, the guests were down to a trickle. "European people finished," he said. He was standing in a pile of overturned tables.

"We hid in the cellars then," he said.

By the mid-1990s, Kabul had become a battleground of competing warlords. Each held his own corner of the city: Ahmad Shah Massoud, the Tajik commander; Dostum, the Uzbek butcher; Gulbuddin Hekmatyar, the Islamist fanatic. There was a galaxy of lesser hoods and gangsters, ever ready to switch sides for a bigger bag of cash.

Every warlord had a fief, and every fief its own checkpoint, where neither a man's cash nor his daughter was safe. At one point, Kabul was divided by forty-two separate militia checkpoints. Hekmatyar's missiles rained from the outside. For two years the capital was dark, without electricity. Sher Ahmad and his colleagues could only watch from their spot in the hotel.

"Massoud shoot here," he said, pointing at an odd angle out the window.

"Dostum shoot here," he said, gesturing to a hill.

For a time, Burhanuddin Rabbani, a Tajik professor close to Massoud, took possession of Kabul and proclaimed a government. The United Nations bestowed its recognition. Massoud was the real power, though his fighters were beholden to no one. In neighborhood after neighborhood, they plundered and raped. One night, Ahmad recalled, they barged into the Kabul InterContinental.

"Massoud's people, they took carpets, the forks, knives, and plates," he said. "Waving their pistols. Bring me vodka. Bring me whiskey."

Ahmad walked over to one of the few tables still standing and pointed to a plate. "Now, there is just junk.

"I like all the people of the world," he said, his eyes growing sadder. "Just not soldiers."

In 1996, after four years of street fighting, and more than forty thousand civilian deaths, Taliban fighters swept into the city.

"We had five bars, and they tore all of them out of the walls," he said. "They pulled down all the paintings. All the posters. Even the postcards in the gift shop. They burned those, the ones that had people on them."

One of the Taliban men used a cable to slash the faces from

a pair of friezes depicting the giant sixth-century Buddha statues that stood in the central part of the country. The frames
still hung on the walls. At the time, the Buddhas in Bamiyan
still stood, too.

Somehow, Ahmad said, he and the other hotel staffers
managed to save a hundred television sets, dragging them
down into the vault in the basement, where they remained on
the day of my visit. The Taliban militiamen smashed the rest.
The staff rescued a thousand bottles of cognac and wine as
well.

Later in the afternoon, as I sat down to a dinner of cold
lamb and wilted lettuce in the lightless hotel restaurant,
Ahmad reappeared, holding a faded hotel brochure. It showed
a young man, clean-shaven, wearing a red tuxedo and holding
a large tray of cakes and pastries. Behind the waiter stood a
tall, blonde European woman in a tennis dress, and another in
a bikini. The young man was smiling broadly.

"This was me," Ahmad said.

Then he looked at the photo, staring back at it in wonder.

IN THE SAME SHATTERED café, a waiter approached my
table, hands behind his back, bowing slightly.

"What would you like to drink?" he asked. "A screwdriver,
a Bloody Mary? Ha ha ha!"

In Afghanistan, the brutality and the humor went hand in
hand; the knife with the tender flesh. There seemed no collapse of their fortunes in which the Afghans could not find
some reason to laugh.

In my many trips to Afghanistan, I grew to adore the place,
for its beauty and its perversions, for the generosity of its people in the face of the madness. The brutality one could witness
in the course of a working day was often astonishing, the casu-
alness of it more so; and the way that brutality had seeped into
every corner of human life was a thing to behold. And yet
somewhere, deep down, a place in the heart stayed tender.

I sat in a mud-brick hut near Bamiyan, the site of a gnaw-
ing famine, and a man and his family pressed upon me, their
overfed American guest, their final disk of bread.

"Please," said the bedraggled man, his face mottled with white patches. "Please take."

Once I drove into the town of Farkhar in northeastern Afghanistan and rolled up to a collection of brick sheds called, improbably, the Kodri Hotel. During the hotel's long periods of inactivity, its rooms were used to store potatoes, and the place reeked of them. The toilet was a field out back.

As darkness enveloped the town, I heard a knock on my door. It was an emissary of the local warlord, Daoud Khan, who wanted to convey how much prestige this visit by an American reporter conferred upon him. Was there anything he could do to make the visit more comfortable? I suggested that a generator would be most welcome.

Sure enough, after a time, some men carried in a generator, a smoking, clattering thing, and a dim electric light was soon glowing in the darkness. Then the same men carried in a television, an antiquated and overweight Sharp with a seventeen-inch screen. And then they connected it to a satellite dish, which had been sitting all along on the Kodri Hotel's mud roof.

By night's end, amid the rattle of the generator, I sat on the floor of the potato shed with the Afghans watching Michael Jackson sing "Blood on the Dance Floor" on MTV. A soldier, perhaps sixteen years old, appeared at the door, leaned his Kalashnikov against the wall and sat down, rapt before the glow of the television.

"*Khoob,*" he said in Dari. "Great."

MAN, THEY WERE scary. You'd see them rolling up in one of the Hi-Luxes, all jacked up, white turbans gleaming; they were the baddest asses in town and they knew it, too. One of them would be sitting across from you in a restaurant, maybe picking at a kebab, looking at you from across the centuries, kohl under his eyes, and you knew he'd just as soon kill you as look at you. Dumb as a brick, but that hardly mattered. Great cultures are like that. Always have been. The Greeks, the Romans, the British: they didn't care what other people thought. Didn't care about reasons. Just up and did it. The

Taliban: their strength was their ignorance. They didn't even know they were supposed to care.

They pulled me out of a taxi once. I was in Herat. I'd been trying to take photographs of women from the back seat of the taxi. Floating blue ghosts. We'd stopped and I'd popped off a couple of shots and my driver, an Afghan, saw the Talibs and froze. I was banging on the front seat to go, just go, but he froze. The Talibs pulled me out of the taxi and one of them raised his gun to my head so I pulled out a business card, embossed with gothic letters, *Los Angeles Times*, very impressive, a get-out-of-jail-free card. The Talib grasped it, looked at it and threw it in the street. I might as well have handed him a starfish. My interpreter, Ashraf, a Pashtun like the Talibs, thank God, walked around the taxi to the man with the upraised AK and began to murmur something in Pashto. I didn't know what he was saying, but as he spoke, he reached out and grasped the Talib's beard and began to stroke it gently, running it through his hands, like he was putting a cat to sleep. Slowly the Talib relaxed his arms and put down his gun and told us we could go. It was like a magic trick.

You could just imagine the waves of Talibs running into the minefields, exploding and running and exploding. Carried along by some vision, some sweating emptiness. I met Hamidullah under a mulberry tree in Kandahar, sitting on the ground with a bunch of other amputees. He was a Pashtun kid from Kunduz, twenty years old, a Taliban soldier for many years. "We have seen more battles than the hairs on our head," he said. Hamidullah had been with a Taliban unit that was charging one of Massoud's posts when he stepped on a land mine, which blew off his left leg. He held out his right arm to break his fall and it hit another land mine; that exploded, too.

"God knows how long I lay there," Hamidullah said.

As I stood over Hamidullah, he looked up at me with the dreamy eyes of a child. Hamidullah said he'd learned to dress himself with his remaining hand, learned to cinch the knot on his tie-up pants, taught himself to write with his left hand. He was still hoping to get married. He picked up a pen and a notebook and drew a cartoon face with a big, wide smile, but his future kept coming back to him.

"It's Afghanistan," Hamidullah said. "I'm finished."

The old men, the leaders, were walking junkyards, metal and bullets and shrapnel, heaped over with holes and scar tissue. They'd walk in on peglegs with ill-fitting plastic arms, and when they plunked down in their chairs it was like watching the frame of an old car collapse. They had these handsome oversize features, jutting chins and enormous hands. They'd pour their tea from the cup and slurp it from the saucer, loud, because it was cooler that way. They'd look at you and you'd think, Jesus, they are not killable. They're from another world. They beat the Soviet Union, and the Soviet Union fell apart.

People loved them—a lot of people did, anyway, at least at first. You'd ask someone about the Talibs and the first thing they'd say is they tamed the warlords. You couldn't drive across town, they'd say. The warlords would be fighting it out in the middle of the city, slugging it out for turf, like gangsters do, for the right to tax and steal. Massoud's men would defeat Dostum's men, set up their rackets and take their revenge. Then Hekmatyar and Sayyaf and Khalili and only the Holy Prophet knew who else.

"It was like a long and dark night," Mohammed Nabi

Mohammedi said one night in Kabul. Mohammedi was a Taliban commander who had fought through the civil war. He sat
in a red upholstered chair in a small room off the lobby of the
InterContinental Hotel.

"Afghanistan was divided into fiefdoms," he said. "Each
commander was only accountable to himself. They were
fighting for power, they were fighting for plunder. The real
purpose of jihad had been forgotten. The people had lost all
hope."

Mohammedi stared straight ahead, avoiding any eyes. He
might as well have been talking to himself.

"The biggest scourge was the checkpoints," he said. "The
commanders, the warlords, they would loot and plunder and
violate all who passed. Rape and violate the women. In this
city, Kabul, the capital, there were checkpoints on every
block. They were a plague on the people."

Mohammedi was an old man, with weathered skin and a
gray stringy beard. But he was tough and hard and honest, you
could see that in his eyes, and he was as straight as a two-by-
four. As I listened to him that night in the little room off the
hotel lobby, I found myself admiring the old warhorse. Anarchy had taken over, and the Taliban were the only guys mean
enough and dark enough to wrestle it back to dusty earth.

"The Taliban heard nothing but God," Mohammedi said.
"They brought order to a country that had become lawless.
Who would have imagined that they would have been victorious over all these commanders, who had become so powerful
and cruel?"

The commander paused, as if wondering himself.

And I felt sorry for him, too. Mohammedi was a hick, a
yahoo from the countryside, and he seemed to know it. And
he seemed to know we knew it, I mean we in the West. He was
like a kid from Appalachia come to the big city, toothless and
staring at the skyscrapers. All he wanted was to be accepted.

Once, in Kandahar, one of the Taliban ministers called a
press conference, and his aides pleaded with the Western
reporters who were in town to come along. When a group of
women reporters showed up, the Taliban minister and his
aides grew flustered and confused. They huddled across the

room. The reporters stood in the doorway. The Talibs were talking and waving their arms. Then one of them walked over to a window and held the draperies in his hand. He motioned with his arm to the women. "Would you mind standing behind the curtain during the press conference?" he asked. The women laughed and walked out. The aides frowned in disappointment.

"We are not drug addicts, we are not illiterate—we can run a government," Mullah Mohammed Hassan, the governor of Kandahar, said a few days after I met Mohammedi. Mullah Hassan had lost a leg fighting the Soviets. He'd hobbled into the room and fallen into his chair, removed his prosthesis and rubbed his stump.

More than anything, what seemed to bother the Taliban leaders like Mohammedi and Hassan was the refusal of the United Nations to extend them formal recognition even though they'd conquered 90 percent of the country.

"Why won't they accept the Taliban?" Mullah Mohammedi pleaded. "I don't know what we have done to earn the enmity of so many countries."

THE BOYS FILED OUT of the school and gathered around me. Their beardless faces shimmered in the morning light, and their turbans framed their faces in diamond shapes. A lone adult male stepped forward.

"Our teachers are all at the front lines," said the young man, named Hassan. He was twenty.

I was in Singesar, two hundred miles from Kabul in the southwestern desert, in the Taliban heartland. The men who had not already gone to war had done so a few weeks before, as the Taliban geared up for its next big offensive somewhere far away. With the men gone and the women shut inside their homes, Singesar was a children's village.

"I have been here since I was five," Hassan said. "We have all come for our religious education."

With his clean-shaven face and innocent eyes, Hassan looked as young as the boys around him. But he was a serious young man, and he was running the madrassa while the adults were away. In sandaled feet, he led me through the village and told us the story of the one-eyed man named Omar.

"He lived in a simple hut," Hassan said. "He was a man of few words."

Hassan pointed to a mud-brick house next to the mosque.

"He would come early in the morning and lead prayers, and then take tea and sit in that room until noon studying the Koran alone," Hassan said. "He didn't talk much, only to his friends."

In the war against the Soviets, Omar was a brave fighter, never more so than on the day he was gravely wounded. The Soviets had laid siege to Singesar, Hassan said, firing a missile into the town's mosque. Shrapnel flew into Omar's right eye.

"Omar just got hold of his eye, took it out, and threw it away," Hassan said. He'd not seen the battle himself, of course; he was too young, but the tale of Omar's eye had the power of a founding myth.

After the Soviets were defeated, Omar returned to Singesar and founded the madrassa where the children were now studying. Omar watched with growing weariness as his country slipped into chaos. When word reached Singesar that two warlords were fighting over the rights to a young boy, Omar decided he'd had enough.

"He had a dream," Hassan said, pausing on a sandy path. "A woman came to him and said, We need your help; you must rise. You must end the chaos. God will help you."

"He only had one rocket launcher and thirteen guns in the village," Hassan said. "That was in 1994."

Omar gathered eight men in Singesar and moved out, attacking the first checkpoint on the highway nearby. He hung the commanders from the barrels of tanks. As Omar's men moved toward Kabul, they lopped off the hands of thieves, beat transgressors with cables, killed adulterers with stones.

Since capturing the capital, Hassan said, Omar had moved to Kandahar, just a few miles down the road. That, more than Kabul, was the real capital of the Taliban. Omar was said to be living in a new house built by his wealthy friend, a veteran of the jihad named Osama bin Laden.

Hassan stopped before a small building. In Singesar, the Taliban had built a concrete mosque on the site where Omar used to pray. It was the village's only monument to its leader.

"It is like the sun is always shining on us," Hassan said.

MOHAMMED WALI, the Taliban's minister for the promotion of virtue and the prevention of vice, hobbled into the Kandahar office on crutches. He sank into his overstuffed chair, exhaled, and looked over his visitors, a group of Western reporters. He gave a small, constipated smile. Wali had the uncompromising face of a scold, but his injury gave him a touching vulnerability. He said he'd stepped in a hole and twisted his ankle.

"Welcome," he said. "You are guests here."

Someone asked him to describe his duties.

"We try to promote virtue—being nice to neighbors and widows and orphans," Wali said. Then he paused, as if he had run out of things to say on the subject. It was clearly the other part of his portfolio, the vice, that he wanted to talk about.

"Everything we forbid is forbidden by the Holy Koran: liquor, gambling, drugs; if a woman is without purdah, that is also a vice."*

An aide placed a bowl of sugar-coated nuts on the table between us. Wali ignored them.

"We also try to prevent the taking of pictures of human things," he said. "Though sometimes there is a need."

Passports, for instance, Wali said.

"We also prevent music and dancing, these kinds of things," he said. "Watching of television and of VCRs."

I thought of Wali's foot soldiers, the young men in white turbans who cruised the streets in their Hi-Luxes.

"We also ask men to grow beards," said Wali, who had a large beard himself. "Men should grow a beard, and they should trim their mustaches."

Trim their mustaches?

---

*"Purdah," which means "curtain" in Farsi, refers to the practice of shielding women from the view of men, by clothing or other means.

"The mustache should not cover the lips," he said.

Wali shifted uncomfortably in his seat, taking the weight off his bad ankle.

"We also get hold of men who do not have beards," he said.

Wali talked about his life a little. Like his fellow Taliban leaders, Wali had fought against the Soviet invaders and helped crush the warlords later on. For thirteen years, during and after the fighting, he had studied in Pakistani madrassas, mostly memorizing the Koran and learning the principles of modern jihad. Seven of those years, he said, were at the Darul Uloom Haqqania, one of the largest madrassas in Pakistan and a school attended by hundreds of Taliban fighters.

The subject turned to women. What about the burqas? someone asked.

"A woman must cover her beauty," Wali said. "If she goes to the market, then the violation is intentional. And she must be punished."

What was the penalty for that? he was asked.

"Maybe," he said, "we beat her with a stick."

White socks, Wali said, were off-limits, too.

"They draw attention to the ankles," he said.

And music? Nobody could understand that, I said.

"Whenever the Holy Prophet, peace be upon him, heard music playing, he would put his thumbs in his ears," Wali said. "This is in the Hadith, the record of the Prophet's life. This is well-known.

"Whatever the Holy Prophet did," Wali said, "we must follow."

We moved on to petty crime and matters of the heart.

"There are certain serious sins," Wali said, turning in his chair, bothered by his ankle again. "A thief, for instance. Islam says that you have to amputate his hand."

I thought of the men in green hoods. An aide came into the room and whispered something in Wali's ear. He picked up as if there had been no interruption.

"Adultery—if the couple is unmarried, then eighty lashes," Wali said. "If they are married, then *rajim*—they must be stoned to death."

Until that point, September 1998, the Taliban had found it necessary to stone to death only one pair of lovers, a forty-year-old woman named Nurbibi and her lover and stepson, Turyalai, age thirty-eight. The pair were each buried up to their necks on a Friday in Kandahar. Taliban guards made separate piles of stones for each.

And until then, as far as Wali knew, the Taliban had prosecuted only five cases of homosexuality.

"We push a wall on top of them," he said.

The wall-push method was unique in that it contained an element of mercy. If the condemned survived, he or she was allowed to walk away.

"Two of them survived," Wali said. "If someone survives, he survives. If he is killed, he is killed."

The most serious offense, Wali said, was murder, and I'd already seen the punishment for that.

"A murderer has to be punished with death," Wali said. "If a person commits a murder, then he will also have to meet the same fate at the hands of the victim's family."

Wali introduced an Arabic word, *qisas*, meaning "revenge." His eyes brightened. Life for life, he said.

"For you, there is life in *qisas*," Wali said. "In revenge there is life."

Wali turned back to the subject of virtue.

"We try to promote virtue," Wali said. "We try to persuade people to pray five times a day. We are asking people to be kind to each other, and to widows and orphans."

It was here, he said, that the Taliban played a vanguard role.

"The Koran says, Among the believers, there must be a group of righteous leaders. I think I am part of that group."

Wali acknowledged the burden his task entailed, but he couldn't imagine doing anything else.

"On the surface, it looks like I have a difficult job," he said. "But I am willing and happy in my work."

With that, Wali lifted himself out of his chair and hobbled out of the room on his sprained ankle.

Talking to Wali that day, and Mohammedi and the other Talibs, it seemed obvious enough that what lay at the foundation of the Taliban's rule was fear, but not fear of the Taliban themselves, at least not in the beginning. No: it was fear of the past. Fear that the past would return, that it would come back in all its disaggregated fury. That the past would become the future. The beards, the burqas, the whips, the stones; anything, anything you want. Anything but the past.

AT THE KHYBER PASS, I flagged down a crumpled white Lada from another age. A driver named Javed, wearing a hajj cap but no turban, took off, driving into the craters, mountains staring down. At the checkpoint, the Talibs poked and pawed and waved us through. Soon Javed tossed his hajj cap onto the dash, reached under the seat and found a cassette. He removed the tape already in the player, koranic readings, slipped in the new one and turned up the volume. Hindi Pop was now blaring through tiny speakers. Our eyes met in the mirror.

Dissent was best expressed in cars. Cars were among the few places you could feel safe talking to people. "Educated people don't fight," Humayun Himatyar, a shopkeeper in Kandahar, said from the driver's seat of his parked car. He was looking straight ahead. I was in the back. "That's why there are no schools. If you're educated, you won't fight. All the Taliban wants is war." He wasn't doing badly, he said, clearing a dollar a day. It was much worse before. Seven militias had controlled different parts of the city. "They put a tax on everything— meat, milk, bread. Even for parking your scooter they charged a tax. If you resisted, they beat you. Now the militias are gone, and if you go out at midnight, you will have no fear."

Himatyar kept half turning to speak, correcting himself, and looking ahead. "If you don't show up at the mosque, they'll go out looking for you, they'll come and get you and drag you to the mosque. Maybe they'll beat you," he said. "My daughters can't go to school. My sons—they'll come one day and take them to the fighting." A pause. I could hear him breathing. "That's the worst thing."

Sometimes on the street a woman would pass and you'd hear something from behind the vent in her burqa. Sometimes it was light and flirtatious, sometimes a little darker.

"I was a teacher of Persian," one of them said once from behind her vent. "This is like a death."

ONCE I WENT IN by air, in a propeller-driven airplane. Looking down, I could practically see the border, where the world ended and the unknown began. The earth turned darker and more bare, the veins of snow tracing the mountainsides, everything shrouded in clouds and mist.

I was with Bill Richardson, America's ambassador to the United Nations then, and he had come to see if he could persuade the Afghans to stop fighting. We flew first to Kabul, where Richardson met with the Taliban leader Mullah Rabbani, the second in command. Richardson came out after a couple of hours and said he thought he had a deal. He said something about the rights of women.

Then we flew in our plane to Sheberghan, where we were met at the runway by Abdul Rashid Dostum, the Uzbek warlord. Dostum had fought for every side over the past twenty years, even ran a militia for the Soviets, and he helped raze Kabul after the Soviets left. He was the warlord who tied the horses to the boy's limbs, or so they said. When the Taliban came to power, Dostum vowed he would not submit to a government under which "there will be no whiskey and no music."

Dostum wore a black suit and a tie that day. He had a flat, Central Asian face, cropped hair and a black mustache; he looked like a cross between a professional wrestler and a funeral director. "I heard you were a cigar smoker," Richardson said, stepping off the plane and holding out his hand.

Sheberghan was on the Afghan steppe, flat as a tabletop and treeless as far as you could see. Next to our plane sat a pair of MiG-21 fighter jets, Soviet made, rusty and tan with the green triangle of the Afghan flag. We drove in slowly toward the middle of town on a winding road, and as we did we passed a row of Bactrian camels, the kind with two humps, each jutting off at oblique angles. The camels eyed us as they walked together.

Richardson seemed eager, and he had an old CIA hand with him, Bruce Riedel, of the National Security Council.

Dostum led us to the stadium, where we sat for a match of *buzkashi*, a kind of polo game played with the carcass of a goat. The horses roared up and down the field, and the militiamen beat and savaged one another, at one point nearly crashing into the viewing stand. Richardson played along, being the diplomat, and Dostum laughed and guffawed and rocked back and forth in his seat.

Then they went to Dostum's villa, ornate and monstrous as you would imagine. I waited outside. As I loitered in the street, I met a group of women who had been gathered there to greet Richardson when he came in. There were five of them, physicians it turned out, and they had walked over from Jozjan Hospital. They wore their white medical coats and the casual head scarves that Uzbek women wore that barely concealed their hair. They were hoping to meet Ambassador Richardson. They seemed genuinely frightened.

"You know what will happen if the Taliban come to Sheberghan," one of them said.

Her name was Habiba Muyesar, a gynecologist. She was thirty-four. She was modest but self-possessed, and she wore red lipstick and a black head scarf. She looked at me with pleading eyes.

She'd been trained in the Soviet Union, she said, at a medical school in Kazakhstan, and had flourished during the Soviet occupation. Dr. Muyesar had practiced in Kabul, working at the Malali Maternity Hospital, stayed through the civil war and fled to Sheberghan as the Taliban entered Kabul. She had four children.

"We have an arrow in our hearts," she said.

The sun was getting low. The security guards were talking hurriedly among themselves. Darkness was not a good time to be moving in Afghanistan. The front lines were not far away.

Just then Richardson stepped out of the palace wearing a buoyant look. Dostum stood at his side, still in the black suit, glancing around.

"I believe we have an agreement," Richardson said.

It was a cease-fire, Richardson said, to be followed by face-to-face talks between the Taliban and their foes.

"It shows our sincerity, not our weakness," Dostum said, looking at no one in particular.

With that, we piled into our cars and raced to the landing strip. We were on the steppe again, and the ruby-red sun was sinking into the great flat horizon. As the engines on our Beechcraft started whirring, Dostum's men loaded enormous handwoven maroon carpets into the hold of the plane. The warlord gave us a wave as we climbed inside. It was just dark.

"I looked into the eyes of the Afghan people today and saw that they want peace," Richardson said.

A few minutes later, as we were gaining altitude, the interior of the cabin began to flash and sparkle. There were great booms of light coming from the outside. I thought we had flown into an electrical storm.

"Lightning," I said aloud.

"Artillery fire," a colleague said.

I leaned toward the window. Enormous orange explosions illuminated the scene. I could see them but not hear them from inside the plane, big orange flashes unfolding slowly below. There were silhouettes of mountains and men.

The Taliban overran Sheberghan a few months later, roaring across the steppe in their Hi-Luxes. I took a photo of Habiba Muyesar that day, and I still have it with me: the loosely covered hair, the red lipstick, the bright, pleading eyes.

CHAPTER 2

Forebodings

AHMAD SHAH MASSOUD sat in the grass and talked of escape. His enemies were closing in, as they had been for most of his life. He'd run out of territory; though this, too, was hardly new. His ragtag army was surviving on child soldiers and old Soviet helicopters. The Taliban, just down the road, would be coming soon.

But here in his mountain hideaway in Farkhar, in the far north of his country, on the sacred holiday of Eid, Massoud put aside his present crisis and allowed himself a moment to reminisce. Sitting in a white plastic chair in the green grass, he remembered it all over again: the seven Soviet invasions of his native Panjshir Valley, the seven narrow escapes. The retreat from Kabul in 1996, when the Taliban had him surrounded, and when, for all that, Massoud had slipped away with his army intact. And the Taliban offensive of only two years before, which had very nearly wiped him out. Massoud had gone to Friday prayers then and given a rousing speech, which echoed from mosque loudspeakers up and down the valley.

"I said that if anyone surrendered to the Taliban, his name would be recalled in the mosques for generations to come," he said.

When Massoud finally got around to talking about his current predicament, he no longer looked like the dashing young warrior he used to be. He still wore the signature flat woolen cap, cocked at an angle, which gave him the look of an artist.

He still lapsed into French, which he'd learned at a Kabul lycée many years before. Turning to the battle at hand, Massoud looked instead like the aging general he was, living off the past, and hoping against the ache in his bones that he could rally his men one last time.

He leaned over and sketched the front lines on my map.

"Here, here and here," he said, scribbling with a pen. "In a very short time the Taliban will attack."

Massoud spoke of a new tactic: pouring nails in the roads to flatten the tires of the dreaded, onrushing Hi-Luxes. On a sheet of paper, he sketched a three-pronged nail with which he would blanket the roads. And then leaned back in his chair. It seemed a fanciful thing; a desperate musing—nails in the roads. And then Massoud spoke of an older, proven tactic: drawing the invaders into the valleys and cutting off their ways of escape. "In this way we can hold out forever," he said.

He took a final sip of tea and tossed the dregs over his shoulder.

"If there had never been a war," he said, "I would have been a very good architect."

Massoud knew his end was near. I could see it in his eyes, in the nostalgia. He did not know, of course, how the demise would come, or when it would come. He could not foresee, for instance, that in just two years a pair of Tunisian men sent by Al-Qaeda would come to his camp posing as journalists and, not far from the white chair and the green lawn where he now sat, explode a bomb inside a camera, two days before the September 11 attacks.

The battle had changed fundamentally in the past couple of years, Massoud said, his face growing serious. The Taliban were still fighting, but they were being sustained by foreigners: Pakistanis and Arabs. The Taliban machine would have collapsed long ago without Pakistani advisers, money and volunteers. And the Arab fighters were the toughest, most fanatical of them all, many of them holdovers from the jihad against the Soviet Union.

"The Arabs are just across the front lines," Massoud said. "We can hear them on the radio at night. Arabic and Urdu."

I was sitting in the grass. I must have looked skeptical.

"Would you like to see the Pakistani prisoners?" he asked.

We drove in an old Russian jeep along a dried riverbed strewn with boulders. The way was treeless and bleak. At nightfall we arrived at a squat stone building where a man named Rahmatullah greeted us holding an oil-burning lantern. The place was called Lejdeh, he said.

Rahmatullah held up the lantern and there was a rustle of bodies. And then the glow of many eyes. The prisoners were huddled together under dun-colored blankets. There were 106 Pakistanis and 55 Afghans, Rahmatullah said, captured in different battles over many months.

I felt as if I were peeking into one of the madrassas in Pakistan, filled with young men being exhorted to fight. Except it wasn't in Pakistan, it was here, in the far north of Afghanistan, twenty miles from the border of the old Soviet Union. They had come a long way.

I'd come a long way, too. When I'd arrived in the Indian subcontinent a couple of years before, I hadn't given much thought to militant Islam. So many other things seemed more urgent, more interesting. The militant Islamists were dangerous and busy; four Americans were murdered in Karachi not long after I landed. But until that evening in the stone prison,

I'd never felt the force of the faith, had never seen its power to inspire men to move hundreds of miles from their homes just so they could fight.

Rahmatullah picked out five Pakistanis and led them to a smaller room. They sat before me, listless and blank, their faces slack with resignation. I goaded them to speak.

"The moment I stepped off the plane, I was captured," said Abdul Jalil, a Pakistani from Baluchistan, the oldest among them at thirty-seven. He was still befuddled by his strange journey.

"I never fired a shot," he said.

The mullah at his mosque had pushed him to fight for the Taliban, he said. Go and fight for God's law, the mullah said. And so Abdul Jalil, an illiterate laborer, boarded a bus bound for Quetta, the provincial capital, found a Taliban soldier and signed up for the cause. The Talibs packed him off to Mazar-i-Sharif. He'd been in prison for two years.

Then there was Faiz Ahmad, seventeen, wearing a pair of wire-rimmed glasses, a hajj cap and no beard. He seemed listless like the others, but when I asked him a question, he came alive.

"It is written in the Koran that we must kill the nonbelievers," Ahmad said. "My teacher taught me this."

Ahmad's teacher happened to be his father; he taught at a madrassa in the Punjab that had been sending boys to Afghanistan for years. One of Ahmad's brothers, Zahid, had died fighting the Soviet Union. When Ahmad told his parents that he wanted to avenge his brother's death in the new jihad, they blessed him and sent him on his way. Ahmad said he'd fought in many battles before his capture near Kabul a few months before. He seemed about as close to a perfect specimen as the Taliban could imagine.

"There is no end to the jihad," Ahmad said. "It will go on forever until doomsday."

After that, there wasn't much to talk about. I got up and the jihadis filed back into their cell. Rahmatullah walked me out, holding the lantern. For a jailer, he seemed a decent man, holding no grudge against the men in his charge. The International Committee of the Red Cross, he said, had even inspected the place. "We are all the children of Adam and Eve," he said.

IN THE SUMMER of 2000, Kabul was filled with chatter about the Arabs. About how they were taking over the Taliban. About how Osama bin Laden was keeping the movement afloat with his money—with bags of American dollars his men carried into the city every month. Another story going around had it that the Arabs were running a training camp for jihadis outside of Jalalabad—a place where they practiced the black arts of assassination and hijacking. My favorite story concerned volleyball: every Friday, a group of Arabs would meet for a game at a court outside of town.

One day I walked into one of Kabul's few upscale groceries, a small corner shop on Chicken Street that carried imported cheeses and meats. I was wandering down one of the aisles when my Afghan interpreter, Farid, grabbed me by the arm, pulled me outside and rushed me down the street.

"There were Arabs inside," Farid said. "If they had seen you, they would have killed you. The Arabs here are crazy—crazy."

I believed Farid, who assured me—in the privacy of my hotel room—that he loathed the Taliban. Farid was a young physician; he had somehow managed to get a medical degree in the rubble of Kabul University. Translating for the Taliban was the only job he could find. I believed the stories about the training camps. And I believed the stories about the Arab volleyball game and about Osama's bags of cash. But after several days in Kabul, I still had not seen any of the Arabs myself.

Then one day Farid and I stood in line at Kabul International Airport waiting to board a commercial jet to Kandahar. By the summer of 2000, Ariana Afghan Airlines was down to two planes: a decrepit Boeing 727 and a Soviet-made Antonov-24, which because of international sanctions, were flying without the benefit of spare parts. Two other planes had crashed. The airport itself, a favorite target of Massoud's rockets, lay in ruins.

As Farid and I waited in line for our tickets, we found ourselves next to a group of a dozen women. They were dressed in the mandatory head-to-toe burqas, which rendered them invisible, except for the shoes that peeked out from the bottoms of their suits. And what shoes they were: stylish, expensive shoes, high heels, low heels and flats, of the latest Italian styles. Possibly Ferragamos. The women were speaking Arabic, with Saudi accents.

"I could be shopping in Paris, but instead, I am here, in this awful place," one of the women said to another through the vent in her burqa.

The other women nodded in agreement.

"Yes, my husband has to be the tough-guy warrior, fighting for Islam," another huffed. "He thinks it brings him closer to God. And so here I am."

"We are stuck here," a third woman said, "in this cursed place."

All the burqas nodded.

Third World

I CAME OVER on a ferry. I'd left my car in the street in Wee-hawken; didn't even bother parking it. The police weren't let-ting anyone onto the ferries that day; they were only taking people off of Manhattan, not into it. After some persuading on my part, a policewoman waved me aboard. If I hadn't known something terrible had happened I might have guessed, just by the looks on people's faces. The men and women were drawn and silent, and remarkably well dressed, like they were coming from some formal disaster. Nobody was looking back over their shoulder; even though, by early afternoon, there was much to see. The whole sky.

By the time I reached Manhattan the initial shock had passed. A middle-aged woman sat on a curb in Midtown sob-bing, her black purse with a gold snap sitting next to her. I looked into one of the temporary hospitals that had been set up in a storefront north of Canal Street and saw that it was empty. Stretcher after empty stretcher. The volunteers trying to busy themselves. All the empty beds: only later did it occur to me why.

Walking in, watching the flames shoot upward, the first thing I thought was that I was back in the Third World. My countrymen were going to think this was the worst thing that ever happened, the end of civilization. In the Third World, this sort of thing happened every day: earthquakes, famines, plagues. In Orissa, on the eastern coast of India, after the cyclone, the dead were piled up so high and for so long that the dogs couldn't eat any more; they just lay about waiting for their appetites to come back. Lazily looking at one another. Fifteen thousand dead in that one. Seventeen thousand died in the earthquake in Turkey. In Afghanistan, in the earthquake there, four thousand. This was mass murder, that was clear, it was an act of evil. Though I'd seen that, too: the forty thousand dead in Kabul. I don't think I was the only person thinking this, who had the darker perspective. All those street vendors who worked near the World Trade Center, from all those different countries, selling falafel and schwarma. When they heard the planes and watched the towers they must have thought the same as I did: that they'd come home.

It took me several hours to reach the site, getting around all the police checkpoints. I had to walk over to the East River, then down along FDR Drive, and then I looped down around to the southern end of the island, near Battery Park, and walked in that way. It was nearly dark by the time I got there. I remember how quiet it was those last few blocks walking in, everything covered in the thin white dust, the heart of Wall Street, empty and silent. It was as if all the sound had been pulled into the hole in the ground a little farther up.

As I moved in closer, my eyes went to a gray-green thing spread across the puddles and rocks. Elongated, unrolled, sitting there, unnoticed. An intestine. It kind of jumped out at me, presented itself. It's amazing how the eyes do that, go right to the human flesh, spot it amid the heaviest camouflage of rubble and dirt and glass, as if it were glowing green in an infrared scope. I saw the same phenomenon later on, at a suicide bombing in Tel Aviv, the Orthodox volunteers with their spatulas and bags, frantically running and scooping every bit of flesh, no matter how tiny, to save the various souls. Down here, in what had been an intersection south of the Twin Towers, I stood and looked at the gray-green mass, thought about whose it was, how it got here; whether, for instance, it had come from one of the airplane passengers, or from one of the people inside one of the buildings. Or even, against the odds, from one of the hijackers. Above me stood one of the airplane landing struts, maybe thirty feet high, snapped off and lying at an angle in the street, looking like the collapsed wing of some enormous bird. The tire was still filled with air.

In the glare of the spotlights and the fire I could see several dozen firemen standing atop an enormous slag heap, perhaps eight stories high, of metal and wreckage and I couldn't tell what else. The firemen were pulling things out and peering inside, on their knees, talking to German shepherds. I started a conversation with a fireman who was getting a cup of water. The fireman was maybe in his midfifties, Irish, with a large, square jaw. He didn't look the least bit tired. He had settled down and had a good pace going, I think; he was not as frantic as I imagined he had been a few hours before, when his buddies had died by the hundreds. Maybe he didn't know yet. He said they'd discovered some sort of cavern, an air pocket in the giant heap of slag. They couldn't get in there themselves, the fireman said, so they were sending dogs in, and the dogs had cameras attached. In case there was someone still alive in there. "We're seeing a lot of spinal cords," he said.

I went into the building marked One Liberty Plaza, just across the street. The inside was well lit from the fire outside. There were racks of cashmere top coats and woolen sweaters, the fall line; I was in Brooks Brothers. I groped in the dark of the stairwell and walked up to the second floor into some sort of an office, perhaps a law firm. It looked like a scene in a movie where the reel had stopped dead. A bagel with a bite taken out of it, the cream cheese still on the end of the white plastic knife. A telephone fallen from its cradle. A Styrofoam cup tipped over, the coffee stain spread across the desktop. A pen next to a half-written telephone number. I think they survived, the people up here, probably ran out in a panic. I walked over to the bay windows, which were blown out, of course, and stepped out onto the ledge. I was looking right into the thing, now just an unintelligible mass of fire. I stood there for a while looking in, wondering about the battery in my cell phone, and realized I was not alone. There was another person on the ledge with me, a photographer, standing quietly, long blond hair. He was snapping pictures in a casual way, raising the camera and bringing it down to his waist, like he was shooting families at a picnic. We stood together for a while and watched the fire.

I walked around some more that night, dodging the cops, calling in a few things to the newsroom on my cell when I could get through. I walked up into One Liberty Plaza again and into Brooks Brothers and toward the back, by the fitting rooms. It was 3 a.m. I lay down in a corner on the carpeted floor and tried to sleep but couldn't; it was too cold. I had run out of my house in a gallop that morning and hadn't brought a jacket. I got up, looked into one of the racks and pulled out a gray cable-knit sweater, size XL. The sweater hung over me like a potato sack, way too big, but it wasn't like I was going to try on another size.

Later that night I was awoken many times, usually by the police. Once when I came to, a group of police officers were trying on cashmere topcoats and turning as they looked in the mirror. There was lots of laughter. "Nice," one of them said, looking at his reflection, big smile on his face. "Look at that."

CHAPTER 3

Jang

ON A CLEAR DAY you could see the B-52s overhead, their contrails marking the sky in long, white streaks. They seemed to float up there, so high above; sometimes, given their altitude, they took half an hour to traverse the whole horizon. The exhaust plumes hung in the air long after the planes had moved on, so on some afternoons the whole sky would be looped and crisscrossed, white against the blue, like a work of abstract art.

It wasn't just the bombs they dropped that were so unnerving; it was the lumbering, dissociative way they let them go. One of the bombers would make an appearance, usually at thirty thousand feet, a tiny gray V in the sky, all the way from Diego Garcia in the Indian Ocean three thousand miles away. Gliding like a crane. Then, without warning, the sharp, titanic bursts, the clouds tumbling upwards, the ground moaning as if something crucial in the world had broken off and fallen away. And then you'd look up and there the plane would be, arcing, plodding, moving across the great blue sky.

Sometimes at night, working late in the mud-brick hut, I'd hear the faint *wup-wup-wup* and rush outside and if I was lucky I'd see a blackened silhouette against the star-flecked night. A helicopter without lights, here then gone. The Americans were here, the Afghans said, but I didn't see any of them until much later.

On the morning the bombing started, the windows in my

house clinked and rattled for minutes on end, like a tea service in an earthquake. I drove as fast as I could as far as I could, forded the Kokcha River on a horse, ran crouching through the muddy Northern Alliance trenches, reached the most forward post and peeked my head over the top. The Taliban positions were just in view, only three hundred yards away. A rolling green field lay between. Up and down the Taliban trench line, the blasts from the bombs had left gigantic circles of blackened grass, like the footprints of some huge beast, fifty feet wide. Blackened hoof after blackened hoof, concentric and overlapping. The bombs had hit the trenches precisely, gone directly inside. And there, across the field, rose the turbaned head of a Taliban soldier, looking to his right, then to his left; amazed, perhaps, that he was alive.

I felt sorry for those Taliban fighters, I really did. Just sitting in their trenches. Trapped. Uncomprehending. Waiting to be bombed. I was right about that, right about what they'd felt. I saw the Taliban prisoners afterwards, dirty and frightened, and all they talked about were the bombs. For the Taliban, the waiting was the worst. A B-52 would appear in the sky, drop a bomb or two and then begin its great U-turn toward its home on Diego Garcia. The B-52s took forever to make that turn, arcing slowly and grandly, turning like an aircraft carrier. And just when I thought the B-52 was finally headed south, headed home, it would keep turning, keep circling back, and then I knew that it was coming back for another run. Sometimes it would take half an hour. And then I'd imagine the Taliban guys in their trenches, fiddling with their prayer beads, looking up, waiting.

In the end they just ran. Up near the Tajik border, where I was. The Americans bombed every day for three weeks, and when the Northern Alliance commanders fired a few tank rounds and sent their men out of their own trenches to go and fight, the Taliban held on for a couple of days, even counterattacked. And then finally they just gave up and ran. I never saw it, never saw the Talibs running, but I walked through their empty positions later on. Stepped on the charred grass, walked into the craters, picked up the odd rifle. It wasn't hard to imagine what the Talibs were feeling when they finally climbed out of the trenches and ran. Glorious, horrifying release.

The whole war was about the B-52s, at least in the beginning. A few weeks later, at the siege of Kunduz, the last of the Taliban units started surrendering, driving out of their own front lines, and all their trucks were smeared with mud. Doors, hoods, even windows, covered with mud. To hide them from the B-52s. Driving across northern Afghanistan soon after, I saw the wreckage everywhere: the Hi-Luxes and the old Soviet Kamaz trucks, the tanks and the Toyotas, over-turned inside the craters, shoes and shreds of clothing splayed in every direction. Boom.

THE HILLS AROUND Kunduz were glowing pink when the silhouette of a solitary man appeared on the horizon. He was barely visible in the setting sun, a speck, yet even so he had captured the attention of the Alliance soldiers. They watched him. He was walking from the Taliban lines, toward the Northern Alliance lines, alone. The city he was walking out of, Kunduz, was under siege, with thousands of his brethren trapped inside. It might have been the scene from a Saturday afternoon matinee: the lonely sheriff walking determinedly out of the sunset.

As he got closer we could see him a little better: black hair spilling over his shoulders. Hollow cheeks. Wide, deep-set exhausted eyes. Billowy white dishdasha* running to his shins. No gun. Finally the man crossed into their ranks, and the men put down their guns and gathered round him. "Welcome, my friend," one of the Alliance soldiers said, wrapping his arms around the hollow-eyed man. He put his arms on the man's shoulders, then his hands to his cheeks, like he was an old friend. "It is good to see you after so long."

People fought in Afghanistan, and people died, but not always in the obvious way. They had been fighting for so long, twenty-three years then, that by the time the Americans arrived the Afghans had developed an elaborate set of rules

---

*A dishdasha is an ankle-length garment, usually white, which resembles a robe.

designed to spare as many fighters as they could. So the war could go on forever. Men fought, men switched sides, men lined up and fought again. War in Afghanistan often seemed like a game of pickup basketball, a contest among friends, a tournament where you never knew which team you'd be on when the next game got under way. Shirts today, skins tomorrow. On Tuesday, you might be part of a fearsome Taliban regiment, running into a minefield. And on Wednesday you might be manning a checkpoint for some gang of the Northern Alliance. By Thursday you could be back with the Talibs again, holding up your Kalashnikov and promising to wage jihad forever. War was serious in Afghanistan, but not that serious. It was part of everyday life. It was a job. Only the civilians seemed to lose.

Battles were often decided this way, not by actual fighting, but by flipping gangs of soldiers. One day, the Taliban might have four thousand soldiers, and the next, only half that, with the warlords of the Northern Alliance suddenly larger by a similar amount. The fighting began when the bargaining stopped, and the bargaining went right up until the end. The losers were the ones who were too stubborn, too stupid or too fanatical to make a deal. Suddenly, they would find themselves outnumbered, and then they would die. It was a kind of natural selection.

One of the Afghan militia commanders with whom I traveled, Daoud Khan, was a master of this complicated game. He was portly and well dressed, and he ate very well. The Afghans spoke of him in reverent tones, but he didn't seem like much of a warrior to me. He'd never fought for the Taliban himself, but thousands of his former soldiers were now in the Taliban ranks. Why kill them when he could just bring them back to his side?

Khan captured his first city, Taloqan, without firing a single shot. He did it by persuading the local Taliban leader, a man named Abdullah Gard, to switch sides. Gard was no dummy; he could see the B-52s. I guessed that Khan had probably used a lot of money, but he never allowed me to sit in as he worked the Taliban chieftains on the radio. The day after Taloqan fell, I found Gard in an abandoned house, seated on a blue cushion on the floor, warming himself next to a wood-burning stove. His black Taliban turban was gone, and he had replaced it with a woolen Chitrali cap just like that of Ahmad Shah Massoud. "All along, I was spying on the Taliban," Gard said, his eyes darting. No one believed him, but no one seemed to care.

The commanders were vain but rarely pompous. Pir Mohammed, an Uzbek commander, was a dead ringer for Genghis Khan; on our first morning together we shared a breakfast of roasted sheep hearts. (Daoud Khan's breakfasts were far more lavish.) Pir had a bullet hole in his face, and two more in his stomach, which he revealed to me by pulling up his shirt, in the style of LBJ and the scar over his gallbladder. I met Pir at his mountain base on the overlook to Taloqan, his hometown, which had fallen to the Taliban fourteen months before. He'd set up a television set in his bunker, kept it going with a car battery, and one Friday we sat together and watched a flickering game of women's tennis beamed from Russia. A few weeks later, after Taloqan fell, I saw Pir again, this time at his old home in downtown Taloqan. "Welcome back," one of the Taliban soldiers had painted on the wall inside. Pir laughed, but not a lot.

Even the fighting, when there was fighting, had a desultory feel. Artillery duels typically consisted of a Taliban shell sailing into the Northern Alliance lines, and then a response; a rocket or two, fired by the Alliance half an hour later. I saw the first such duel while still in Tajikistan, standing on the banks of the Amu Darya River with the Afghan frontier on the other bank. "This isn't fighting," Asrat Pulodov, a Russian border guard, said, watching a Taliban shell sail errantly into the dirt. "This is a joke."

On the first night of the long-awaited offensive against the Taliban, carried out at the urging of the Americans, the Alliance commanders bombarded the Taliban lines and then, as night fell, sent their men forward. Yet when I arrived the next morning, the Alliance soldiers stood more or less where they had the day before. They'd run, and then they'd run back. No one seemed surprised. "Advancing, retreating, advancing, that's what you do in war," Yusef, a twenty-year-old Alliance soldier, told me with a shrug. He was sitting in a foxhole.

It wasn't that the Afghans were afraid to fight, it was that they'd fought too much. And now, given the opportunity, they wanted to avoid it if they could. "My dear, I am your brother, you know how much affection I have for you, there is really no point in resisting anymore," Mohammad Uria, a Northern Alliance commander, said into his radio to a Taliban commander a few miles away.

Of course, there were plenty of Taliban soldiers who wanted to fight forever. Fight to the death. They were the Pashtuns from Kandahar, for the most part, a different breed. "I've seen them run right into the minefields—they want to die," Pir Mohammed said, shaking his head in awe. But where I was, in northern Afghanistan, many if not most of the Taliban soldiers weren't from Kandahar, they were from the north—Tajiks and Uzbeks who'd switched sides when the fearsome Kandaharis rolled in. Now the northerners wanted to quit. The one group of people who really took fighting seriously were the foreigners—that is, the Americans and Al-Qaeda. They came to kill.

"Kunduz has been captured!"

The cheer went up through the ranks of the Northern Alliance soldiers, and everyone started piling into cars.

They'd cut a deal, and there would be no bloodshed. Kunduz had fallen. The Taliban had given up. The Alliance soldiers, hundreds of them, marched along the main road toward Kunduz, now just a few miles away. I was on a hill, overlooking the approach, standing near Daoud Khan, the well-fed warlord. His men were just outside of Kunduz when the rockets started vaulting out of Taliban lines. You could hear the explosions through his radio. Khan's face suddenly lost all its color.

"I don't know what is happening," Khan said, jerking his head about. "We made contacts with commanders in the city. They told us they would embrace us."

General Khan scampered down the hill, jumped into his sedan and sped away. Taking their cue from their commander, hundreds of Alliance soldiers began to retreat, running, throwing their guns, falling down, falling under car wheels, yelling and shouting, trampling each other in a panic to get away.

"Let me on, let me on!" soldiers yelled, leaping onto the back of our truck. What seemed like an orderly Afghan-style surrender had, in Kunduz, been a double-cross. And the double-cross had turned to a rout. Men were run over by trucks in the pandemonium, caught under the wheels. The bodies of the rocket victims were left behind in the road. The retreat stretched more than a mile, a broken line of cowardice and confusion. I was in my Toyota Hi-Lux. Perhaps thirty men had jumped onto our truck and we drove at whatever speed we could gather. Finally we were stopped by a Northern Alliance soldier firing his Kalashnikov into the air. "Anyone who passes I shoot!" he said.

I found Pir, my Genghis Khan look-alike, a few days later. His cheeks were more sunken than usual. Four Taliban commanders he'd been negotiating with no longer answered their radios, he said. Pir dragged a finger across his throat. Refugees coming out of the city were saying the same thing; that the Al-Qaeda fighters who had crammed into the city— Arabs, Chinese, Uzbeks—were killing anyone who even spoke of surrendering. Kunduz, it turned out, was different. There would be no pickup basketball. It would be a fight to the death.

"All the trucks are full of foreigners, and every truck has a translator," Ibrahim Hoxar, a refugee who walked out of the city, told me.

With a little help from the Americans, the Afghan way reasserted itself a couple of weeks later. The B-52s and now F-16s pounded Kunduz; every morning, I sat on a hill and watched the bombs. It took about two weeks. Whatever the foreigners might be doing in there, the Taliban units started surrendering again. One sunny afternoon I stood at the outskirts of the city, in an abandoned town called Amirabad, and watched a dozen muddy Toyota trucks rumble out, each of them filled with Taliban soldiers.

Mullah Abdullah, one of the surrendering Taliban chieftains, stepped from his truck and embraced Daoud Khan. His men did the same.

"Hi, how have you been?" a Northern Alliance soldier said to a Taliban fighter, a tank driver named Mullah Gulmir, age twenty-seven. The two men embraced.

"Fine, thanks," Gulmir said to his old friend, "and you?"

Gulmir said he'd first become a soldier in 1992, at the age of seventeen, when the mujahideen entered Kabul and took it from the collapsing Communists. Then, Gulmir had signed on with one of the most famous of warlords, Rasool Sayyaf. When the Taliban threw the mujahideen out of Kabul in 1996, Gulmir left Sayyaf and joined them.

"I joined the Taliban because they were stronger," Gulmir said. "I'm joining the Northern Alliance because they are stronger now."

As the Taliban and Northern Alliance soldiers embraced and hugged, one of Khan's deputies, Mohammad Uria, looked on and gave a knowing smile.

"Yesterday, my enemy," Uria said, "today, my brother."

THE BODIES OF the Taliban soldiers lay stiff and straight at odd points across the intersection of Khanabad Road and Chugha Street. The big toes on their bare feet were tied together, in the Islamic burial tradition, and their white turbans had been unfurled to reveal bullet holes through the tops of their heads. Their eyes were frozen open wide, staring upward. Their mouths were parted slightly, giving their faces improbable looks of surprise.

"They didn't have a car," said Muhammad Ashraf, twenty-five, standing over the body of a Taliban soldier whose name nobody knew. Kunduz had fallen the night before. "They couldn't get away, like the rest of them. When the Northern Alliance soldiers came, they killed them."

Not far away, a Taliban fighter named Abdul Hadid sat on a curb and looked up in terror as a crowd of soldiers encircled him. Only minutes before, Hadid had been shot through his left ribs at the Kunduz fruit market. He was barefoot and trembling. It was nearly dark.

"Where are you from?" one of the soldiers shouted. "Where are your friends? Where is your gun?"

Hadid's robe was soaked with urine. He tried to say something but the soldiers shouted over him. He looked up at a pair of Westerners.

"I have a friend in Germany," he said.

A Northern Alliance commander put Hadid into a horse-drawn wagon and took him away. He said he was taking him to the hospital.

In the Kunduz town square, Alliance soldiers were herding the Talibs into the backs of their trucks. They bound their hands and pushed them in. It was too late for deals. A crowd had gathered round to jeer and cheer.

"Long live the Northern Alliance!" they said.

"Short life for Mullah Omar!"

"Short life for Osama!"

A cheer went up, though I was not sure whether it was for themselves or for their new masters. The uncertainty hung on everyone's lips like a secret; I finally found someone who explained it.

"Well, the Taliban are finally gone," said Zulgai Zabihul-lah, a twenty-one-year-old medical student. He said he'd gone to school without his turban for the first time in four years. "But I do not think I will celebrate today. Not yet. Maybe tomorrow. Maybe I will celebrate tomorrow."

"Why wait?" I asked him, but he just shook his head.

In the street in front of Zabihullah, a group of Northern

Alliance soldiers were manhandling some Talib prisoners into the back of a Hi-Lux. The hands of the Talibs were bound with strips of clothing. In the front of the truck, in the driver's seat, sat a youngish-looking man with a beard and turban and flowing hair. He had a gun. I said hello, and to my surprise he recognized me.

"My friend," he said.

It was Mullah Abdullah, the same Mullah Abdullah I had met two days before in Amirabad, when he was a Taliban commander. Two days before, Mullah Abdullah had taken three hundred of his Taliban soldiers out of Kunduz and crossed into the lines of the Northern Alliance and surrendered. Now he was helping take his erstwhile comrades prisoner.

"They are Taliban and I'm Northern Alliance now," Abdullah said. He gave a sheepish grin.

It had happened that fast: Abdullah quit the Taliban, went behind the Alliance lines, got some sleep and joined the attack. He might never have left his Hi-Lux.

"I'm waiting for the order from my commander, and I will kill them," he said.

I walked around to the back of Abdullah's truck and chatted with one of his former comrades, a young Talib named Amanullah, now a prisoner. His arms were bound behind him. A large crowd had gathered around Amanullah, and some were beginning to taunt him. He was biting his lip.

From the bed of the truck, Amanullah told me he'd joined the Taliban at the urging of his religious teacher, Mullah Agha, when he was a student in Ghazni. The mullah, he said, urged him to help wage jihad against the heathens. The heathens, the mullah said, were near Kunduz. And so Amanullah joined up and made his way here.

"He told me to fight the nonbelievers," Amanullah said.

As the taunting grew louder and the truck prepared to take him away, Amanullah said he had reconsidered the concept of jihad. "The Taliban are believers, and the Northern Alliance are believers, too," he said.

"Only I am a nonbeliever now," Amanullah said, looking at his hecklers, "because I allowed myself to be tricked."

The truck rumbled away.

. . .

IT HAD BEEN an unusually warm November day, and now, after the sun had set, a breeze was carrying the sounds through Taloqan's streets. They were the words of Ahmad Zahir, an Afghan singer of romantic reputation who bore a remarkable resemblance, in life and in sound and even in his thick black pompadour, to Elvis himself.

> *Laili Laili Laili, dear*
> *You've broken my heart*
> *You never came back to me*
> *You've killed me with longing . . .*
> *You've broken my heart.*

The song seemed to carry a decade's worth of dashed hopes, and the Afghans tilted their ears toward it, rocked their heads to its steady beat. The Taliban had held this city in its grip for fourteen months, though not long enough, I gathered, to corrode the television sets and cassette players the locals had wrapped in plastic and hidden underground. By nightfall, the machines were out of the ground and sending forth a gleeful cacophony.

I chose one melody and followed it a little way into Habibullah's Restaurant, then up to the counter and then overhead and then to a false wall that had hidden the cassette player for so many months. The music was pouring out of its tiny, tinny speaker, and it was so loud that I could scarcely hear Habibullah himself, who was seated cross-legged on a pillow. The cassette player had sat inside the secret cabinet during the whole of the occupation. "I haven't listened to music in two years," he said. I found another man, Asif, who had just hooked his battered Emerson television to a gasoline-powered generator and slipped a bootleg videocassette of *Titanic* into its built-in player. The opening credits were flickering on the screen when Asif looked at me, and he appeared younger and somehow lighter-looking than anyone I had seen in a long time. He had taken off his turban, and his beard was already gone. There wasn't much to say. He laughed and turned to his movie.

I walked into the street and the breeze was still wafting, pushing open the burqas of the women who were walking by themselves and with each other, unaccompanied by the men. I listened to their friendly murmurs as I walked past them, then stepped into Aman's barber shop. Aman was standing shin-deep in a pile of beard cuttings. There were four other customers waiting their turn. "All day long, they've been coming," Aman said, clipping, circling his customer. "It is the best day I have ever had." One of the Taliban's rules had decreed that while they would not generally quibble with the length of a man's hair it was imperative that his bangs not cover too much of his forehead, lest such hair get in the way when the man knelt and pressed his head to the ground to pray. Halfway was the limit. So, Aman explained, the vice and virtue police would sometimes sit in his shop and check on the forelocks of his customers. Occasionally, they would drag a man off for a beating or a night in jail.

The last customer who took the chair was Ismail Isat, who looked like just another bearded Afghan but who was soon revealed to be, after twenty minutes of Aman's work, as handsome and chiseled as a movie star. Isat thought so, too; for several minutes after his cut and shave he remained in the chair, moving his hand across the freshly clipped beard, amazed at the face he saw in the mirror. Then he swiveled round and spoke to everyone in the room: "I've got nothing against beards, you know; in fact, I used to wear one myself. The problem is when someone tells you that you have to grow one," he said. By now it was past closing time. Isat and a couple of other men lingered for a while as Aman swept up a small mountain of beards. Then the owner stopped, realizing that there was one thing that he had forgotten to do. "Tomorrow," Aman said, "I am going to cut off my own beard."

DOSTUM, THE UZBEK warlord, was standing amid the bodies. There were hundreds of them, Taliban and Al-Qaeda prisoners, shot down and bombed after they'd rioted at the giant fortress prison called Qala Jangi. The Taliban had surrendered a couple of days before, offering themselves at the gates of the city. Dostum wore a jacket of soft black leather, and he'd wrapped his face in a blue silk scarf. Only his eyes showed.

The prisoners, about two hundred of them, lay about in angular, improbable poses: legs stuck up in the air, arms twisted around necks, fingers curled over palms. Dead horses lay with them throughout the yard, frozen and arched. Soldiers from the Northern Alliance were examining the human corpses with care, prying boots from feet and rings from fingers.

Dostum unfurled the scarf, revealing his face. The eyes were brutal, but he looked younger than his forty-seven years. After the September 11 attacks, when the Americans had decided to take out the Taliban, they had gone first to Dostum. "Dostum fights," one of the Americans told me. With the B-52s above them, Dostum had captured Mazar-i-Sharif, the first city to fall. Now among the bodies, Dostum seemed at ease, even a little exhilarated. He was back. A television crew was pushing its way through the crowd.

We'd rolled into Mazar-i-Sharif when the riot was still unfolding. It had happened like this: after the Taliban had given up, the Northern Alliance had corralled the prisoners into Qala Jangi and, with the help of CIA paramilitaries and Special Forces soldiers, had begun to interrogate them. The presence of the Americans agitated the Arab prisoners, and some of them pulled guns and grenades that had gone undiscovered. One of the Americans, Johnny Mike Spann of Winfield, Alabama, was killed. The riot spread, and the Alliance guards in the towers opened up with their guns. The Americans called in the F-16s.

Now, with the riot crushed, the walls of Qala Jangi were pockmarked from bullets a thousand times and toppled from the bombs. I did not know it at the time, but as Dostum surveyed the carnage, about eighty more prisoners were hiding in the basement below. One of them was John Walker Lindh, the jihadi from northern California. Bursts of machine-gun fire echoed through the yard.

Dostum was chatting with his aides when Catherine Davis of the BBC came close. She pressed her microphone into his face. Are you not shocked by the number of dead? Davis demanded of Dostum, of the ferocity of the fight inside the fortress? What is your explanation?

Dostum seemed stunned at first, but he quickly recovered.

"*Jang*," he said with a shrug, using the Dari word for "war."

"*Jang.*"

I CAME TO A HOUSE in a ruined part of town. The sky was gray and the yard was strewn with rocks and old metal and wires. It was one of the makeshift prisons that had popped up across Mazar-i-Sharif when the riot at Qala Jangi began. The place was being guarded by Hazara militiamen who, curiously, were wearing camouflage uniforms that looked brand-new. It was a strange pattern for camouflage, dark green with bright yellow splotches.

I found Nasir inside, in a room without windows. He was on the floor, shirtless and shivering, covered by an old blanket. A bullet wound festered in his right arm. He was from Saudi Arabia, the other prisoners said.

I didn't have a lot of time. The war was winding down and people were scattering and disappearing. Things and people that were here today would soon no longer be. "After we talk to them," Syed Wasiqullah, one of the Northern Alliance commanders, told me, "they're finished." He dragged a finger across his throat.

I crouched next to the prisoner on the floor. He looked very young. His eyes were floating and he was groaning under the blanket. A slice of stale bread sat on a green plastic plate on the floor next to him. "He needs some fruit," one of the prisoners said.

"Dying," I wrote in my notebook.

"My name is Nasir," he said, "and I am twenty-one." He was an Arab, with dark skin and full lips. But his face and limbs were long and thin, giving him the delicate, elongated look of a man painted by El Greco.

Nasir had grown up in a middle-class neighborhood in Riyadh, he said, graduated from high school, even had American friends. In Riyadh, he used to meet the Americans at the

Pizza Hut near his home. "The Americans were my friends," Nasir said. "I talked with them. I stayed with them. Some of them were speaking Arabic to me."

He'd been on Hajj, he said, the Muslim pilgrimage to Mecca, when a fellow Saudi who called himself Abu Mali approached. It was the spring of 2001, only six months before. The war against the infidels, Mali called it; would you fight against the infidels? Nasir said yes, he would go to Palestine to fight the Jews. Abu Mali said yes, of course, we will send you to Palestine. So Nasir went to the bank and withdrew 3,000 rials—about $800—and called his father to tell him.

"He was very angry with me," Nasir said, staring upward from his place on the floor. "He forbade me from going."

Nasir had never defied his father before, but this time he did, eager to do something special with his life and make his family proud. Before fighting in Palestine, Abu Mali told him, Nasir would have to go first to Afghanistan to receive his training. So Nasir used his 3,000 rials to fly to Karachi with four other recruits, and he rode on the back of a motorcycle across the border into Kandahar.

There on the floor, Nasir resumed his groans and winces.

"I am in much pain," he said. His voice squeaked and he began talking in gasps. I reached into my bag and handed him a banana and an orange. His eyes didn't follow them, and he left them on the plate.

Once his military training began in Afghanistan, Nasir said, he discovered that he lacked the zeal to be a soldier of the jihad. He wanted to go home, he said, but he was out of money. He asked Abu Mali about Palestine. Soon, Abu Mali said, and Nasir carried on.

Then the day came, Nasir said, that he was pronounced a soldier in Kandahar with several other Arabs. They were gathered together in the training camp when a tall and long-limbed man, another son of Saudi Arabia, stood before them and spoke.

"I didn't know the face of Osama at the time," Nasir said. "People pointed to him. They said he was a good man."

"Very quietly he spoke," Nasir said. "Osama said, This is the way of jihad. If you are killed—in Palestine, in Chechnya, in Kashmir—you will help these people become free."

It was not long after that, Nasir said, that Abu Mali left for Saudi Arabia. The leaders who remained told Nasir that he would not be going to Palestine, after all. It was September 2001, and there was a jihad to be fought right there in Afghanistan.

"I told them I wanted to go home," Nasir said. "I told them I did not want to fight against other Muslims."

Still, Nasir went along, packing his bags and riding to Kabul in the back of a pickup truck. From there, he flew aboard a Taliban plane to Kunduz, which Northern Alliance troops were by then rapidly encircling. Once in Kunduz, Nasir said, he volunteered for unimportant jobs to keep him away from the front lines.

He'd been in Kunduz for ten days when the Taliban surrendered. A truck carried him with the others to the Qala Jangi fortress in Mazar-i-Sharif. And then the riot broke out, and after hiding in a horse stable for two days, he scaled a wall and ran. "Home," he said to himself as he zigzagged through the bazaar. Then he was shot.

Lying on the floor, Nasir said he had given up his dreams of the jihad. He said he did not care for bin Laden. More than anything, Nasir said, he wished he were the naive young man he had been only a few months before.

"You can tell them, I will never come back here again," Nasir said. "All I want is to sit with my mother, and my father and brothers and sisters."

A guard entered the room, one of the Hazaras. "Leave now," he said. Nasir took my pen and notebook and wrote his name and address. "Nasir Fahd Al-Riaz; Al-Dakhl Al-Mahdood, Al Saudia Arabia." He wrote it himself in English; even used the semicolon.

"Can I ask anything of you?" Nasir said from his spot on the floor. "Before they kill me, could you please get in touch with my parents?"

He moaned again, and the guard motioned for me to leave.

I never found Nasir after that, never found a record of his name—not in any of the Afghan prisons or even at Guantánamo Bay. After I left the country, I called one of my colleagues in Saudi Arabia and gave him Nasir's name and address. He never found the family.

THE VALLEY FLOOR was flanked by escarpments and scattered with yellow canisters the size of Pepsi cans. Smooth yellow cans, folded in the snow, lethal to the touch. Cluster bombs, the mess left behind. A pair of Afghan men walked among the unexploded cans, picking up pieces of shrapnel. Metal scavengers. "Osama was living there," Mohammad Zaman said. He pointed to a crater. "This was Osama's camp."

The camp, known as Melawa, had been a mujahideen base in the 1980s, a place the holy warriors had used to attack the Soviets. Melawa lay within a rugged stretch of valleys and caves called Tora Bora. In the 1990s, when Osama came back to Afghanistan, he'd come back to Melawa. Then, in December 2001, when the Americans had him cornered here, he departed again.

"I saw Osama many times," Zaman said. Zaman was long and thin and slightly haggard, not unlike the man he was describing. "Osama was rich like a king. He did not allow any of the villagers to come here. He did not give us jobs. As a result most of the people did not like him."

Zaman carried on with his work, stepping around the yellow canisters with the grace of a big cat.

I stepped into the crater. It contained the remnants of a building: a collapsed roof, splintered beams, fallen walls, papers and rubbish. Rummaging around, I found a shoe with a melted sole, a green jacket, a belt with bullets. I picked up a paperback with seared pages that was the size of the New York phone book. It was Al-Qaeda's training manual, written in Arabic. The book was a how-to on waging a terrorist campaign; there were diagrams for shooting down an airliner, blowing up a bridge, cleaning a rifle. I rustled in the wreckage and pulled out a notebook. This one was handwritten, in Uighur, a language of the Muslims of western China. Every page was filled with calculations, every letter carefully drawn, all the lines perfectly straight—the author had been a serious student. Throughout the book were diagrams that contained the English initials "TNT." On the inside front page, the student had jotted down some notes to himself. "Don't ask when the class is going to end," he wrote. "Always be honest."

I walked for a couple of miles across the Melawa valley. The landscape rolled out barren and sandy like a beach in winter. The only water came from a small stream that curled back up into the escarpments. Most of the caves were little more than tunnels, barely high enough for a man to crouch in.

I came to a group of men picking through splinters and bricks. One of the men, Sahar Gul, was holding up pieces of his home and looking them over as if they were relics from another age. Until recently, the rubble had been a hamlet called Khan-i-Merajuddin. "Everything is finished," Gul said, glancing up at me from the rutted ground where he stood. Six members of his family had died here, he said.

Osama had come on horseback to Khan-i-Merajuddin the night of November 30, Gul said. He came with a dozen Arabs to see a friend, Merajuddin, who'd kept the camp at Melawa supplied with food and mules. By then, the bombardment of Tora Bora was already well under way. The news about Osama that day reached the nearby bazaar. Then it reached a local warlord. Then it reached the Americans.

The bombs fell on Khan-i-Merajuddin at 4 a.m., a few hours after Osama had galloped off. The villagers were waking up for their Ramadan meal; some of them were already outside, which is what saved them. "I heard he was here for dinner, but I never saw anything with my own eyes," said Gul Nabi, another of the survivors. Nabi was sitting on a brick that had been part of his home. Most of his family—two wives and seven children—was dead, he said. Nabi had buried them in a new cemetery a few steps away. There was a son who survived, Ahmad, with a single leg. The cemetery contained forty-six graves, each marked by a plank of splintered wood. It was impossible to know who was in which tomb, Nabi said. "All these people in pieces," he said. "Six legs, six hands." The two men, Gul and Habi, stood at the head of the graveyard, wrapped in blankets against the cold wind.

A few days after the bombing, a helicopter landed in Khan-i-Merajuddin, Gul said. An American had gotten out. He had a beard. He took some photographs of the village, of the cemetery. Then he got back in the helicopter and flew away.

IN THE AFTERNOONS, I started running laps around the track at the Kabul sports stadium. It was the same stadium where I'd sat at midfield nearly four years before and watched the Talibs put a man to death. Running around the track, I tried to recall that scene, find some evidence of it in the grassless patch in the center. But by then the field had been taken over by men playing soccer, who trampled the spot over and over without giving it a moment's heed. From the stands, rising above us, stood a giant, larger-than-life mural of Ahmad Shah Massoud, the guerrilla leader with an architect's dreams. The Afghans would gather in the bleachers underneath it, wearing Chitrali caps just like his.

Massoud's men were in Kabul now, and one of them, Dr. Abdullah, had become foreign minister for the new government. Abdullah had become famous with reporters as the Afghan official with just one name—it used to drive the editors crazy back home. We need a second name, the editors would say, and so, in many newspapers, Abdullah became Abdullah Abdullah, the deputy foreign minister of the Northern Alliance. Abdullah was an ophthalmologist by training, yet with his pale face and dark beard and three-piece suits, he looked more like a silent movie star.

"There were times when I wasn't sure we were going to make it," Abdullah said, seated at the desk in his new office in the Foreign Ministry building. He was still getting used to his new circumstances. "We had nothing, you know. So many years. Even the satellite phones, we couldn't pay for them. There was no money. Nothing. Massoud and I, in the bad times, we used to wrestle. Massoud liked to wrestle. That was what we did. We wrestled each other on the floor. We would really go at it, really test each other on the floor. We were like children." Abdullah smiled, recalling the moment, and then he started to weep.

In the stadium years before, during the executions, the orphans would gather at the entrance and surge and squeal, and the Taliban guards would beat them back with switches and whips. Now, when I went running in the stadium, young boys were offering to shine my shoes. "Hey mistah! Hey mistah!" they called, and sometimes I thought they remembered me from before. When my newspaper opened an office in Kabul, we put two of the kids on the payroll. We called them "Team Shoeshine," and our only condition of employment was that in the morning they go to school. Kabul is a muddy city, and we had a lot of reporters, and the two boys cleaned our boots every afternoon and lined them up in rows outside the front door.

PART TWO

Baghdad, Iraq,
March 2003-

CHAPTER 4

Land of Hope and Sorrow

I'D BE TALKING to one of the Iraqis—about the situation, say, or about their lives, anything—when the conversation would take a turn. Just like that, without warning. And if I didn't try to steer the conversation back to where I'd started, if I just listened, they would tell me everything.

One day, a couple of years after the invasion, I met Yacob Yusef, the headmaster of Baghdad College, an old Jesuit high school on the northern edge of the capital. I found Yusef seated behind a wide desk, the kind you'd imagine a headmaster would have. He looked like a principal, too, with a slightly stiff demeanor and a coat and tie where everyone else was more casually dressed.

I'd gone to Baghdad College to flip through the old yearbooks, to ask about some of the school's long-departed students, Ahmad Chalabi and some of the others, who were vying to become prime minister in the new Iraqi state. It was December 2005. And Yusef was telling me what he remembered from the old days, before the Baathists had expelled the Jesuits. He told me about the old priests, Father O'Callaghan and Father Cronin and the rest, many of whom were buried in the yard outside. And he told me about Saddam's sons, Uday and Qusay, how they'd carried themselves around the school. "Qusay was very vulgar," Yusef said. "He wore his shirt unbuttoned to his waist and walked around like a bandit." On one of

Qusay's exams, Yusef said, he'd managed a score of 4 percent. "I could hardly read his handwriting." Yusef started telling me about the son of Barzaan al-Tikriti, one of Saddam's senior henchmen, when he suddenly started talking about his brother. Just changed the subject without notice, possibly in midsentence.

"One day, my brother disappeared, you know," Yusef told me. "Saadi. He vanished. 20 March 1988. I was searching everywhere for him. I could not sleep. My mother was in a panic. It was a terrible time.

"Three weeks later, I got a phone call," Yusef said. "I was taking my dinner. There was a man on the other end, a government official. He said, 'Are you Yacob?' Yes, I told him. And he said, 'Come and get the body of your executed brother.'

"You see, someone had written that Saadi was doing suspicious activities. It was nonsense, of course, but . . ." And he shrugged.

"So I drove to Kut, a two-hour drive from Baghdad, and I went to the state security building," Yusef said. "And Saadi's body was there, in the back of a refrigerated truck used to distribute agriculture products. The man who I had talked to on the phone was there, and he said to me, 'You are very lucky. Most people, they never get a body. You should be very grateful to us.' He waited for me to thank him. So I thanked him.

"And then this man said to me, 'I cannot release your brother's body just yet.' Why? I asked the man. And he said to me, 'Because you must pay for the bullets that we used to kill him.'"

By this time, Yusef's formal demeanor had collapsed and his cheeks were covered with tears.

"Two bullets they used to kill Saadi. Two bullets. And I paid for them. One hundred fifty dinars. And this man gave me a receipt. 'Here is the receipt for the bullets used for the execution of your brother.'"

Iraq was filled with people like Yacob Yusef. They weren't survivors as much as they were leftovers. The ruined by-products of terrible times. Once I was sitting with Mowaffak al-Rubaie, the national security adviser, and we were talking about the role of Islam in the new Iraqi constitution, how extensive it would be, whether the constitution would say that Islam would be "the source" of legislation or merely "a source," an issue that was considered quite important at the time, when Rubaie wrapped himself into a ball to show me how he had been hung from the ceiling. He'd been rolled into a ball by his interrogators and hung from the ceiling and spun like a fan. "For many hours," Rubaie said. They forced him to imitate a dog, too, to walk around his cell on all fours and bark.

Rubaie left Iraq after his imprisonment to become a neurologist in London. He didn't need to return to Iraq. Sitting in his shabby office in Baghdad, he used to complain with laughter at the pay cut he had taken to become national security adviser. "My children are bankrupting me," he laughed. One day I visited him in his home inside the Green Zone and noticed in his study an enormous bronze bust of Saddam's head in the corner, taken from one of the palaces, its eyes turned directly toward Rubaie's desk. I never asked him why.

Some days I thought we had broken into a mental institution. One of the old ones, from the nineteenth century, where people were dumped and forgotten. It was like we had pried the doors off and found all these people clutching themselves and burying their heads in the corners and sitting in their own filth. It was useful to think of Iraq this way. It helped in your analysis. Murder and torture and sadism: it was part of Iraq. It was in people's brains.

Sometimes I would walk into the newsroom that we had set up in *The New York Times* bureau in Baghdad, and I'd find our Iraqi employees gathered round the television watching a torture video. You could buy them in the bazaars in Baghdad; they were left over from Saddam's time. The Iraqis would be watching them in silence. Just staring at the screen. In one of the videos, some Baath party men had pinned a man down on the floor and were holding down his outstretched arm, while another official beat the man's forearm with a heavy metal pipe until his arm broke into two pieces. There was no sound in the video, but you could see that the man was screaming. None of the Iraqis in the newsroom said anything.

I tried to recall these things when I got impatient with

the Iraqis. Sometimes, when readers from America sent me
e-mails expressing anger at the Iraqis—why are they so
ungrateful? why can't they govern themselves?—I considered
sending them one of the videos.

A FEW DAYS after Saddam fell, when Baghdad was in flames,
I asked an Iraqi I had hired whether he knew of any interrogation centers. He shrugged and steered his battered Toyota to a
three-story dun-colored building nestled among a row of spa-
cious homes in Karada, a neighborhood a mile from my hotel.
The building was called Al-Hakemiya.

As we pulled up, other Iraqis were coming, Iraqis who had
spent time inside. They were coming back to see the place
where they had been tortured. Most of Al-Hakemiya was
taken up by ordinary-looking offices, with linoleum tiles and
gray file cabinets. Files were strewn about the floor, and many
of the desks were overturned and the windows smashed. But
the Iraqis I saw were roaming quietly through the halls, not
looting or smashing anything, as people were doing in the rest
of the capital at the time.

Upstairs, accessible by a back stairway, were about a hundred cells, dark and windowless, smelling of urine. In one of
the cells a red light protruded from the ceiling; the walls and
ceiling and floor were likewise painted red. At the end of a
hallway lay a pile of bindings and blindfolds.

The only elevator led to the basement and more cells.
There were shackles in one room, long cables in another. On
another floor I found a small operating room, with trays of
cutting instruments. Out back stood three portable morgues,
metal containers the size of toolsheds, with freezer units for
cold air. Inside each were six aluminum trays, each about six
feet long.

I followed an Iraqi man, Masawi, as he walked through the
building. He was an ordinary-looking man, with a mustache, a
checked shirt and slacks. He ran his hands along the walls. He
walked to the back and through a door and then up the stairwell that opened onto the corridor with the cells. Masawi
stopped at number 36.

"Here it is," Masawi said. "My cell."

The iron door had been pried open; Masawi stood at the edge but did not step inside. He lit a cigarette and told me he'd been an importer of luxury goods, jewelry and the like, a prosperous man, he said, when the secret police had come to his door one night, blindfolded him and brought him here. Al-Hakemiya was a first stop in the Baathist detention network, a place where Iraqis were tortured and interrogated before being sent to prisons like Abu Ghraib. But the files strewn about the floors suggested something else. There were receipts for funds and stock certificates and bank ledgers. There were files of title certificates and change-of-ownership forms. Whatever else it was, Al-Hakemiya was a shakedown operation. Masawi's family paid $25,000 to get him out. After six months.

"Being here gives me a doomed feeling," he said.

It carried over, the trauma. There was a tendency among Iraqis to see conspiracy everywhere, to reject the official version of whatever was said—to never even believe their own eyes. I'd go to car bombings, and all the Iraqis would be screaming, and usually I could find the engine block from the exploded car right away, smoldering in its own crater. Then I'd start talking to the Iraqis, and one of them would say it was the Americans who had blown up the building; an Apache helicopter had swooped down and fired a missile. And then the answer would spread through the crowd like a fever and within a few minutes the whole crowd would be saying it: the Americans did it, the Americans fired a missile. After a time, the Iraqis started becoming violent, and I had to stop going to bombings altogether.

It wasn't that the Iraqis were incapable of warmth or joy. Quite the opposite. There was no entering an Iraqi home, no matter how hostile your relationship with its host, without being embraced by a hospitality that would shame anything you could find in the West. Glasses of tea and sweets and fruits; your host would see you looking at something in his sitting room, a painting or a jacket hanging from a chair, and he'd pick it up and hand it to you. "A gift," he'd say. It was just that the past always seemed to overwhelm the present. In those first months, anyway. Before the present became unbearable, too.

One of the most popular people after the invasion was Khalid al-Ani, the keeper of the files. Ani had been the superintendent of the secret cemetery at Abu Ghraib. The cemetery was surrounded by a fence. The guards would bring the bodies out at night. Always at night. Ani kept the death certificates.

When Saddam's regime fell, Ani took all of his death certificates, hundreds and hundreds of them, to his home on Haifa Street in central Baghdad. And there, for many months after the invasion, Iraqis whose sons and daughters had disappeared lined up outside Ani's house to see if there was something he could tell them.

One of the people who went to see Ani was Abdul Razzaq al-Saiedi. His brother, Sadoon, had disappeared a decade before. He was an army officer and a mechanical engineer—his loyalty had never been questioned. But Sadoon's family was Shiite; Saddam's dictatorship was dominated by members of the minority Sunni sect. One night, Baath Party men were waiting outside his apartment as he came home from work. He was thirty-eight, the father of three children.

Razzaq searched frantically for Sadoon. The two were especially close: their father had died when Razzaq was two, and Sadoon had stepped in to raise his younger brother. "He was a knight," Razzaq said. "He dressed me in the morning; he made sure I had my books before I went to school."

Some time after his brother vanished, Razzaq discovered that Sadoon had listened to a cousin denounce Saddam for his reprisals against the Shiites following the 1991 Gulf War. The secret police had arrested Sadoon's cousin. And they took everyone he had talked to.

Pleading and working whatever connections she had, Sadoon's wife, Sundos, persuaded one of Saddam's assistants to meet her. It was ten months after Sadoon had been taken away. Sundos pleaded with the official for help; he seemed a decent man. At one point, he picked up a telephone and ordered the execution of Sadoon to be canceled—if it had not already been carried out. Sundos's heart leaped, but the Baath Party man couldn't hide what he believed to be true. "I don't know if he is alive or not," he told her.

Nine years later, following the collapse of the regime, Ani, the file keeper, reached into his archives and found the certificate marked with Sadoon's name. He'd been hanged six months after he was taken—which meant he'd been dead for four months on the day that Sundos had made her appeal. On the death certificate was his grave number, 303, in the cemetery behind the prison. Ani looked at Razzaq's other brother, Qassim, and asked for forgiveness. "I had no authority," he said. The next day Ani drove with Qassim to retrieve Sadoon's bones. They identified them by a chipped tooth.

Following Saddam's fall, Iraq became a theater of revenge, each murder inspiring another and then another. On Razzaq, the death of his brother had an unusual effect. He became the most gentle of souls: generous, humane, forgiving. But he walked with saddened eyes and stooped shoulders, like a man for whom life weighed too much.

I DROVE INTO Iraq from Kuwait on the day the invasion started in a rented GMC Yukon. The border had been locked down by American and Kuwaiti soldiers, but by midafternoon I was rolling into Safwan, a frontier town on the Iraqi side. I was enthusiastic and happy, eager to meet these new people whom the Americans had freed.

When I had ridden into the villages and towns in Afghanistan only months before, men threw off their turbans, kids dug up television sets. It was easy to believe that Iraq would be the same; that the people would be grateful, that they'd be pleased, that they would cheer when we arrived.

Safwan was broken and dirty and dead. The trees were gone and the grass had disappeared, and the buildings and the roads were the color of sand. As I drove in, the Iraqis stood on the roadside: slack-jawed, gaping, uncomprehending. Some of them were crying, some started moaning and cooing and ululating. A few of them cheered. Together the noises made for a feeling of grim ecstasy, happiness and sorrow rising together. People were calling to me in long guttural cries.

"Oooooo, peace be upon you, peace be upon you, oooooo," moaned Zahra Khafi, a sixty-eight-year-old mother of five. "I'm not afraid of Saddam anymore." Her face was dry and drained. The abaya draped over her body was as ragged as an old black flag.* Khafi threw her arms around me and looked up, the cheer on her face turning to shadow.

"Should I be afraid?" she said, mumbling and wiping her eyes. "Is Saddam coming back?" She started sobbing and calling out for her son.

Khafi was right to doubt her deliverance. In 1991, following the expulsion of Saddam's army from Kuwait, the Americans had goaded the Iraqis to rise up, and they did, across the Shiite south. And Saddam's troops had come in with their tanks and helicopter gunships and strafed and shot until their hold on the region was again secure.

Khafi's son, Massoud, vanished two years before. Age twenty-six. "Help me find my son," Khafi pleaded, clinging to my clothes. "Please help me." I sat with her for a while in the dirt outside her mud-brick home, and after I got up and walked around the town she trailed after me.

I had not gotten very far when another Iraqi approached. He was young and short with intelligent eyes.

"Help me," he said. "There, there are Saddam's men, and if you leave me they will kill me right now." His name was Najah Neema and he was trembling. That very morning, Neema said, he had been an Iraqi soldier. He'd torn off his uniform, thrown down his gun, and run away as the American army had poured in.

A crowd of Iraqis had filled in behind me. They were laughing and cooing and frowning, like a Greek chorus.

"Where are Saddam's men?" I asked Neema.

"There," Neema said, pointing a shaking hand. "Right over there. He is Mukhabarat."†

A middle-aged Iraqi man stood fifty paces away. He wore a checked short-sleeved shirt that seemed to have just been ironed and had a small trimmed mustache. I turned to walk over to him, and Neema, astonished, padded after me. The crowd turned and followed.

*A black overgarment worn by women.
†The Iraqi secret police.

"That guy over there says you are going to kill him," I said to the man in the checked shirt. He was a proud man, not used to such questions, and he gave me a look up and down and introduced himself: "Tawfik Muhammad," he said. "I am the headmaster at the school here." I could feel the breathing of the Iraqis behind me. Are you Mukhabarat? I asked him.

Muhammad turned and looked back and gave a little wave. "God willing," he said, "the Mukhabarat will return."

The crowd behind me gave a nervous laugh; I was not sure for whom.

One of the men stepped from the chorus and offered to talk. He seemed more sure of himself than the others, perhaps more educated. He lit a cigarette. "The name is Haider," he said in English. The chorus appeared uncomprehending.

"Let me tell you something, my friend. If Saddam's government came back, believe me, many of my friends here standing around me would turn me in. In Iraq, we have learned. I don't trust even my own brother."

The Americans were pouring into the town, in trucks and tanks and troop carriers, young and overfed and heavily armed. They were kids mostly, nineteen-year-olds from Kansas and North Dakota. It was the first day of the invasion, and they were having a good time. They used their Ka-Bar knives to slash the canvas Saddam posters, and they tied ropes around his statues and used their Humvees to pull them down. "Feels good," said Oscar Guerrero, nineteen, from San Antonio, running his blade through a canvas likeness of the Iraqi leader. "I wish he were here in person."

The Iraqis stood by watching in their dumbfounded way as the Americans tore up the Saddams. Not one stepped forward to help. They looked more like children then, standing back and watching the teenagers have their fun, enjoying the spectacle but preserving their deniability should their parents come home. "How would you like it if I were to cut up a poster of President Bush?" one of the villagers asked me, but he was drowned out by catcalls.

A crowd of Iraqis descended on Safwan Elementary School, carrying out the desks and tables and blackboards. One of them pried an air-conditioning unit from a wall and

loaded it into a cart. The Americans looked on and did nothing, looking at them and looking at me and giving a shrug. By sundown the Americans were gone.

WIJDAN AL-KHUZAI's cell phone would ring and a sinister voice would promise her a terrible end. Drop your campaign for the national assembly, the voice would tell her, or you are going to end up like the others. "Terrorists," Khuzai would say as she snapped her cell phone shut. Sometimes as she drove around Baghdad to campaign for votes, Khuzai would glance into the rear mirror and notice a car trailing behind.

And then she would get on with her campaign. It was the winter of 2004 and hope was still thriving, even in the ruins. The first election for the new National Assembly was only a month away. There was a new secular constitution and a quarter of the seats were being set aside for women.

Khuzai, forty-seven, belonged to the Independent Progressive Movement, one of the many parties with earnest-sounding names that had come together as the elections approached. She was one of those people found in dreadful countries the world over, fearless and determined and unwilling, for reasons always unclear, to make the same calculations of personal safety as everyone else. In the 1990s, Khuzai founded her own aid organization, a center for widows and mothers in Hillah, a Shiite city south of Baghdad. It was a brazen act; Khuzai neither asked for the government's permission nor received it. And sure enough, Saddam's men visited Khuzai after not very long and suggested with kind faces that she become a government informant. Khuzai could hardly have refused, so she fled to Kurdistan instead, which was by then under American protection. There she waited, for eight years, busying herself with her five children, until April 2003, when Saddam's regime came crashing down. Khuzai returned to Baghdad and, like many Iraqis, took up the promise of liberation. She wasn't alone; 7,471 Iraqis signed up to run for the 275 seats in the new parliament. Not many of them, though, were brave enough to campaign openly, like Khuzai, or to travel without armed guards. It wasn't like she didn't know what she was up against. "These people," she told her family, "I am their worst enemy."

An American patrol found her body on Christmas Eve 2004, on the road to Baghdad International Airport. Khuzai had been shot five times, once in the face. Her shoulder blades had been broken, and her hands had been cuffed behind her back so tightly that her wrists had bled. "The police said she had been tortured," her brother, Haider Jamal, told me.

I visited the Khuzai family at their home in Ghazaliya, which even then was one of the most dangerous neighborhoods in the capital. It was twilight, and people were milling about the street, looking at me and whispering as I climbed out of the car. "Quickly," my driver, Waleed, told me. I sat with three of Khuzai's sons, her brother and her sister. Sitting upright with perfect posture in a row of chairs, serving me sugary tea, Khuzai's sister, Nada, and the rest of Wijdan's family expressed confidence that the Iraqi police would track down Wijdan's killers. Their optimism struck me as tragic, perhaps not unlike Wijdan's. They were less optimistic about the country itself. "My sister figured that if she didn't do it, then no one would," Nada said.

People ask me what happened in Iraq, and I tell them the story of Wijdan al-Khuzai. Iraq might have been a traumatized country, it might have been broken, it might have been atomized—it might have been a mental hospital. But whenever the prospect of normalcy presented itself, a long line of Iraqis always stood up and reached for it. Thousands of them, seeing the opportunity in the events of April 2003, had set out to build an ordinary country with ordinary ways: newspaper editors, pamphleteers, judges, politicians and police officers. "Every morning, I come to work with a passion to serve my country," Aladeen Muhammad Abdul Hamza, a new policeman in the town of Diwaniya, told me in the summer of 2003.

And they went to the slaughter. Thousands and thousands of them: editors, pamphleteers, judges and police officers, and women like Wijdan al-Khuzai. The insurgents were brilliant at that. They could spot a fine mind or a tender soul wherever it might be, chase it down and kill it dead. The heart of a nation. The precision was astounding.

EARLY ON IN THE OCCUPATION I drove to Falluja after an American helicopter had gone down in a bean field. When I arrived I could see the remains of it, gnarled pieces of torn metal scattered across the rows of beans. It had been a big Chinook, the kind with two rotors. Sixteen American marines and soldiers had been inside, on their way to their midterm leaves. The insurgents had hit it with a missile. I was standing at the edge of the bean field, with a bunch of Iraqi schoolkids, trying for a better look. The Americans had cordoned off the crash site, and a pair of Humvees rumbled up on the same dirt road where we were standing. As they rolled by, one of the Americans reached into a bag and threw out a handful of candy.

"Don't touch it, don't touch it!" the Iraqi children squealed. "It's poison from the Americans. It will kill you."

The children jumped back as if the candy were radioactive.

Falluja was like that from the start, even before the big battle in November 2004. Anything the Americans tried there turned to dust. The Americans repaired a brick factory and the insurgents blew it up. The Americans painted a school and the insurgents shot the teachers. The Americans threw candy to the kids and the kids called it poison.

A few weeks after the helicopter crashed, I drove out again on the strength of a story I'd heard. It went like this: A group of American soldiers who had been on patrol ran into an angry mob. Rather than confront the mob, they ducked into the walled compound of Sadoon Shukar Mahmood, a forty-eight-year-old father of seven. The crowd passed and the Americans thanked him.

The next day, the Americans came back, pulling up in their armored personnel carriers. They wanted to thank Mahmood a second time. They handed some candy to his children. Months passed, and then, one morning, the first of many leaflets appeared under Mahmood's gate. "For your traitorous actions we will kill you," one of them said.

One day sometime after that, Mahmood stepped into the street to buy eggs and cream for breakfast. A yellow sedan without license plates pulled up next to him and two masked men inside opened fire. Mahmood died in the street.

I showed up a few days later. It had been a misunderstanding, Mahmood's family told me.

"People thought he was cooperating with the Americans," Dari Abu Hassan, a cousin, told me in the sitting room of Mahmood's home. "But he was not. He was not."

And so, three months later, as I drove into Falluja, I was not expecting much. The Americans, who were still formally occupying the country, had called on the Iraqis to hold caucuses to select representatives for provincial councils. It was an entirely American idea: the councils would have neither power nor money but somehow, the Americans figured, the Iraqis would take to them just the same. The Iraqis in Baghdad who were advising the Americans dismissed the idea as fanciful. "The word 'caucus' does not exist in Arabic," one of the Iraqis told me.

I drove in on Highway 10, the main drag that ran into the center of the city, and jotted down the graffiti that appeared on the walls. "Anyone who helps the Americans in any way is a dirty traitor," it said on a wall of the Falluja Primary School, "and that person is worth killing."

As I pulled into the Falluja Youth Center to witness the caucus, I was surprised to find not a tiny gathering but hundreds of Iraqis, lawyers and doctors and army officers and engineers, pushing and squeezing to get inside. By 10 a.m. two hundred Iraqis had made their way into the auditorium. Many of them were dressed in their best clothes.

One of the first candidates to speak was Sabah Naji, who climbed up onstage and gave a modest address.

"If you believe that I am the better candidate, then I ask that you vote for me," Naji said. "And if you think my opponent is the better man, vote for him."

For a moment, I felt as if I were back in Miami, at the county commission that I'd covered once as a reporter. For a moment, I wondered about the fate of the country I was in.

After Naji's opponent, Saidullah Mahdi, gave a similar speech, the chairman of the caucus, Muhanad Ismail, took the stage to make an unexpected announcement.

"An objection has been raised by someone in the audience that Mr. Naji was a high-ranking member of the Baath Party," Ismail said. Naji, he said, had risen to the party rank of a *shuba*, which made him a senior member of the party and technically barred from holding any kind of government post in the new Iraq.

A murmur swept through the crowd. Ismail had more to say. "But I also have in my possession a Baath Party document listing the names of party members who were regarded as disloyal and unenthusiastic," he said. "And Mr. Naji's name is here on that list." He held the paper up over his head.

Another murmur. A man stood up in the audience.

"And Mr. Naji was expelled from the Baath Party just before the war," the man said. "I know that to be true."

With that, Ismail, the presider, called for a vote. Each man in the room wrote down the name of his preferred candidate on a ballot, a piece of plain paper that carried the official seal of Anbar Province. One by one they rose and dropped their ballots into a metal box.

When the votes were tallied on the blackboard, Naji had bested Mahdi by a wide margin. Afterward, many of the lawyers and engineers said they had chosen Naji for his youth and energy, and that his ties to Saddam's party didn't matter so much.

"What's the big deal?" Abdul Satar, one of the lawyers, told me afterwards in the lobby. "Just about everyone here was a member of the Baath Party. And anyway, they kicked him out."

The lone unhappy man at the Falluja Youth Center was Ghazi Sami al-Abid, a rotund Sunni sheikh who had come dressed in a kafiya and a flowing white robe. Abid owned hundreds of acres and an ornate mansion on the Euphrates with a dock and two Jet Skis. Whenever he drove to his office in Baghdad, he wore expensive Western suits.

Abid had won one of the early rounds of voting and then lost in his bid for one of the council seats later in the day. And so it turned out that this powerful sheikh who had gotten wealthy under Saddam would not be sitting on the Anbar Provincial Council after all.

"I am a wealthy man, a rich man. I deserve to be elected," Abid told me after the vote at a lunch in his house. "And then some little money changer comes along and beats me."

Abid paused, and then smiled as if some revelation had come to him.

"I guess that's American-style democracy, isn't it?"

Two months later two SUVs carrying four American contractors drove into an ambush a few blocks from the Falluja Youth Center. The insurgents opened fire at close range on two Mitsubishi Pajeros, killing all four contractors. A crowd gathered, men with guns and without, fathers with children, and they dragged the corpses from the Pajeros, finally stringing up the blackened remains of two of them on the bridge that spanned the Euphrates. Television cameras captured the Iraqis cheering, some of them slapping the bodies with the bottoms of their shoes—in that part of the world a terrible insult. A few days later, American marines attacked and then retreated, handing Falluja to a group of gun-wielding Islamists who set up something called the Mujahideen Shura. Overnight, Falluja became its own little Islamic emirate, and a car-bomb factory to boot. The Americans waited seven months, then invaded Falluja and destroyed it.

Sometimes I wonder what happened to all those Iraqis who crowded into the Falluja Youth Center that winter day. Probably they fled or were killed, but I don't know. All those lawyers, editors, army officers, politicians, police officers, filling out their ballots with their official Anbar stamps. All those hopeful little pieces of paper.

CHAPTER 5

I Love You

March 2003

T HE FACES OF the Iraqi soldiers were veiled by orange
dust from the passing storm. Old mattresses and tins
of unopened food mingled with their bodies in the
trench. The Iraqis had been waiting on the side of the highway for the American convoy to drive by, and they'd opened
fire. It didn't last very long: a couple of shots from one of the
big American guns and then silence.

Dr. Wade Wilde, an American doctor, walked around the
air-conditioned tent the Americans had erected with amazing
speed on the side of the highway. It was already filled with
wounded Iraqi soldiers. Wilde was a soft-spoken man from
Cheyenne, Wyoming, and a pediatrician in Virginia. Some of
the Iraqis were already on their elbows, watching him. "The
officers threatened to shoot us unless we fought," one of the
Iraqis said. None of the others protested. "They took out
their guns and started shooting."

Wilde stepped outside. It was early morning in the Iraqi
desert, the invasion six days old. A layer of clouds shrouded
the sky in pale gray. Wilde nodded toward a green blanket on
the ground next to the tent. The blanket was full and still.

"We think he was shot by his own," the doctor said.

Under the blanket lay an Iraqi soldier. By the rise and fall
of the blanket I could see he was still breathing. His head was

swathed in a pillow of gauze Wade had made for him, and so his face was invisible. The gauze around his head was so voluminous that he looked like an alien from space. The marines had found him after the firefight in one of the Iraqi trenches. There was a bullet lodged in the back of his head. A small-caliber shell, Wilde said, probably a pistol, fired at close range. Much of the Iraqi's skull had come apart.

"If he had been hit by an M-16, it would have taken his whole head off," Wilde said, looking over at the blanket. "Seems like it was an Iraqi gun."

The Iraqi had reached a state of human existence that Wilde referred to as "expectant," meaning that although he was still alive there was nothing the doctors could do to save him. Wilde had been unable to extract the bullet. He had given the soldier an injection of morphine and laid him down in a quiet spot next to the tent.

"We've tried to make him as comfortable as possible," Wilde said, "and let the wound run its course."

I DROVE NORTH toward Baghdad in my rented SUV. The burning oil wells glowed orange along the far horizon. On the side of the highway I counted the little heaps of Iraqi army uniforms left along the way. Tanks and trucks lay abandoned; the trenches had gone barren.

I came upon a group of marines who'd taken three Iraqis prisoner. They'd deserted some weeks before, they told the Americans, and had been living on tomatoes and sleeping under a bridge. They had been waiting for the Americans to come. The marines were driving up the road when they spotted the three men waving a long stick with a dirty bedsheet tied to it. The Americans had spread out blankets inside a ring of barbed wire, and had given the Iraqis peanut butter and crackers.

"We are not cowards, but what is the point?" Ahmed Ghobashi, an Iraqi colonel from Baghdad, told me through the barbed wire. "I've got a rifle from World War II. What can I do against American airplanes?"

Colonel Ghobashi talked on for a while, detailing his participation in Saddam's wars. "War upon war," he said. He called himself a professional soldier and a family man, and he said he had not joined the military to engage in fanciful adventures.

"He doesn't give us enough to eat, he doesn't pay us. Then he starts this thing with the Americans and tells us to defend the country against the invader. Tell me what is the sense in that?"

Colonel Ghobashi bit into one of the American crackers and shook his head.

"I believe Saddam is an American agent," he said.

A GROUP OF IRAQIS WAS MOVING along a road that ran along the Euphrates. Cobra gunships were circling a few hundred yards away over the middle of the city the Iraqis had fled. The reports were confusing but an American supply truck had taken a wrong turn and driven directly into Nasiriya. Iraqi militiamen had killed some of the Americans and taken the rest prisoner. Among them was a nineteen-year-old from West Virginia named Jessica Lynch. The Iraqis walking out of the city were Shiites, the people the Americans told themselves they were liberating, but the Iraqis snarled as they approached an American checkpoint.

"No Iraqi will support what the Americans are doing here," a man who called himself Nawaf said. "If they want to go to Baghdad, that's one thing, but now they have come into our cities, and all Iraqis will fight them."

"Yes, yes!" the crowd of Iraqis behind him said.

Mustafa Muhammad Ali, a medical assistant at Saddam Hospital inside Nasiriya, shoved his way to the front of the pack. He said he'd spent much of the morning hauling dead and wounded civilians out of buildings that had been bombed by the Americans. He said he had no love for the Iraqi dictator, but he said the Americans had forfeited his support.

"I saw how the Americans bombed our civilians with my own eyes," Ali said, and he held up a bloodied sleeve. "I dragged them into the ambulances myself."

"You want to overthrow Saddam Hussein's regime?" he asked me. "Go to Baghdad. What are you doing here?"

One of the Americans manning the checkpoint, First Sergeant Michael Sprague, stepped in. "You'll get your country back," he said.

Someone translated and the crowd hissed.

Then a man named Mohsen Ali stepped forward and pointed at my notebook. Despite his reduced circumstances, he carried himself with greater pride than the others. Write this down, he instructed me.

"Saddam is a knight—he is a knight," Ali said, and the other Iraqis quieted considerably on hearing this. "There is no one like him in the world."

I reminded Ali that Saddam had killed tens of thousands of his fellow Shiites a dozen years before, in the uprising after the first Gulf War. Many thousands in this very city, I said. He practically spit on me.

"In Iraq if there is a leader who is fair, he will be killed," Ali said. "He must be tough, or he will be killed the very next day."

AT THE BASE CAMP of the Fifth Marine Regiment, just outside of Diwaniya, two sharpshooters sat on a berm and swapped tales of combat. They'd just climbed off a helicopter, and their eyes were aflame.

"We had a great day," Sergeant Eric Schrumpf told me. "We killed a lot of people."

"Yeah," Corporal Mikael McIntosh said.

All up and down the highway to Baghdad, the shooters said, the Iraqi fighters were mixing with the civilians, jumping out of houses and cars to shoot, then running away. Some of the fighters wore strange black uniforms. Fedayeen Saddam was what the officers were calling them, a militia of irregular fighters.

"These soldiers don't even have socks," McIntosh said.

Schrumpf and McIntosh said they were frustrated by the fedayeen's practice of using unarmed women and children as shields. "Cowardly but effective," Schrumpf said. He was only twenty-eight. Both men said they had declined to shoot several times for fear they might hit civilians.

"It's a judgment call," Corporal McIntosh said. He was twenty. "If the risks outweigh the losses, then you don't take the shot."

Schrumpf nodded.

But in the heat of a firefight, the calculus sometimes changed. A shot not taken in one set of circumstances might suddenly become a life-or-death necessity. There were a few of those moments today.

"We dropped a few civilians," Sergeant Schrumpf shrugged, "but what do you do?"

To illustrate, the sergeant offered a pair of examples.

"There was one Iraqi soldier, and twenty-five women and children," he said, "I didn't take the shot."

But more than once, Sergeant Schrumpf said, the odds were in his favor. One of the fedayeen fighters would be standing among two or three civilians. Usually it worked out: Schrumpf shot him. Not always. He recalled one such moment, in which he and some other men in his unit opened fire. He watched one of the women standing near an Iraqi soldier drop to the ground.

"I'm sorry," Sergeant Schrumpf said, shaking his head. "But the chick was in the way."

TOMMY SMITH sat alone in his ambulance, in the driver's seat, staring ahead into the distance. The streets were quiet, scattered with bullet casings and broken glass. Most of the other marines, thousands of them, had continued toward Baghdad.

"All the stretchers were full of blood," Smith said. "I was shooting guys with morphine. Pretty much all of them had gunshot wounds."

With blond hair and a boyish voice, Smith was twenty-one but looked even younger. He was from Brooklyn, with a slight accent, and we talked about New York for a bit. Then he walked around the back of the ambulance and opened the door to the cabin. "I just got done cleaning it a few minutes ago," he said. "It was full of blood."

At the outskirts of Baghdad, Smith's battalion had run into an ambush. An American tank, hit by an Iraqi rocket, had burst into flames and blocked the road. Then the driver of Smith's ambulance, Corporal Luke Holden, took a bullet in the middle finger of his left hand.

Smith took over, with Holden in the passenger seat, when he was shot again, this time in his right hand as he hung it out the window. With bullets zinging past, Smith carried Holden to the cabin, then weaved his ambulance in and out of gunfire, stopping to pick up wounded marines. In the middle of the firefight, Smith picked up eight of his bleeding comrades; one of them, a captain, had been shot in the face. Then Smith felt a bullet hit his own chest. It felt like someone had punched him, he said. When he recovered, he looked down and saw a hole in his tunic where the bullet had gone in. It hit his Kevlar vest. The hole was there still.

"I didn't think we were going to make it," he said. "They hit us with rockets. You don't know where they're coming from."

Smith's voice was so gentle, and he seemed so young, that I felt moved to comfort him in the way that I would a child. I wanted to hug him, but I couldn't very well do that, so I handed him my satellite phone. It was a Saturday morning in Brooklyn.

"I'll have some stories for you when I get home," Smith said into the phone. "I love you, too, Ma."

THE MARINES HAD smeared war paint on their faces, flat black and olive green. They had given their daggers a last lethal edge. And by the time they crossed the Diyala River they had left nothing untouched. The landscape was littered with smoldering Iraqi bodies. The air stank from the smell of so many things afire. Only the stray dogs, nosing around the flesh and flames, appeared to be alive.

My truck crept down a narrow lane marked by little flags, a path through a minefield. Shards of metal and bullet cases cracked under the wheels. On the left, the bottom half of a corpse lay in the dirt; a few feet away, a human head. It was twilight.

The bodies of three Iraqi soldiers lay at the foot of a stone wall. They were pressed tight against it, cheeks and arms in a tangle together. They had been running when the bullets found them, and as they went down they had kept moving for-

ward. Pressed against the wall, the three men looked as if they had been trying to crawl inside of it, to become one with the stone.

All through the desert, the Iraqis had run backward. In a few places they had stood and fought, one shot, two shots, and then they had run. Here, at the outskirts of the capital, the three Iraqis had tried to flee, but there was nowhere left to go. So here they lay together, in a last contorted pose.

Over against the fence were piles of black boots and old military uniforms, discarded by deserters. I picked up a small piece of paper blowing in the breeze.

"Oh God, creator of all things in the world," went the handwritten note, "please bind up all my wounds."

With the fighting over, the marines were suddenly not so buoyant anymore. They had taken off their war paint and they were no longer joking. "It's a little sobering," Captain Sal Aguilar told me, looking at a field full of dead Iraqis. "When you're training for this, you joke about it, you can't wait for the real thing. Then when you see it, when you see the real thing, you never want to see it again."

I felt as though I'd seen something the marines did not want me to see. As night fell the colonel came over and told me in a voice that was not negotiable that I was no longer welcome. "Get out of my unit," he said, so I drove back through the darkness and across the river and behind the lines.

It was a beautiful night. The landscape was still. The dead were no longer visible. I lay in the road, next to a box of bullets and the corpse of a dog, and fell asleep.

AS THE AMERICANS streamed toward Baghdad, the Iraqis were fleeing south. They were crammed into buses, cars and taxis, all flying southward on Highway 6. One Iraqi was driving himself and his family on a motorcycle and sidecar, another in a clattering 1954 Dodge pickup with everything he owned stuffed inside. A third man, standing in the bed of another pickup, raced down the highway shouting what appeared to be the only words he knew in English.

"George Bush!" he cried, whizzing past.

Even some Iraqi soldiers, hoping to make their escape, had jumped aboard the backs of trucks. Many Iraqis, eyeing the American convoys, waved white flags, some fashioned out of bedsheets or T-shirts. One woman waved a pair of boxer shorts.

"You have saved us from him," exclaimed Alawih Hussein, pausing as he drove his battered red Toyota out of the capital. "It is finished. It is finished. We want you to kill him, as he has been killing us."

Hussein's wife, who sat next to her husband, was so effusive in her joy that she paused several times to suck on a pocket inhaler.

"I love you," she said in English, panting and weeping. "I love you."

CHAPTER 6

Gone Forever

I WOKE UP in the shadowy cool of a palm grove in the
southeastern corner of the capital and drove in at dawn.
The marines had been expecting a fight but by sunrise it
was clear there wasn't any Iraqi army at all. I left the marines
in the palm grove. After a few minutes I spotted some Iraqis
and spun the car in their direction; they'd converged on the
United Nations headquarters on the edge of town. It looked
like the aftermath of an outdoor concert: paper strewn about
the floors, desks overturned, windows smashed, walls punched
out. The Iraqis were carrying off refrigerators and ceiling fans
and boxes of UN rations, which included split-pea soup and
strawberry shortcake. They were piling the stuff into the
trucks the UN had left behind and they were stealing them,
too. The last Iraqis were bounding up the stairs with the desperate looks of shoppers at Christmas worried there'd be
nothing left.

I found an American colonel on the second floor. He was
walking slowly and without much purpose; bewildered, perhaps, by the disappearance of the enemy he'd prepared for.
For a time, the colonel watched the Iraqis as they carried off
the last of the merchandise, and then, when it was gone, he
ordered his men to close up the building. The colonel walked
to the road and looked at the stream of Iraqis pushing carts
laden with the offerings of a nearby department store. They
were waving happily to us. "There obviously is a vacuum of

public authority," he said. Then he offered a small smile. "I wonder if they like us, or if they are just happy to loot the stuff."

I kept driving, weaving through the throngs, without much idea where I was going. Plumes of smoke rose along the horizon. I felt the strangeness of a place in the first minutes of momentous change. I passed what appeared to be a bank; people were pawing at clouds of Iraqi dinars spiraling in the air. I stopped at the Oil Ministry. There was an American tank parked out front, making it the only government office I found that day to receive any sort of protection. Even so, the Iraqis were helping themselves, carrying off desks and lamps. The Americans looked on. The Iraqis were working together, smiling and amazed. Not everyone, though. I found myself standing next to an elderly, well-dressed man. He was shaking his head; he was already from another era. "I am here to collect my paycheck," he said. His name was Hassan Ali. He looked at his countrymen carting out the furniture and twisted his face. "I am angry. Very angry."

I pulled into a Sunni mosque called Al-Ani, and a throng of Iraqis backed me up against a wall and started shouting. "You've unleashed these people, the lowest people," a man yelled into my face from three inches away. His breath was buffeting my face. He was referring to the looters, who he said had come from the neighborhood next door, Saddam City, a sprawling Shiite slum that contained nearly half of Baghdad, and which by the end of the week would be renamed for a famous ayatollah. "It is their religion to steal," said a man named Ali Nasr. "This is what they preach in their mosques." Another voice rose from behind. "Only for oil," he said. Soon, driving some more, I came upon Ibrahim Hussein, a sixty-one-year-old taxi driver, seated in a plastic chair outside his home and taking in the view. Beyond him, the street lay abandoned, strewn with glass and metal shards. Across the road lay the Ministry of Telecommunications, smoldering from air-strikes. "These people need someone tough," Hussein said, not rising from his chair. "A soft man will not be able to govern. He will need a stick."

I drove some more. The faces of the Iraqis showed as much surprise as happiness, a sudden lightness in a new world none of them yet understood. Two men, Haider Jasser and Malik Salem, walked the street together and looked on at the unfolding excitement. That very morning, Jasser and Salem said, they had woken in a Baath Party jail, nursing scars from beatings they had received for crimes they claimed not to remember. An American tank had come to the prison gates, the men said, and a soldier had climbed out and told them to go home. Jasser and Salem, now free, tried their English phrases on me, tossing them out like little thank-you notes. "Hello mister," Haider said. "Okay okay. Thank you very much. Thank you, George Bush."

I encountered a blacksmith, Muhammad Abbas, standing with his two young children at the base of a sixty-foot statue of the Iraqi dictator. A crowd had gathered round the green copper likeness along with some American soldiers. Abbas's eyes tilted upward in blinkered wonder as a group of marines tied a noose around the statue and began to pull. The metal Saddam was pointing upward and out.

"Good," Abbas said, his eyes showing both pleasure and fear.

The marines gunned the engine on their personnel carrier, to which the metal Saddam was tied, and the statue tilted and bent. Abbas, warming to the exercise, urged the marines to pull harder.

"All the way down," he said, eyes flashing.

And then Saddam snapped at the knees, and he came crashing down, and the crowd that had gathered, and Abbas, too, cheered and whooped and clapped.

"Very good," Abbas said, reaching for his daughter and son. "A good day."

A couple of miles away, thoroughbred racehorses were bursting out of their stables and rearing up, their eyes bulging with terror. They were tall and sleek, of great strength and the highest breeding, and their coats shimmered in the afternoon light. A crowd of Iraqis were circling, trying to corral them, and they were leading them away. "For my family," one of them cried, hand on the reins, and the others laughed with him. I could only imagine what they meant.

The building from which the horses were escaping contained the office of the Iraqi Olympic Committee. Despite its name and the Olympic rings on its archway, the building had served as the personal fief of Uday, one of Saddam's sons and the one with the most deranged reputation. Uday had brought his women here, whom he sometimes kidnapped from weddings. He also brought his prisoners here, sometimes athletes whom he tortured for losing their games. He had his parties at the Olympic Committee's bar, waving his guns and cavorting with his imported prostitutes; the videos of those parties started showing up in Baghdad's bazaars only a few weeks later. And it was the place where Uday kept the racehorses that were now rearing and screaming.

The Iraqis who were not chasing the stallions were carrying off the contents of the office: computers and rolled-up carpets and even things they appeared not to understand, like computer switchboards. One man carried a polo mallet and helmet and a pair of leather jodhpurs. A set of horseshoes dangled on his forearm. He pushed an office chair that carried a desktop computer.

Watching this scene from a few paces away was a platoon of American marines. A young lieutenant stood with his men, looking on with a troubled expression. I asked him why he was letting the Iraqis destroy the building, destroy the city. "I don't have orders," he said, shaking his head. "No orders."

The lieutenant watched a little while longer and, growing more agitated, he began running back and forth along a row of his men. He said something to one of his sergeants, then something to someone else. I approached again.

"Not now," he said. He was lining the men up in a row. I stood back. Something was going to happen. He gave an order.

"Ready, front!"

About forty marines stood at attention, looking ahead, past the Olympic Committee headquarters.

"Present, arms!

"Order, arms!"

The lieutenant turned and looked toward the Olympic Committee.

"Forward, march!"

The marines began to march toward the Olympic Committee in a wide row. The lieutenant was darting back and forth, calling "two-three-four-march." The men carried their M-16s at their sides, pointing them at nothing.

The column of marines moved not into the crowd but past it, with none of the marines turning their heads. Their boots struck the ground in rough unison. It was like a parade, one meant to scare the Iraqis away. As the marines passed, a couple of the Iraqis glanced over, and one or two stopped working. The rest continued plundering.

"Column, halt!" the lieutenant shouted.

The marines stopped. Next to them, a group of locals were standing in the bed of a truck, lifting an office table inside.

"About face!" the lieutenant yelled.

The marines turned on their heels.

"Ready, front!"

"Forward, march!" and the men began again, marching past the party, whose members now, on the second pass, did not bother to look up.

THE LOOTERS POURED into the cluster of clinics known as Al-Kindi, disappearing down its corridors and reemerging with medicines and beds and surgical instruments. As the men departed with their booty, new looters took their place. They came in waves. En masse they turned to one of the last untouched hospitals, a one-story building called Al-Wasiti. The mob surged then stopped at the metal gate and banged on it—bang, bang, bang, bang. They could have easily kicked it open.

Yasir Mousawi, a young doctor, sleepless after many days, was sitting quietly in a plastic chair. Hearing the banging, he rose and walked to a supply closet and took out a Kalashnikov and walked outside and fired a single shot into the air. In a few seconds the crowd was gone.

Al-Wasiti was a filthy, chaotic place, and, on this chaotic day, the best Baghdad had to offer. It was filled with patients, gun-shot, broken and deathly ill, led there by nurses and doctors from the city's other hospitals, many of which had ceased to function. The beds were filled and dozens lay in the lobby, on tables and stretchers, wailing and gasping. Various liquids mingled on the tile floor.

In one bed lay a young man, Amran Adnan, nineteen, shot through the head while he sat on his front porch. No one seemed to know what had happened; perhaps, his parents said, it was the neighborhood men celebrating the return of electricity by firing their guns. Adnan lay in his bed, blinded, his head and face covered in gauze. His parents sat at his side, while Adnan's thirteen-year-old brother, Muhammad, waved away the flies.

"His eyes burst," Dr. Nuis Hassab said, looking on.

His parents turned to me. "Can you take him to America? In America they can restore his vision. Can you take him?"

In another room was Abdul Wali, fifteen, whose intestines and stomach had been shredded by an American cluster bomb. Doctors said he would recover. Still, the frustration among the doctors seemed to be swelling with the disorder in the halls.

"We are using medicines here that are of only historical interest in the West," Dr. Ahmed Abdullah said. He was slumped behind his desk. "And without electricity we have no water, and we cannot sterilize our instruments. The nurses, they hand them to me and tell me they are clean, but I don't believe them.

"I don't believe anything," Dr. Abdullah said, shaking his head. "I don't believe anything."

At 1 p.m. a man was carried inside the hospital's lobby bleeding from his neck and shoulder. The orthopedists and plastic surgeons sprang toward the new patient. With no emergency room, they began working on the man in the lobby itself, amid the wailing patients who had filled it to overflowing.

The man's name was Kamal Sultan. The doctors flailed about with their outdated equipment. They massaged Sultan's chest, and his heart murmured and skipped. They soaked up his blood with bandages and napkins, but it kept spilling onto the floor.

"Electricity!" one of the doctors shouted, his hands and forearms soaked in Sultan's blood. "Where is the electricity?"

Amid the chaos, one of the orderlies wheeled a suction machine to the foot of Sultan's stretcher, hoping to clear his lungs of water and blood. But the plastic machine refused to start without the electricty. Where is the generator? someone asked.

Sultan, with one shoe on and the other on the floor, clung to the last bits of his life. The orderly wheeled up another suction device, trailing a tangle of extension cords and plugs and exposed wires. He knelt down to find a connection.

"Where is the electricity?" the doctor yelled again, as the nurses beat and worked Sultan's chest.

In twenty minutes, Sultan was dead.

"Finished," one of the doctors said.

I discovered that Sultan had been sitting in his car at an intersection in Baghdad when an unidentified man approached and fired. In Sultan's pockets, the doctors found $4,500 in American bills, an impossible sum for an ordinary Iraqi.

Sultan's sister entered the hospital, spotted his body, threw herself on top of it and began to wail.

I saw a couple of Iraqis step toward the door, and I followed them outside. It was a father and his daughter. Halla Ibrahim, age six, had fallen down while playing in her yard, and her father had brought her here to have a splint placed on her tiny arm. Al-Wasiti was, after all, an orthopedic hospital.

"I've been trying to calm her down," Hamad Ibrahim said. "She is terrified of the dying. She is terrified of the soldiers and their guns. She is afraid of the bombs."

He ran his hand through his daughter's hair. Halla was holding her father by the pants leg.

"She is a quiet girl," Hamad said, himself thirty-five. "I'm an old man, and these things I can't bear."

AMAL AL-KHEDAIRY STOOD in the ruins of her waterfront home and cursed the people who had rained the bombs on her. Hers was a full-throated, almost lunatic fury, sharpened by the Western-educated voice that carried it. For years, Khedairy had run Baghdad's most luminous artistic center, one that flourished under Saddam. It was a place dedicated to bringing the worlds of Occident and Orient together.

"This is our American liberation!" said Khedairy, seventy, as she waded through the half-burned books of her second-story library. "I never thought you would do it. I went to the American School. I believed in your moral values. And every night you bombed. Every night, I ran through the streets, an old woman in my nightgown. Look at my library!"

In a city of flat, squat buildings spare of trees and greenery, Khedairy's home was a luxurious island: two levels, floor-to-ceiling windows, a garden full of jasmine and bougainvillea and date palms. The Tigris River meandered past her back-yard.

Khedairy's house was in Suleik, one of Baghdad's wealthier enclaves, known for its intellectuals. The house was filled with cultural artifacts, or it had been. I thumbed through record-ings of Beethoven and Wagner among the antiquated LPs; there were collections of Turkish and Arabic music as well. A handcrafted wooden grille formed one of the walls of the sit-ting room, and the books on her shelves included works on Oriental architecture and French literature.

Khedairy's house sat just across the Tigris from the head-quarters of the Mukhabarat, the Iraqi secret police, and this was her misfortune. Night and day for weeks the bombs fell there, most of them finding their target, some of them not. At least one had missed; the back end of Khedairy's house was splayed open to the world. The windows were shattered, the rain had come in and the LPs and the books had been blown apart and scattered.

"I want you to come and see what they have done to my institute," she said, tugging on my shirt. The institute was downtown, a mile or so away. "It's all gone: the paintings, the piano, the carpets, the music. All looted by these animals. Our liberation!"

For weeks, Khedairy said, she fled her home when the bombing started, dashing to a friend's house blocks away, where she felt safer.

This was not the first time Khedairy had returned to her home since the invasion, now a week old. Nor was it the first time she had seen the wreckage. During the invasion, she had returned every day to her garden to water the plants and palms. Perhaps it was my unexpected entrance into her home, the appearance of an American, that had set her emotions tumbling. As I stood by, she ranted and wept amid the ruins of her home, picking up a tattered book here, a record album there.

"We will kill them all one day, Rumsfeld and every one of them," she said. "Look at what they have done to my library."

I felt bad for Khedairy but I wondered how she had flourished under Saddam. Perhaps this was unfair, perhaps it was malicious of me, but I couldn't help but wonder. The Mukhabarat building lay just down the street. I meant to ask Khedairy, but she was lost in misery and confusion and I thought that it was perhaps not the best time to inquire.

We sat on her couch. Khedairy was a graduate of London University, a professor who had taught the literature of Britain and France. The bombing of her house, the ransacking of her cultural center and the looting of the national museum were all connected, Khedairy said. They were evidence of an American plan to deface her country's culture and steal its treasures.

"Why else would they do this?" she asked.

For all the bombs, Khedairy's house—and Khedairy's neighborhood—had not yet been looted. But the thieves were coming closer. For the past two weeks a group of her neighbors, armed with guns, had stood guard over their houses. But Khedairy believed that her home would not be safe for much longer. In recent days, she said, American soldiers had moved closer to her neighborhood, and Khedairy was convinced that they would allow the looters to roam freely through her home.

"They follow the tanks," Khedairy said. "The Americans come in, and they let the looters do as they wish. That is what they did at the museum. That is what they did at my institute. My neighborhood is next."

Not all of Khedairy's anger was directed at foreigners; she had saved a good deal of it for her fellow Iraqis. As we arrived at the steps of her cultural center, she surprised a half-dozen Iraqi men picking over the last of the artifacts and paintings that had not been stolen.

"My God, I'll kill you!" she growled, and the young men

scampered out the door. In her anger, Khedairy picked up a piece of broken pottery and hurled it into the back of one of the men. "How could this nation produce such sons?"

The devastation wrought by the looters was complete: books and sheet music lay scattered across the floor, lamps and fans had been torn from the ceiling. Upstairs, a recent exhibit of artwork by Iraqi and Japanese children lay in tatters.

Khedairy paused before a decorative wrought-iron door, one of the few things that appeared intact. She fingered it, studied it, swung the thing on its hinge.

"I will have to save this," she said, "before someone takes it."

I PULLED UP TO the gates of the presidential palace in Tikrit just before the marines. It was a stately, magnificent place, taking up two miles along the Tigris. There were ninety buildings in all, including homes, offices, hotels and servant quarters. For all the upheaval outside, swans and ducks were still swimming in its lakes.

I stepped into Saddam's personal study, a wide room of marble floors, cathedral windows and magnificent carpets. The room was empty and quiet. There, on a shelf, sat *The Collected Works of Saddam Hussein*, volumes 1 through 10, barely cracked. In the next room was a tablet of paper, imposing in its plainness, labeled simply "The President." In the bathroom were signs of a hurried exit: a cabinet door open, a crumpled towel on the floor, a pair of men's boxer shorts still hanging on the rack.

I was joined by a group of Iraqis, locals who'd never set foot in the place.

"All my life I have dreamed of this palace," said Ahmed Farhan, a twenty-two-year-old student. He looked at a chandelier and ran his hands along the books. "We were never allowed to see this."

Farhan and I walked together down a long marble hallway; I tried to see the place through his eyes. He wore a white dishdasha and sandals. He said his father owned a small farm about a mile away. Farhan walked wide-eyed down the corridor, stopping here and there to admire something.

"I didn't know anyone could lead such a life," he said.

He spotted an Arabic romance novel, with a pouting, large-breasted brunette reclining on its cover, and he picked it up. He pocketed some AA batteries for his shortwave radio. But that was all.

The first marines came trickling in. For a few hours, everyone walked together amid the splendor, Americans and Iraqis, everyone wearing the same astonished looks. There were cavernous ceilings, massive chandeliers and dining tables long enough to seat a hundred people. All of it was plated in gold or bedecked in sequins or spangles or panels of oak.

"Wow, this looks like Las Vegas," a young American captain said, standing on a balcony and looking out on the panoramic grounds.

Within a couple of hours, the serious looters arrived. They carried away carpets and stoves, paintings and gilded chairs. I found an Iraqi man, Maaruf Hussein, loading his car. He had been rummaging around one of the palace's meeting rooms. He had come to furnish his house. Into his battered taxi he had loaded a half-dozen Persian carpets and several boxes of lamps and fixtures. His prize, though, was a refrigerator, which he had strapped to the roof of his car.

"I never had a refrigerator, and today I took one," Hussein told me. "I'm going to put cold water in it for my wife. Maybe I will take the day off tomorrow."

Hussein said he would not allow himself to be burdened by guilt for taking the Iraqi president's belongings.

"Nobody likes to steal, and everyone would like to live in a wealthy country," Hussein said. "But he never made us feel like we were part of the country."

Which brought Hussein around to the carpets he had put on top of his car.

"I am going to put them down in my house," he said, "and whenever someone comes and walks on them, I will tell them that these came from Saddam Hussein's palace."

THE CROWD WAS STILL gathered round the Abu Hanifa mosque. The battle had ended hours before. Whoever it was the Americans had been trying to kill had fought ferociously and driven away. One marine had been killed and twenty more people wounded. The Americans said they'd found a meeting of "regime leadership," which was shorthand for Saddam Hussein. The Americans were gone. It was April 10, 2003. Twilight. The regime had collapsed the day before.

"Saddam was here, and I kissed him," an Iraqi man said, stepping out of the throng. He spoke in a gravelly voice and his eyes were rimmed with blood. He was surrounded by a group of men with matted hair and matted clothes. "He got out of his car. We shook hands and kissed him. There were two hundred people here."

The Iraqis looked on warily, keeping their distance. I sensed their hostility and kept the car's motor running after I'd stepped into the street. The neighborhood, Adamiyah, bore fresh marks from the battle in the shattered windows and the shot-up storefronts. In the distance, I saw an American boot. Adamiyah had been a neighborhood favored by Saddam's officers.

The Iraqi man continued in his hoarse voice. Saddam had arrived yesterday, in the afternoon, in a convoy of thirty cars that included his son Qusay and the Iraqi defense minister, Sultan Hashem Ahmed. The Americans were still in the center of town, seizing the ministries, and had not yet made it to the northern end. Saddam had climbed onto the top of his sedan, then stepped into the adoring crowd.

"Then the Americans came and Saddam fought like a knight," another man said. "They retreated like women."

In my left ear I heard a high-pitched sound growing louder with the seconds, moving fast, and as I turned toward the whistle I saw a black line, a black streak moving, streaking into Abu Hanifa's dome. I felt the air suck me in and away and then out and back and the minaret disappeared in a cloud. The ground shook from the explosion and I fell backwards and so did the Iraqis. I was stunned and they were, too. The Iraqis looked at me and I looked at them and they looked at their beloved Abu Hanifa and a voice rose from the crowd: "Do you see what your country has done!" I was already diving into the car, and the crowd was throwing cans and rocks as I sped away.

. . .

THE GROUND WAS parched and without life and the sky held no clouds, only the sun. Saddam Hussein's family gathered round the graves in an open field in the dictator's hometown. Some wore kafiyas to shield their skin. There were two hundred men, and by their broken-down cars and shabby clothes they looked like the poor relations of a powerful family. They stood in unhappy silence as one of the leaders of Saddam's tribe delivered the eulogy.

"O God, welcome Uday and Qusay as martyrs on the day of judgment," intoned Sheikh Ali al-Nida, the head of the Bani al-Nasiri tribe. "Give them a soft place to rest in the earth, open the grave wider for them, and let each become your son."

The bodies had stunk and the faces had been unrecognizable when the Americans took them from their refrigerated containers and handed them over earlier that day. It wasn't just the bullets and shrapnel the Americans had poured into the house in Mosul where the brothers had fled with Qusay's fourteen-year-old son, Mustafa. It was also the freakish funeral-parlor restoration job they had done on their faces, in a sorry effort to convince the Iraqis that the sons of Saddam were dead. So the metal coffins were closed, the faces of Uday and Qusay without burial shrouds.

"In Islam, this is not the way you bury a martyr," Nida told me. "The Americans have not allowed us to have a proper ceremony."

American soldiers had spent the morning turning away Iraqis who had tried to attend the funeral, but the moment the ceremony got under way the Americans departed. The Tikriti soil was baked so hard from the heat that an Iraqi man connected a jackhammer to a gasoline-powered generator and made the graves that way. Then the pallbearers lifted the coffins, and Saddam's friends and family could no longer contain themselves.

"Our blood, our souls, we'll sacrifice for Saddam!" the family members cried, repeating the line again and again.

The bodies went into the ground and the men gathered

around, all of them pressing in. Each of them leaned over and picked up one of the bricks of hard-rock earth and threw it on the coffins. The rocks banged off the coffins and fell into the graves. Some of the men stood back.

"O Uday and Qusay, angels will be visiting you in your house in Heaven," one of the men said. "They will ask you, 'Who is your God?' and you will tell them Allah, and Mohammed is his Prophet."

The Iraqis crouched on their knees and lined up in prayer to mark the end of the ceremony. As they finished, one of them rose from his knees and cried out, jabbing his finger at me and Tyler Hicks, the photographer who accompanied me.

"Death to America!" he shouted, with roars of assent from the others. "Death to America!"

The men rose and the crowd began to move, and it was growing louder, rapidly approaching the moment when it would transform itself into a beast, its individual parts absolved by the actions of the whole. I heard angry chatter all around me.

"Let's go kill some Americans," one man said to his friend. "Just like we did before."

As Tyler and I made for the car, one of the Iraqis stopped me and put his hand on my shoulder.

"We will make the Americans leave this country on their knees," he said. "Just you watch."

Video

THE ARMORED CARS were wheeling up to the office building where the insurgents were trapped. The Americans began firing their cannons before they had even braked, encircling the building fast as if they thought it was going to run away. The insurgents were shooting back. I could feel the wind of their bullets flying up the street. I moved in closer.

A Humvee was burning. It was sending up billows of flames and black fog and crumbling into itself. The soldiers had parked it in the middle of the street in the middle of the day in the middle of Karada, as nice as any neighborhood in Baghdad, and gone into Al-Warda to shop for candy and sodas. It was like a 7-Eleven in the United States. The insurgents had been waiting for them in the office building across the street, on one of the high floors. When the soldiers cut the engine on their Humvee the insurgents fired their rocket-propelled grenade from an open window and the Humvee exploded.

"Hey this guy's legs have been blown off!" a soldier yelled as he ran behind an armored car. Two more soldiers came in crouched behind him, dragging the bloody mess.

The insurgents had stayed put. They'd ambushed the Americans and then waited for more soldiers to arrive so they could fight it out with them and then die. I walked in closer, pressed against the windows of the shops, which were pulsating against my flattened palms. Bullets were flying in every direction, yet when I looked up I saw the locals immersed in their routines. A woman was hanging laundry from her window, sheets and T-shirts. An ice cream shop was selling cones.

I slipped into a video store to get out of the shooting and

found it filled with young Iraqis. They were dressed in tennis shirts and a couple of them were discussing a videotape to rent. They looked frightened at my presence so I went back into the street and as I did an American soldier who was sticking out of the hatch on his armored car turned around and looked at me and waved his arms at me to get back, get back. I kept moving toward him and he fired his gun over my head. "Get the fuck back," he shouted. I stopped, not retreating but not moving forward, and he turned back to the battle.

In a couple of minutes the shooting stopped and the Americans drove away, leaving the neighborhood burning and smoking. They towed the Humvee but left the building aflame, belching and sputtering like a spent Roman candle. I stepped back into the video store. Everyone was still there.

"Me, I love the American people," Atheer al-Ani, the owner, told me. He stood behind the counter. Like others hanging around his shop that day, Ani spanned many worlds. His mother and sister lived in Chicago. He stocked mostly American films. He was wearing a yellow Izod tennis shirt. "These people who do this have no minds, no minds," Ani said. "They're stupid."

Still, Ani was flustered by the firefight that had just unfolded in this normally lovely neighborhood. He turned to a friend.

"Who are they fighting for, Saddam?" he asked his friend. "Saddam is finished. Right?"

"Right," said the friend. "Finished."

The Kiss

I PULLED ON my running shoes and stepped into the street. It was a Thursday in July, twilight and well over 100 degrees. I was feeling a little reckless. If this ended badly, the only thing anyone would remember was how stupid I was.

We'd set up *The New York Times* office on Abu Nawas Street; there we lived and worked. It was an Ottoman-style house, with a gated yard and a veranda on the second floor that looked out on a boulevard that tracked the eastern bank of the Tigris River. In those first days, we didn't fortify the place: no razor wire or blast walls, no watchtowers or machine guns mounted on the roof. Cars motored past our front yard on their way to the Jumhuriyah Bridge a couple of miles up the road.

In the beginning, Baghdad wasn't that threatening. The other houses around us were either abandoned or rented by foreigners: the French Embassy and the BBC were around the corner. And the Iraqis in the neighborhood were unusually friendly, waving whenever we passed. Running at night seemed reckless, but given the otherworldly heat, running during the day was impossible.

So I set off. The reaction of my neighbors was immediate. Men looked up and waved, they held up bottles of water as I ran by. "Good, good!" one man said in English. "America good!" Abu Nawas was lined with fish restaurants that overlooked the Tigris; as I passed, men held up chunks of *masgouf*, their beloved bony fish, and asked me to join them. Children stopped their soccer games and ran after me; even the stray dogs gave pursuit. I felt I was living the scene in *Rocky II*, when the character played by Sylvester Stallone goes for a training run in his Philadelphia neighborhood and all the children clamor after him.

I started running that same route every evening after that, usually well into twilight, but early enough that the streets were still filled with people. My reception was always the same: cheering crowds, squealing children and happy stray dogs. In an odd but real way, my five-mile runs up Abu Nawas Street made me wonder what the war in Iraq was about. All day long reporting in the country I encountered hostility and chaos, which was intense and growing and real. And yet at night when I hit the streets, in the fall of 2003, I could not find a trace of it. It was as if the city, in the heat of the afternoon, had exhausted itself, only to lighten with the setting sun.

One day early on, a young Iraqi boy ran up alongside me. He had been kicking a ball along Abu Nawas, and as I came running he left his friends and started running next to me in his bare feet. The locals sometimes did that, but usually they dropped off after 50 yards. The Iraqi boy, who was perhaps nine years old, kept running the two and a half miles to the Jumhuriyah Bridge; as I turned to run back on a trail along the Tigris, he dropped off to wave goodbye.

A few days later, at twilight, the same boy appeared again, picking up the trail along the Tigris. His name, he said, was Hassan. We ran together for a while, me in my running shoes, he in his bare feet. Hassan motioned across the Tigris, toward the sprawling compound that once housed Saddam Hussein's Republican Palace and which was now the headquarters of the American occupation. The Green Zone.

"Saddam house," he said.

We ran together some more, and Hassan motioned again across the river.

"Now, Bush house."

One night, without warning, a wall of razor wire went up across Abu Nawas Street. Somebody somewhere had decided that the Sheraton Hotel, which sat just 100 yards away, was too easy a target for the car bombers, who had just begun striking the city. A barricade now stood between me and the rest of the neighborhood. All traffic ceased.

A few days later, sensing the disruption they had caused,

the Americans made an opening in the razor wire so pedestrians could walk through. I resumed my running, but I never saw Hassan again.

One afternoon later in the summer, another Iraqi youngster pulled alongside me as I made my way down the street. She, like Hassan, was about nine years old. Her name was Fatima, she said, huffing next to me and looking up with enormous brown eyes. She wore sandals, and she was very dirty. She kept up the pace.

Fatima and I ran for a couple of miles, her sandals making a scraping sound on the pavement. After a time, she indicated that she needed a rest. We stopped at one of the open-air fish restaurants. Everyone seemed to know Fatima; she seemed to know them.

A man walked out onto the sidewalk, put a hand on Fatima's shoulder and ran a finger across his neck. "Mother, father finished," the man said. He pointed to the sky, as if to suggest they had been killed by bombs.

"Fatima live here," the man said, gesturing with his hand to encompass the restaurant and its environs.

Then a second man walked up, twisted Fatima around and gave her a long and ugly kiss on her lips. He laughed and walked away. Fatima looked at me with very sad eyes, and I suggested that it was time to go.

We ran some more and then, after a time, Fatima stopped. She looked up at me one last time.

"Bye-bye. Tomorrow, OK?" Fatima said, and she turned and walked up the street. I never saw her again.

CHAPTER 7

A Hand in the Air

IN THE FIRST SUMMER of the American occupation, I found myself riding along the banks of the Euphrates River with Lieutenant Christopher Rauch, a twenty-two-year-old army reservist with a drawl nurtured on the chicken farm where he'd grown up in Lexington, South Carolina. Only four months before, Rauch had been working as a clerk for the state government, processing applications for unemployment insurance. Now he was overseeing the reconstruction of a half-dozen dams on the Euphrates.

Rauch wanted me to know right off that he didn't know much about dams themselves. But as the holder of a bachelor's degree in agriculture, he was, he said, the closest thing his unit had to an expert. So here Rauch was, driving along the wide green waters of one of history's great rivers, doling out dollars and advice. And, in his own estimation, not doing half bad. The Iraqis were gobbling up whatever Rauch had for them. In the few months since Rauch had taken over, he'd developed a solid rapport with his Iraqi counterpart, Hussein Alawi, the provincial minister for dams. "When it comes to engineering," Alawi said, "the Americans really know what they are doing."

The Iraqi dams were in terrible shape. The gates were crumbling, the copper on the electric motors was worn away and the spillways no longer channeled the water flow. In just a few months, Lieutenant Rauch had given away tens of thousands of dollars to make them work again. He was pleased with the progress he'd made so far, not just in rebuilding dams but in winning the trust of the Iraqi people. "We've made friends here," he said, his hands on the wheel of his Humvee. "They were wary at first, but when we started paying for things they started coming forward with requests."

We pulled up to the Habbaniya Dam, got out of the Humvee and walked out along the top. Alawi, riding in his own car, came out to meet us. "We need two generators," Alawi said, standing atop the dam and pointing down at the broken gates. The Euphrates ran below. "We don't have spare parts." Rauch rubbed his chin through the strap on his helmet. "What do you think that will cost?" Rauch asked. "I'm thinking $7,000 each."

I knelt down and read the inscription on one of the copper plates, green from years of oxidation. "Royal Air Force Cantonment. June 1947." A British-made dam. Rauch shook hands with Alawi and a couple of his assistants and walked back to the riverbank. I stayed behind and asked Alawi what he thought of the Americans in Iraq. He didn't hesitate to answer.

"I take their money but I hate them," Alawi said. "I am cooperating with the Americans for the sake of my country. The Americans are the occupiers. We are trying to evict them."

Rauch was motioning to me from his Humvee.

"No one likes to be told what to do," Alawi said. "You just saw that right now."

There were always two conversations in Iraq, the one the Iraqis were having with the Americans and the one they were having among themselves. The one the Iraqis were having with us—that was positive and predictable and boring, and it made the Americans happy because it made them think they were winning. And the Iraqis kept it up because it kept the money flowing, or because it bought them a little peace. The conversation they were having with each other was the one that really mattered, of course. That conversation was the chatter of a whole other world, a parallel reality, which sometimes unfolded right next to the Americans, even right in front of them. And we almost never saw it.

. . .

THE MOST BASIC BARRIER was language itself. Very few of the Americans in Iraq, whether soldiers or diplomats or newspaper reporters, could speak more than a few words of Arabic. A remarkable number of them didn't even have translators. That meant that for many Iraqis, the typical nineteen-year-old army corporal from South Dakota was not a youthful innocent carrying America's goodwill; he was a terrifying combination of firepower and ignorance.

In Diyala, east of Baghdad, in the early days of the war, I came upon a group of American marines standing next to a shot-up bus and a line of six Iraqi corpses. Omar, a fifteen-year-old boy, sat on the roadside weeping, drenched in the blood of his father, who had been shot dead by American marines when he ran a roadblock.

"What could we have done?" one of the marines muttered.

It had been dark, there were suicide bombers about and that same night the marines had found a cache of weapons stowed on a truck. They were under orders to stop every car. The minibus, they said, kept coming anyway. They fired four warning shots, tracer rounds, just to make sure there was no misunderstanding.

Omar's family, ten in all, were driving together to get out of the fighting in Baghdad. They claimed they had stopped in time, just as the marines had asked them to. In the confusion, the truth was elusive, but it seemed possible that Omar's family had not understood.

"We yelled at them to stop," Corporal Eric Jewell told me. "Everybody knows the word 'stop.' It's universal."

In all, six members of Omar's family were dead, covered by blankets on the roadside. Among them were Omar's father, mother, brother and sister. A two-year-old boy, Ali, had been shot in the face.

"My whole family is dead," muttered Aleya, one of the survivors, careening between hysteria and grief. "How can I grieve for so many people?"

The marines had been keeping up a strong front when I arrived, trying to stay business-like about the incident. "Better them than us," one of them said. The marines volunteered to help lift the bodies onto a flatbed truck. One of the dead had already been partially buried, so the young marines helped dig up the corpse and lift it onto the vehicle. Then one of the marines began to cry.

In the beginning, the Americans tried to compensate for their lack of Arabic with the usual high-tech gadgetry. Once during the invasion, I accompanied a group of marines into an open field where they had spotted some Iraqis. A group of farmers had walked in off the plains at sunrise with their camels. They were carrying a white flag.

The marines had no translator, but one of them carried a small box the size of a video camera. As the Iraqis approached, the American held up the box, dialed a knob and pressed a button.

A tinny voice crackled.

"We are here to help you," the machine said in Arabic.

The marine pressed the button again.

"Put your weapons down."

The American smiled. He turned the knob again.

"Do you speak English?" the machine said.

"I need to search your car."

The Iraqis twisted up their heads and stared at the instrument. The two sides stood staring at each other with nothing to say. As it happened, I had brought a translator into Iraq, an Egyptian named Mandy Fahmi. She struck up a conversation with the Iraqis. One of them was named Khalid Juwad, and he turned out to be quite friendly.

"I have come to get water," Juwad said, staring into the rifles of several young marines. "I am willing to cooperate."

It turned out that Juwad had come in hopes of persuading the Americans to restore water to the canals that irrigated his farm. A large valve on the farm's big pump was rusted in place.

"Sure, I think we can turn your pump on," Major Mark Stainbrook, one of the marines, told him.

And, sure enough, Major Stainbrook did. Before noon, the water of the Euphrates was flowing into Juwad's farm.

. . .

I DIDN'T SPEAK ARABIC myself. Once, while I went to interview a powerful Sunni sheikh of uncertain allegiance, he launched into a long conversation with my translator, Warzer Jaff, before he said a word to me. Jaff was Kurdish, a former guerrilla fighter, and his English and Arabic were perfect. He'd already saved my life many times, and I trusted him completely. The two talked in Arabic for many minutes as I sat quietly by, not two feet away. I had no idea what they were saying, though at one point the conversation grew tense. After a while they quieted down, and Jaff turned to me and said, "Okay, ask your question." And so I did. The rest of the interview proceeded smoothly.

During the ride back in the car, still puzzled, I asked Jaff what he and the sheikh had been talking about before the interview got going.

"He wanted to kidnap you," Jaff said, allowing, as he usually did, an unlit cigarette to dangle from his lips. "He was proposing that both of us kidnap you and hold you for ransom, and split the money. I told him I didn't want to do that, and that my tribe was much bigger than his tribe, and if he tried anything I would hold him and his tribe responsible. He apologized after that and everything was fine." Jaff laughed.

The Americans naturally gravitated toward Iraqis who could speak English. There were never enough of them. Sometimes, when I encountered a local who spoke English, no one else around him could. In that case I could have my own secret conversation, in a parallel world of my own, right in front of the Iraqis.

Once, in the spring of 2004, I ventured into the Al-Askari neighborhood in Falluja after a gun battle between the marines and some insurgents. Falluja was the most hostile city in Iraq from the beginning, and it was easy to assume that everyone hated the Americans. That same afternoon, I had gone to Falluja General Hospital to check on the civilians the Iraqis said the marines had killed and wounded. A man stood at the hospital door holding a pistol. "Any American that comes in here dies," he said.

After that, I went to Al-Askari to see if I could figure out what had happened. As was often the case in Falluja, the locals were offering only partial accounts of what they'd seen—versions that seemed hedged and tentative, and unlikely to get them into trouble with either the insurgents or the marines.

The most talkative among them was a man named Qassim Ubaid, an electrician, whom I'd stopped in the street. In a calm way, and in precise English, Ubaid offered me a detailed description of how the fighting had unfolded. The marines had come into Al-Askari on foot, Ubaid said, and the insurgents had been waiting for them. The insurgents fired first, killing one of the marines, and the marines had fired back and then embarked on a series of door-to-door searches. Ubaid's version matched that of the marines.

As Ubaid told his story, a number of Iraqis gathered around him. Back in the early days of the occupation, when American reporters could still go to cities like Falluja, we always drew big crowds. The Iraqis gathered behind Ubaid and strained to understand what he was saying; it was not clear that any of them did. Toward the end of the interview, Ubaid told me that a majority of Al-Askari's residents opposed the insurgents but that they were too afraid to say so, fearing they would be killed. "Most of the people here, they support the Americans," Ubaid told me.

It was a startling thing to say. It was quite possibly untrue. But I felt for a moment that Ubaid was offering an insight into how Iraqi public opinion actually functioned behind the backs of the Americans. Indeed, the crowd that had gathered around Ubaid seemed to suspect that he had told me something he should not have, even if they did not understand exactly what he had said. A man in the crowd said, "Come on, Ubaid, speak in Arabic so we can understand you."

"No," Ubaid said, glancing at them. "I prefer to speak in English. It's safer."

Then he looked at me.

LANGUAGE WAS NOT the only barrier; it was not even the biggest. From the beginning, any number of Iraqis realized that they could tell the Americans pretty much anything they wanted, and there was a good chance that the Americans would believe them, if only because they were too over-worked, too lazy or just unable to check out the stories. By and large, the Iraqis were right. It was the two conversations: tell the Americans what they want to hear and they will go away, and we can carry on the way we want. And the money will keep flowing: to repair the dams, to paint the schools. It was a game the Iraqis rarely gave away. But sometimes they did.

In late 2005, when the first reports of Shiite death squads were beginning to circulate, I visited the home of General Bassem al-Gharrawi, the commander of an Iraqi police unit called the Volcano Brigade. The Volcano Brigade was one of the most feared armed groups in Iraq, especially in the pre-dominantly Sunni neighborhoods of western Baghdad.

When the Americans began their crash effort to train and equip the Iraqi security forces, they set up a constellation of armed groups: army divisions, police forces and a hybrid corps of gunmen known as "police commandos." The commandos were heavily armed, mounted on trucks and almost entirely Shiite. It wasn't long after the Americans set up these units that I started hearing reports that they were swooping into Sunni neighborhoods and killing civilians and kidnapping them. Every morning, more and more young Sunni men were turning up dead, in ditches and trash dumps, hand-cuffed, drilled with holes, burned with acid, shot in the back of the head. Among the police commandos, the Volcanos had one of the meanest reputations.

General Bassem, as he called himself, was a short and gregarious man, with an improbable Saddam-style handlebar mustache over his upper lip. His office was filled with distractions, among them a life-size Elvis Presley doll that sang Elvis songs and a wide flat-screen television tuned at high volume to an Arabic music channel. Bassem had an assistant with thin lips and a hard face, who was ordered to sit in the back of the room with my translator, Ahmad. General Bassem and I spoke English.

I got nowhere with the general. Each time I asked him

about the allegations of torture and summary executions, he laughed and lit a cigarette. "I am so peaceful," he said. "We have not killed a single person. Not a single person. We have not even fired our guns!" I laughed along with the general, jabbed and pressed, and he kept laughing and denying. And as we were laughing, my translator and the general's thin assistant were laughing as well. Not with us, but between themselves.

Afterward, driving home, I asked Ahmad what he and the commander's assistant had been joking about. And he laughed again. "Sir," Ahmad said, "when General Bassem told you that the Volcano Brigade had never killed anyone, he whispered into my ear and said, 'I personally have killed fifty people during our operations. And that's just me.' Ha ha ha, sir. It is very funny."

FROM THE BEGINNING, Iraq was a con game, with the Iraqis moving and rearranging the shells, and the Americans trying to guess which one hid the stone. In April 2003, a couple of days after Baghdad fell, the American military prepared for a final battle. They would sweep north and capture Tikrit, Saddam's hometown, about a hundred miles north of Baghdad. If the Baathists were going to stand and fight anywhere, the military figured, it would be in Tikrit. So, with Baghdad still in flames, the Americans assembled a task force of several thousand marines and rushed north, only to find that most of the enemy fighters had disappeared.

"There wasn't a lot of resistance," Major Chris Snyder told me from a marine command post set up inside Saddam's presidential palace. It was late morning on the first day of the attack, and the enemy had failed to materialize. The streets of Tikrit were empty. "We're not sure where they all went."

A clue of sorts appeared in the streets outside the palace. Three local men approached me and introduced themselves. They were dressed in street clothes. They had spent the last two nights in Tikrit and agreed that the fighting had been minimal. When I asked them what they did for a living, they answered in unison.

"We're in the Republican Guard," they said.

The men, who claimed to share tribal bonds with Saddam, said they had fought for many years in the Iraqi army, in Kuwait and elsewhere. When the American invasion began, they had been stationed in Radwaniya, near Baghdad. They'd found the American bombing so intense that they decided to go home to Tikrit. They were still soldiers, the men said, but when they heard that the Americans were also coming to Tikrit, they peeled off their uniforms and sat down on the curb.

"We're not cowards," Borhan Abdul Karim told me, within earshot of one of the American soldiers roaming the streets. "But there's no point in fighting when the Americans have this aviation, and there is no way we can win. We would just be killed."

The other two men nodded in agreement. Were there other Republican Guard soldiers wandering the streets of Tikrit?

"Oh yes," Karim said. "Hundreds. They are all around us. Just look."

The insurgency: it was everywhere and it was nowhere. The Americans would bring in the heavy artillery and the troops, they would roll into Iraqi towns ready for a fight, and they would discover, invariably, that the enemy had disappeared. Often, the people they were looking for were standing a few feet away.

Over the course of the long war, American officers often spoke in acronyms like "AQI" (Al-Qaeda in Iraq) and "AIF" (Anti-Iraqi Forces). We reporters did likewise, using terms like "insurgents" and "guerrillas" as if these were distinct groups, as if they were wearing uniforms and carrying flags. They almost never were. The insurgents were Iraqis; the Iraqis were insurgents. Sometimes they fought; the rest of the time they were standing around like everyone else.

It drove the Americans crazy. They would drive through a village and spot an Iraqi man standing on the roadside, marking the convoy's time and speed as it passed. Working for the insurgency, no doubt, but how do you shoot a guy for looking at his watch? Then the Americans would spot a guy on a

rooftop, fifty yards away, tracking the convoy's route. It wasn't just that the insurgents lurked in the shadows; they actually were the shadows, flitting and changing with the light.

And no one ever saw a thing. If you were ever lucky enough to get one of the Iraqis to answer, he'd tell you almost without exception that the guys who fired the missile or planted the bomb or fired from the rooftop had come from somewhere else: outside the village, outside the country. He rarely said, It was that guy, right over there, third house on the left.

It wasn't just that the Iraqis lied. Of course they lied. It was that they had more to consider than the Americans were ever willing to give them credit for. The Iraqis had to live in their neighborhoods, after the American soldiers had gone home. The Iraqis had to survive. They had their children to consider. For the Iraqis, life among the Americans often meant living a double life, the one they thought the Americans wanted to see, and the real one they lived when the Americans went home.

IN AUGUST 2004, I stood outside the forty-foot-high gates of the Imam Ali Shrine in Najaf and watched the remnants of the Mahdi Army file out in tatters. The Mahdi Army was the militia of Muqtada al-Sadr, an anti-American cleric with a huge following among the Shiites of Baghdad and southern Iraq. The militia had taken over the shrine, prompting the Americans to go in and flush them out. As the Americans moved in closer, blasting everything in their way, the country's pro-American Shiite leaders cut a deal to let the Mahdi Army fighters vacate the mosque and go home. And so, at dawn on August 27, the fighting stopped. I watched the fighters walk out through the shrine's high doors.

"In the name of Allah, my brothers in the Mahdi Army," the voice intoned over the shrine's loudspeaker, the one ordinarily used for prayer. It was a message from Sadr himself. "I beg you, if civilians are in the shrine, walk out with them, and leave your guns behind."

And so they did, bloodied, bedraggled and starving, leaving behind their guns, wearing ordinary clothes and disappearing into Najaf's teeming streets. By midmorning the shrine was empty, and the Mahdi Army had scattered.

"Who is the Mahdi Army?" a man named Arkan Rahim asked me with a quizzical look, as we witnessed the procession together. "It is the Iraqi people. Nobody can say the Mahdi Army is finished. It is the Iraqi nation!"

There was no way to know. You had to accept your ignorance; it was the beginning of whatever wisdom you could hope to muster. As the fighting between the Mahdi Army and the Americans unfolded in the days before the truce, the Iraqi residents of Najaf, caught in the grip of Muqtada's militia, had professed in near unison their undying love for the young rebel. Every souvenir shop and every pilgrim hotel carried photos and posters of Muqtada on their walls. It was uncanny. And within hours of the Mahdi Army's evacuation of the shrine, Muqtada suddenly became a pariah to every Iraqi I could find.

"Muqtada and those people around him, they know nothing," said a cleric who had studied under Sadr's father, Mohammed Sadiq al-Sadr. We were a block from the shrine. "Muqtada, he just sat on his father's computer. He is not an educated man."

With that, the cleric began to tell me how Mahdi Army

fighters had threatened him during the tense times of the previous three months. The cleric produced a small handwritten letter. "Some clerics sell their consciences to Jews and foreigners," the letter said. "If you are not careful, you will be killed."

"Tell the truth about Muqtada," the cleric said to me, and then he walked away.

MAJOR LARRY KAIFESH listened patiently as the mayor outlined his desires.

"I just want to inform you that five hundred families are without drinking water," Majid Mahmood, the mayor of Garma, told him.

Kaifesh nodded, but without conviction. A thirty-six-year-old civil affairs officer from Chicago, Kaifesh had come to Garma to inspect one of the many projects the Americans were paying for.

Before the war started, Kaifesh had been an investment adviser for Morgan Stanley in Costa Mesa, California, and he brought a shrewdness to his job that made him a hard man to deceive. In Garma, as in every village in Anbar Province, Kaifesh faced the same paradox: the Iraqis wanted more money, and they were more violent than ever.

"We are all drinking from a ditch," Mayor Mahmood said.

Kaifesh shook hands with Mahmood, waved goodbye and climbed into his Humvee.

"They are all playing us," Kaifesh said, arching his eyebrows.

We drove fast out of Garma, barreling up the road to foil any insurgents who might be trying to set off roadside bombs. The night before, four marines had been killed when their fifty-seven-ton armored personnel carrier had been thrown across the road. The marines had been killed by what the military called an IED, jargon for "improvised explosive device." Kaifesh and I rode together, we spied every pile of trash, every old tire, every dead dog. The temperature was perhaps 120 in the shade. The air was so hot we had to cover our noses and mouths to breathe.

We pulled into Al-Kandari, the next town on our route. There was a group of Iraqi men standing on a street corner. I wondered what they were up to in the heat; usually only the Americans were out in the sun. And insurgents. Kaifesh gave them a wave. No one waved back.

Kaifesh and his convoy of four vehicles were cutting a wide semicircle around eastern Anbar Province. At the center of the arc was Falluja, which at the time was out of American control. In another bit of military jargon, Falluja was being called a "no-go zone." A group of jihadis had seized control and set up their own emirate, replete with religious courts. The Americans had not yet decided to retake Falluja, but they wanted to make a show of their goodwill in the little towns outside of it.

We pulled into the Al-Kandari Women's Center, another American project, where we were greeted by a man named Namir. Kaifesh had come to inspect the job site; he'd forked over more than $25,000 in American money for the new center, which was supposed to provide vocational training for women. But as he examined the half-painted yellow walls and exposed rebar, his face showed frustration.

"Twenty-five thousand dollars—I could have built a house with that," Kaifesh said.

"We will build a place you can be proud of," Namir replied.

Another man, who identified himself as Adel, approached Kaifesh. He was angry. He wanted Kaifesh to get tougher on the contractors. Namir had already disappeared.

"You give them a lot of money and they never do anything," Adel said. "We don't like when you give money to people who don't do any work."

"Neither do we," Kaifesh said.

After a time, we returned to the Humvee. Kaifesh collapsed in the seat and sighed.

"We know everyone takes a cut," Kaifesh said. "It's a gimme mentality. The more you give them, the more they want."

We drove off into the fields. A shell exploded in the dust about a hundred yards away. Kaifesh's men asked over the radio if they could turn around to hunt the perpetrators, but Kaifesh waved them off. He had hardly raised an eyebrow. "Until we get into a fight, we won't worry about it," he said. We drove on through the heat.

"These people know everything," Kaifesh said as the Humvee bounced along. "They know the minute we leave our compound and the minute we come back. They know when there's going to be a bomb."

The convoy approached Zaydon, east of Falluja. Kaifesh stared straight ahead as we rumbled into town. The streets were empty.

"They really hate us here," Kaifesh said.

We pulled into the parking lot of a squat government building. Inside sat a half-dozen Iraqis. They had been waiting for Kaifesh.

The first of them, Nafir Karim, age thirty-five, stepped forward.

"America killed my brother," he said.

Kaifesh shook his head. "I know you, Karim. You've already filed a claim. And we paid you for it."

Karim did not protest. Deflated, he left the room hanging his head. A second man stepped forward, Nasir Salam. He claimed the Americans had killed a relative of his without justification.

"You need to file your claim with the Zaydon city council," Kaifesh said. "There is an Iraqi government now. You're going to have to stop thinking about the Americans."

Kaifesh was reminding the Iraqis who had waited for him at the Zaydon government center that the American occupation had formally ended in June 2004. There was an Iraqi government now, and Kaifesh wanted the Iraqis to start taking their problems there. But the Iraqis in Zaydon were not thrilled about this idea.

"The city council is a bunch of thieves," Salam said. "They will put everything in their own pockets."

As we were leaving, another man approached Kaifesh and started whispering. "I need to speak to you alone," the man said. "I have an idea for an economic project."

As we drove off, I asked Kaifesh whether he had consid-

ered the possibility that he was giving money to the same people who were mounting attacks against him and his men. Or
at least to people who knew the people who were.

"No question," Kaifesh said. "We are giving money to
people who do bad things."

I was a little stunned by his frankness.

"The areas we are dealing with are very tight. Everybody is
in everyone else's tribe. The people I am giving money to may
not be attacking us, but they know who is."

In Kaifesh's mind, the American money he was doling out
might not be putting an end to the attacks. But the alternative
was even worse.

"Think about it," Kaifesh said. "Can you imagine if we
weren't doing this, how bad it would be? This money is buy-
ing goodwill."

As we rode out of Zaydon, our convoy prepared to take a
left onto a road flanked by rice paddies. As the first Humvee
began to turn, I looked ahead and saw a young man standing
in the middle of the street with his hands in his pockets. Just
standing, watching us. I knew immediately that we were in
danger.

The Humvees continued making their lefts, and I fixated
on the kid in the middle of the street. Some of the marines
noticed him, too. As our Humvee, the last in the convoy, completed its turn, I twisted my head around and saw the kid take
his right hand out of his pocket and hold it up in the air over
his head. For five seconds the kid stood there with his hand in
the air.

"Incoming!" one of the marines yelled. Mortar shells were
exploding all around us. The convoy swung around to capture
the kid. He was already gone.

IT WAS DRIZZLING in Mosul when I arrived. Broken glass
was splayed across the pavement. The truck had been towed
away.

Two American soldiers with the 101st Airborne had
climbed into a regular SUV, no armor, and driven off the base
and into Mosul at rush hour. They were supposed to have

known better than to go out alone. One of the soldiers was Jerry Wilson, forty-five, of Thomson, Georgia, the brigade's command sergeant major, meaning he was the unit's senior enlisted man. The other was Corporal Rel Ravago IV, twenty-one, from Glendale, California.

The insurgents started following Wilson and Ravago the minute they drove off the base. They were in a car just in front of the Americans, and in the heavy traffic they suddenly stopped. Another car trailing just behind the Americans pulled up to their rear bumper. The soldiers couldn't move. The insurgents got out of their cars and, with their Kalashnikovs, shot them in the head.

A crowd of Iraqis had gathered around the executed Americans, dragged the bodies out of the car and stripped them of their watches, jackets and boots. The Americans said initially that the soldiers' throats had been cut, too, which caused a sensation in the United States, because it revived memories of Somalia in 1993. The next day, the military took back the statement.

After checking out the scene of the attack, I walked up the street to the Ras al-Jada fire station, one of the new ones built by the Americans. It was a big brick building, with three wide garage doors and three brand-new, bright red fire engines inside. It was very American. I performed a quick mental calculation and figured the renovation and the new trucks had cost about a million dollars. Milling around the front of the fire station were the firemen themselves, dressed in brand-new flame-retardant suits and boots. They looked very sharp and well-groomed, like firemen in the United States. I asked the Iraqis about their salaries, of which they were especially proud. These had risen tenfold since the Americans had toppled Saddam, they said. And they'd completed a six-week training course to learn how to operate the fire engines.

I asked the fireman what had happened down the street. The firemen had seen the whole thing, they said. Oh, yes, absolutely. All of them had walked down the street to watch with everyone else.

"I was happy, everyone was happy," Wa'adallah Muhammad, one of the firefighters, told me. "The Americans, yes, they do good things, but only to enhance their reputation. They are occupiers. We want them to leave."

The rest of the firefighters chimed in. There were six of them. Not the least bit hostile. Yes, yes, they said, we were cheering when we saw the dead Americans. Who did it? I asked them. The men shrugged. "The Americans are not popular in Mosul," one of the firemen said.

From the fire station I drove to the American base in downtown Mosul, the same base from which Command Sergeant Major Wilson had departed. I wanted to ask the commander about Mosul, since, until then, it had been something of an American success story. The 101st Airborne, under the command of Major General David Petraeus, had spent more money on public works projects than any other unit. The streets were calm. Mosul was the model of how a successful counterinsurgency campaign, with its emphasis on political and economic factors, could be carried off.

"I reject the idea that things have gone bad here," Colonel Joe Anderson told me. He was in command of about five thousand soldiers in the heart of the city. "Most of the Iraqis are glad we are here, and they are cooperating with us."

The Iraqis lied to the Americans, no question. But the worst lies were the ones the Americans told themselves. They believed them because it was convenient—and because not to believe them was too horrifying to think about.

I WENT IN to see the chief, Colonel David Teeples, at his base in Ramadi. It was the summer of 2003. In just three months in Anbar Province, Teeples told me, the Third Armored Cavalry Regiment had remade the city: reopened schools, refurbished the main bridge that spanned the Euphrates, "stood up" a new police department and even, most remarkably, started an Iraqi highway patrol. It was this last achievement that stuck in my mind. A highway patrol in Iraq? It seemed to me that a highway patrol was the sort of thing a country put together when all of its big problems had been taken care of. Adding a highway patrol to a government was like adding a swimming pool to a house. Wow, I thought, they must be very far along here.

"We have a good thing going here," Colonel Teeples said. "We don't need combat forces. We need civil affairs officers and MPs. That's how we are going to win this."

When I finished talking to Colonel Teeples I climbed into the passenger seat of the 1990 Chevy Caprice my Iraqi driver, Mohammed, had bought a couple of weeks before, and we headed toward Highway 10. That was the east–west highway that would take us to Baghdad. We got off the army base but Mohammed couldn't find an on-ramp to the highway, so he took the Caprice across a sandy field that separated us from the road. The Caprice made it to the lip of Highway 10 but fell back into sand. Mohammed gunned the engine, which dug the car into a hole. We were stuck.

I stood on the edge of Highway 10, far enough away from the cars whizzing past, and looked east and west. And lo, a few hundred yards up the road were a group of Iraqi men standing underneath an overpass and leaning against a car. They wore gleaming white shirts. I was a little surprised they had not come over to help us, so, along with my translator, a Jordanian woman named Nadia Huraimi, I started in their direction.

As I got closer to the underpass I could just make out the insignias on their shirts: Iraqi Highway Patrol. They were smoking cigarettes and sitting in the shade, yes, but still, I thought, what a stroke of luck. There were six of them. They looked up as I approached.

"Are you an American?" one of the officers said. "We're looking to kill an American."

I assured him I was not. The rest of them joined in.

"I hate the Americans," Majid, another officer, said. "It's an occupation."

Having just spoken to Colonel Teeples, I mentioned to the Iraqis that they were being paid by American dollars, that those uniforms they were wearing were being paid for by the Americans, too. I felt like a Boy Scout.

"No, it's our oil that is paying," the first officer said. "We are being paid for by the oil the Americans are stealing."

He looked at me again. His stomach was hanging over his belt.

"Are you sure you are not American?"

I looked down the road toward Baghdad. Mohammed had

somehow managed to dig the Caprice out of the ditch. He was waving in the distance. Nadia and I said goodbye and walked quickly to the car.

Perhaps a minute later, as we climbed onto the highway, my satellite phone rang. I stuck the antenna out the window and heard the voice of Qais Mizher, another translator I worked with. Qais was saying in a breathless voice that I needed to come quickly to Habbaniya, a town just east of Ramadi, as fast as I could.

On the approach to Habbaniya, the traffic was backed up for more than a mile in each direction. I got out and walked to the front. And there, smoldering in the road, lay the remains of an American supply truck, one of the big ones called a seven-ton. A crowd of Iraqis had gathered, and they were shouting and waving in great excitement. One of them was holding up the bloody shreds of an American uniform. The body of the American from whom it came lay on top of a stretcher next to the burning truck, a heap of flesh mangled but still moving. The Iraqis began to cheer, quietly at first, almost a hum, then rising to a shriek each time the bloody shirt came up.

Then an American tank appeared, a massive M-1, and it opened fire with the .50-caliber machine gun mounted on its turret. Not at the crowd, but into the field off to the side of the road. Perhaps the crew had seen some insurgents there. The tank, firing, swiveled its turret from side to side, sweeping the tall green grass with its gunfire. A .50-cal. is a horrifying instrument. Boom-boom-boom-boom-boom.

"Look at what the Americans are doing to the Iraqi people!" an Iraqi man yelled at me. "Look at what they are doing!"

I was angry for the bleeding man in the road and for some reason I felt no fear. "That's because they blew up an American soldier, you dumb fuck," I shouted. Nadia told me to shut up, noting that everyone in the Arab world knows that word.

"Death to America!" the Iraqis started cheering, turning to face me. "God is great! The American army will collapse in Iraq!"

After a few minutes, the tank came rumbling our way, a

huge, monstrous thing, clanking and smoking, towing the smoldering truck behind it. The crowd grew quiet. As the tank passed, a young American crewman, his helmeted head peering out of the turret, trained his machine gun on the crowd. He looked angry and afraid, clenching his teeth, hands on his gun.

The cheers went up again.

I walked back toward our car, passing the Iraqis who were still stopped in traffic. As I did, I came to an Iraqi police car. Brand-new, white and blue. Four Iraqi officers sat inside, with their car doors open, relaxing and smoking cigarettes.

Blonde

IN THE MORNING, the captain and I had walked down a road lined with craters. We'd walked slowly, checking for wires, animal carcasses, loose dirt. Bomb stuff. It was a sweltering morning in Ramadi, with the mist of the Euphrates infiltrating our lungs.

Later on, sitting in a walkway of one of Saddam's palaces, the captain started telling stories. We hadn't spent much time together but we'd walked this road and survived, so the air around us for the moment was light and full of trust. We were both from Florida.

"So we came up with this great way to search villages," the captain told me. He pushed his knife into an MRE (Meal Ready to Eat).

"We've got this girl here in the company—blonde, she's hot," the captain said. "This is when we were up in Mosul. We had to search all these villages for guns. Those villages are awful up there. So we went into this village and put the blonde girl we had on top of one of the Bradleys. We just rolled in and put her up there and took off her helmet and let her hair spill out.

"So she's standing there on top of the Bradley, blond hair and everything, and we called out on the loudspeaker, 'This woman is for sale. Blonde woman for sale!' And I'll be damned if every Iraqi male in that village wasn't gathered around the Bradley in about two minutes. You know the Iraqis are crazy for blondes. Crazy for them. They don't have any here."

The captain started eating a strawberry Pop-Tart.

"So she's standing up there on the Bradley, and we'd have an auction. Highest bid gets the blonde! They're going crazy, the Iraqis, offering their goats, trucks, all their money. Children. Everything. I'm standing up there, saying, 'Nope, not enough! Not enough!' And they're bidding more. One of the guys had his hands on the big machine gun just in case it got out of control. The Iraqis were wild. Just staring at her.

"So we're up there having the auction, and during the auction I sent our guys around back into the houses to look for guns. We're having the auction and all the Iraqis are at the auction yelling for the blonde while our guys are collecting the guns from the houses. It was totally quiet in the houses, just the women in there. We got a huge pile of guns. Searched the whole village. No problem."

What happened with the auction? I asked him.

"We just shut it down. Told them the bids weren't high enough." The captain laughed. "The Iraqis were pissed off but it was okay."

I was laughing and the captain got quiet for a second.

"We did that in three villages. Worked every time. We got reprimanded. Somebody found out about it. They didn't like it," he said, chewing on his Pop-Tart. "I thought it was brilliant myself. Smartest thing we ever did."

CHAPTER 8

A Disease

THE CHINOOK LUMBERED across the sweltering sky
as benignly as a blimp. It seemed to float on the heat
rising from the plains. Inside the helicopter was Paul
"Jerry" Bremer, the head of the Coalition Provisional Authority. His aides were crowded into the back. I was riding in a second Chinook, on one of the canvas seats. I turned to the
person next to me.

"So what were you doing before the war?" I asked.

"The 2000 campaign," he said.

It was Chris Harvin, office of strategic communications—
Stratcomm for short. It was the public relations outfit Bremer
set up at the Coalition Provisional Authority, the formal name
of the occupation authority. For this trip, Harvin was Bremer's advance man. In the United States, the advance man is
crucial to political campaigns; he's the guy who visits the site
before the candidate does, to make sure, for instance, that the
television cameras capture the candidate in front of the most
picturesque backdrop. Or to make sure the locals chosen to
greet the candidate say positive things.

"What did you do in the campaign?" I asked Harvin.

"South Carolina primary," Harvin said.

"That was the nasty one," I offered.

"Yeah," Harvin said, nodding.

I asked Harvin, Isn't that the primary where a telephone
bank put out the rumor that John McCain had fathered an

illegitimate child? I didn't say it was the Bush campaign that had done this to McCain.

Harvin broke into a wide smile.

"We kicked their ass," he said.

The Chinooks landed and Bremer climbed out and stepped into the heat. Despite the temperature, he wore a red tie and a blue suit with a pressed white handkerchief tucked into his front coat pocket, set off by a pair of tan army-issue boots. Bremer's chin jutted confidently; he looked like he had come from a lunch in Hyannisport.

We had come to the Mubarqa Maternity Hospital in Diwaniya, a mostly Shiite city in southern Iraq. Bremer had been invited there by Raja Khuzai, a witty and pro-American obstetrician and member of the Iraqi Governing Council, the pseudo–Iraqi cabinet the Americans had set up in Baghdad. The council had no real power, except to tell Bremer what they thought. Bremer followed Khuzai into a room off the lobby. It had been decorated with purple and orange streamers celebrating his arrival and filled with men in kafiyas and mustaches. An Iraqi girl handed Bremer a bouquet of roses. He picked up a microphone.

Bremer began his visit, as he often did, by congratulating the United States.

"We of the coalition are glad that we were able to provide you with your freedom from the dictatorship of Saddam Hussein," Bremer said. "You now have that freedom, and you now have a better hope for the future."

In English, Bremer loosed a stream of statistics suggesting that conditions in Iraq had improved.

"There is eleven times more electricity now than before the war," Bremer told the Iraqis. "All of Iraq's 240 hospitals are now open. . . . In May, when I arrived, 500 tons of drugs were shipped in. Last month, we shipped 3,500 tons—a 700 percent increase in shipments in three months."

The hospital staff gave Bremer a round of warm applause, and then they lined up with requests.

"The electricity plant is damaged," a man who identified himself as "Sheikh al-Khuzai" told Bremer. He was the head of the province's biggest tribe. "The police station has to be up as soon as possible. We need security here. We lack a proper water system."

Others stood in line behind him. "There is no justice in the salary system," another man said.

Bremer listened for a while, then moved upstairs through the hospital's wards, with a retinue of aides and gunmen trailing behind. When he arrived, one of the Americans handed Bremer a clutch of stuffed animals to give to the children. And so Bremer did, taking the animals and touring the hot and stale rooms, handing out fuzzy pink animals to babies and mystified mothers still lying in their beds.

Bremer moved to the ward for premature babies. The newborns were skeletal and malnourished, lying in rows. A baby of about three days sagged incoherently in his mother's arms. A shriveled infant lay motionless on its back, wrapped in red, gazing at nothing. One of the Iraqi doctors smiled and motioned to Bremer, suggesting he give one of the stuffed animals to one of the lifeless babies. Bremer grimaced. "I don't like seeing this at all," he said.

One of the doctors whispered in my ear. "Four babies died in one week."

I broke away from Bremer's entourage and walked downstairs, where I fell into a conversation with some young Iraqi doctors. There had been no electricity in more than a week; it was only running, the doctors said, because Bremer was here. This had not been the case before the war, the doctors said. During the invasion, Mubarqa Maternity Hospital had stayed open continuously. The lack of electricity was killing the babies, the doctors said. Without the electricity the incubators were going cold and, after a time, the babies were going cold, too. The vaccines in the refrigerator were spoiling. So were the bacterial cultures. So was the blood.

As the doctors spoke, Harvin, the advance man, broke in.

"Are you happy that Saddam is gone?" Harvin asked. "Things are better now?"

"Yes," Dr. Kassim al-Janaby said, smiling wanly. "Yes."

"What's the best thing about Saddam being gone?" Harvin asked. He was on his toes now.

"Only one—I think only one," Dr. Mohamed Jasim said.

"Only the free talking. Only only only. But no doing. No doing."

"Do you think over time it gets much better?"

"Yes, we are thinking the next time it gets better," Jasim said.

"Patience, yeah?"

"We need continuous electricity," Dr. al-Janaby said, his smile gone now. "Continuous security. Security in our city also is not until now. That's it. Also the salary."

"But don't you think with time it will get better?" Harvin asked. "What do you think? What can we do?"

"Security," one of the doctors said.

A FEW DAYS LATER, I went back to Mubarqa by myself. Roaming its halls, I stepped into a bare room where I found Hassan Naji, the hospital record keeper. The room was dark from the lack of electricity. Naji was seated at a metal desk, surrounded by piles of paper. A file cabinet stood behind him, all of its drawers opened. I asked him about infant deaths.

"Yes, yes, babies are dying," he said, looking up. Naji's face was drawn but his eyes locked on me in a flash. "Under Saddam, this did not happen. Not like this."

I asked Naji if he could be more specific—if he could show me statistics on recent infant deaths.

Naji dropped whatever it was he had been working on and began sifting through the piles on his desk. It was covered with stray notes, jottings and calculations. He produced a gigantic ledger, an ancient thing filled with numbers and names. He got up and walked to the file cabinet and rifled through it but found nothing. This, too, was different from Saddam's time, Naji said.

"Democracy has ruined this hospital," Naji said. "Democracy has made everyone incompetent. We used to have standards here. In the past, people really worked at their jobs, if only because they were terrified of their supervisors. They worked late. We kept the most accurate records. We had weekly meetings on the worst cases. When a child died, we had a meeting and we really studied it.

"Now, with all this freedom, no one cares anymore," Naji said. "We don't keep records anymore. We don't even have death certificates. We don't have birth certificates. Look at the files: elementary statistics we don't have. The department's work is not getting done. Files and paper are piling up. The whole hospital is this way."

Naji stared into the ledger again.

"Most deaths are in the operating room now," he said. "The sterile ward has collapsed. They used to have their own nurse there. They used to take care of the ward; they kept it clean. The babies would go immediately to the sterile ward. Now it's unsterile. And we don't have any oxygen. If we go on like this we will have a catastrophe. We have babies who gasp. So the babies that are premature go right to the operating room. They die in the operating room.

"Come with me," he said. We walked down the hall and up the stairs, the route Bremer had walked a few days before. We stopped at a bed. A tiny baby breathed from a tube. Naji picked up the chart and read it aloud.

"Mother, Wafa Abid. Baby boy, Hassan."

Naji looked at the gauge on the oxygen bottle next to the bed.

"The tank is empty," Naji said. "Do we have any oxygen? No, we don't."

He put the chart down and started down the stairs again. Records, I told Naji. Records of deaths. Help me show how this has happened.

Naji reentered the office and picked up another ledger at his desk. It was filled with a sheaf of pink papers, forms filled with names and addresses and birth dates and birth weights. He threw it back down on the desk.

"Before the war, you would have the full address written here," he said, pointing. "Everything. But when the war came the printing press was looted. We don't have any forms. This is what we are using, just these." He held up a scrap of paper. "We just write down whatever now, Hamsa District, Nahinder District. I don't know where these families even live. I don't know how the babies died. Look at this. This family came in three weeks ago. The mother doesn't even have a medical chart."

I looked around Naji's office. There were a couple of shriveled plants in the window.

"After the war, with the new regime, everything became a mess," Naji said. "People used to work so they could forget themselves. Now they don't care anymore. People don't use the freedom they have correctly.

"Personally, I'd give them a beating," Naji said. "But it's not my decision."

So you miss Saddam? I asked Naji. You sound like you miss him.

"Never," Naji said, shaking his head. "Never. The Americans did a great thing when they got rid of that tyrant. Things could even get worse here and I would still feel that way. Believe me," Naji said, standing up to see me out, "most of the people in Diwaniya would feel that way."

THE SUN BEAT on the tarmac as Bremer climbed aboard his helicopter and lifted off. We were at Landing Zone Washington, inside the Green Zone, in Baghdad. This time, Bremer was in a Black Hawk, one of three, a soldier manning a heavy machine gun on each door and a pair of Apache attack helicopters flying escort. The Black Hawks did not lumber like the Chinooks that had gone to Diwaniya seven months before; they rocketed out of the Green Zone, dipping and weaving over the rooftops at 140 mph, leaping over the telephone wires. Bremer had overseen the creation of a new Iraqi government; he'd laid out a schedule for democratic elections and he was traveling the country to say goodbye. It was March 2004; in three months he would be gone. Insurgents were everywhere, hence the speed.

The helicopters slowed at their destination, Al-Kut, a provincial capital sixty miles south of Baghdad in the Shiite heartland. Within a few minutes Bremer was sitting at a folding table across from the local officials of the Wasit government. Al-Kut was famous as the place where during the First World War the British lost thirty thousand men trying to lift a siege by the Ottoman Turks. Bremer wore the same outfit as he had in Diwaniya: a blue suit, a red tie, a pressed handkerchief and a pair of army-issue desert boots.

First came the governor, Nema Sultan Bash Aga, who told Bremer that everything in Wasit was running smoothly indeed. "Our situation is not bad at all," Aga told Bremer. "Praise be to God our situation is the most quiet in all of Iraq." His main problem, Aga said, was unemployment; there were too many young men with too little to do. "If we gave people jobs, we would have an end to terrorism," he said. Bremer listened and offered an occasional response. "It looks to us that unemployment in the country has come down quite a bit," he said.

Bremer stood up and the men shook hands and the governor left the room.

Next came Abdul Salaam al-Safaar, the chief of the provincial council. He shook Bremer's hand firmly as he sat down but didn't smile.

"I have a list of issues that I would like to talk to you about," Safaar said.

"Okay," Bremer said. "Please go ahead."

"The main issue is security," Safaar said. "We are on a collision course with the Ministry of Interior, which set up our police force in an arbitrary way. There are many thieves in the police force, there are many terrorists."

Bremer sat motionless in his chair, listening.

Safaar told Bremer he wanted to set up an independent police unit with expanded powers, for which local leaders like him could choose their own men. The ministry in Baghdad was opposed to this, he said.

"After June 30, when the CPA leaves, the police cannot guarantee security," Safaar said. "They cannot."

Safaar stared intently at Bremer. Then he went to the next item on his list, the border with Iran. Many members of the local political parties and police, Safaar said, maintained extensive links with the Iranian government.

"We have evidence that members of the Iranian secret police are working with local political parties here," Safaar said. "This is not healthy for a stable society."

At the heart of the problem, Safaar told Bremer, was Wasit's hundred miles of unguarded border with Iran. "You can cross the border anywhere you want," he said.

Bremer nodded and said nothing.

Safaar pressed on. The political parties were acting in their own narrow interests, he said—so narrow that they threatened the fledgling democratic experiment in Wasit Province. Some of the parties, like the Supreme Council, were allied to Iran, he said. Others, like Muqtada al-Sadr's, maintained their own militias, which were more powerful than the police.

"All of these parties have militias," Safaar told Bremer. "Even God cannot make decisions unless he receives the approval of the political parties. If he does not have their approval, even he will be attacked. As an Iraqi I would like to see democracy in my country, but what we have cannot be called a democracy. Democracy as we know it is a disease."

Bremer finally spoke.

"We understand," he said. "There are problems with the police in many places in many countries. The problem is that we had to call up a police force very quickly. We had to vet these people as they came into the forces. It has been an imperfect process."

Bremer spoke some more and suggested that the meeting was over. But Safaar kept talking. He did not appear angry or agitated. His greatest fear, he told Bremer, was that the Iraqi government, to which the United States was preparing to return full power in less than three months, was not ready for the task. And the Iraqi people would not be ready for the elections Bremer had scheduled.

"Three months is a very short time to ensure that the political process will be good," Safaar said to Bremer. "People need time, they need experience in these things before they just go to the polls. We have to have a longer period."

"People are going to have to learn faster," Bremer said, shaking his head. "Most Iraqis don't want the elections to be delayed."

He stood up.

"Thank you for letting me bring up these issues with you," Safaar said.

And the meeting ended and Bremer flew away.

A month later, al-Sadr launched an uprising against the Americans and the nascent Iraqi government across southern

Iraq. The government building in Al-Kut fell to the rebels. Across Wasit Province, across southern Iraq, government buildings, police stations, civil defense garrisons and other installations set up by the Americans were sacked and overrun. Overnight, the Iraqi police, the Iraqi national guard and the Iraqi army disappeared.

An American official in southern Iraq summed up the situation a few days after the uprising began.

"Six months of work is completely gone," he said. "There is nothing to show for it."

The View from the Air

THE BLACK HAWK skirted the date palms and the mud-colored roofs, the altitude and the movement of the helicopter offering a cubist view of the world below. Green rectangles of farmland shifted as if in a mirror then flattened as they fell into the horizon. The anarchy of the streets carried no sound so high; every haphazardness of the place, the trash, the goats, the fields of junk, seemed, from the distance, planned and carefully measured, like a city by L'Enfant. A farmer stopped his work, cupped his hand over his eyes and waved. Under the spell of the whirring motor I felt suddenly hopeful for the country below. I looked down at the tiny people and imagined them going about their days just as any of us would up here, with fears and desires no greater or lesser than our own, or which, in any case, were not so different that they couldn't be reconciled. It was useful to fly in helicopters for this reason, I thought to myself, useful to think this way, to take a wider view of the world. Too much detail, too much death, clouded the mind.

Not long before I'd been to the scene of a car bombing, stood amid the screaming mothers and the flesh with dirt, and I had thought that this was all there was. In the Black Hawk I wondered whether I needed to stand back, to take a longer view. Perhaps in the hideous present some larger good was being born, struggling painfully and awfully, but coming into the world just the same. And perhaps this new world might one day justify the death and suffering unfolding below, just as the Americans in the Green Zone and the angry bloggers told me back home. Sometimes even Iraqis told me that. Once I sat with an Iraqi nuclear scientist, Ibrahim al-Shakarchy. We had tea in his office. He'd lived through three decades of Saddam and the Baath and the terror, was living through the occupation and the insurgency, and he told me with conviction that I needed to take a more abstract look at the world around me.

"Napoleon's invasion changed Egypt in ways that never would have been possible," Shakarchy said to me. He seemed sure of himself. He was wearing a cardigan sweater. "Sometimes you need to impose new ideas by force. Sometimes there is no other way."

I thought these things in the Black Hawk, looking down on the world.

We were over the capital. Rows and rows of houses, low-slung and the color of sand, spread far and wide. Beds on rooftops. Goats on rooftops. Children kicking a football. The cobalt-blue globes of the Monument of Martyrs shimmering in the white noon. The Black Hawk banked over the Tigris and began to circle the landing area inside the Green Zone. The tidy two-bedroom trailers that housed the Americans were arrayed around Saddam's sandstone palace. Off-duty soldiers laughed and dove in the palace's pool. The Black Hawk came in fast, dropping its tail like an animal, the pitch of its engine falling as it scraped the cement. A marine stood to the side directing the landing with precise movements of his hands. He was shouting something over the whine of the engine that I could not hear. I unhooked my shoulder straps and stepped onto the pavement. Back on the ground.

LEAVING WAS the only time I got the measure of the place. Coming in was too depressing, too intense. There was so much anticipation and so much regret. On the plane in, the pilot, always a South African, would come onto the loudspeaker and get everyone ready. There was never a gradual descent; the jet, a Royal Jordanian Fokker, would fly above the clouds until it was directly over Baghdad International and then drop like a piano, like a dive bomber, not really descending in a corkscrew like the pilot said but falling in long vertical strokes. The dive was designed to protect us from ground fire.

The jet would drop straight onto the runway, pulling up at the last second and slamming down hard and fast before coming to a stop. As I got off, the stewardess, also South African, would smile and say, "Did you see they were shooting at us?" And then I'd meet the Iraqi immigration officers, sullen and corrupt with their thick Saddam mustaches, same guys as before, making a fuss about letting me in, as if anyone would come in if he didn't have to. When I stepped from the terminal, the armed guards would be waiting for me, as would Waleed, my driver and friend, smiling with a hug, and we'd get in the armored car and set out on the airport road, where convoys got hit every day. We'd pass the carcasses of the cars, the sawed-down date palms where the Americans tried to deny the guerrillas cover, the fences and the blast walls. Driving in was an upper and a downer at once, like putting a bullet in the chamber.

No, it was in the leaving that I felt the essence of the place. As much as I hated arriving, I hated leaving more. After so long I'd become part of the place, part of the despair, part of the death and the bad food and the heat and the sandy-colored brown of it. I felt I understood its complications and its paradoxes and even its humor, felt a jealous brotherhood with everyone who was trying to keep it from sinking even deeper. I hugged the Iraqis who worked with me as I climbed into the armored car, letting them lift my bags into the trunk. I saw the envious looks they threw me for leaving. As we pulled out of the compound the guards switched the safeties off their guns. And when the car hit the long flat stretch of airport road my stomach tightened, not from the danger of the place but from the anticipation. From the thought of leaving the world, the big, wide, only world, and moving to the next one. The two worlds. There was nothing in between, no way station, no purgatory, only this world and the other.

The Royal Jordanian plane lifted off and I could see the others on board felt the same. Diplomats, reporters, contractors, guards: tightened mouths and grim faces, nobody smiling and nobody whooping for finally getting out. We'd become Iraq, become the unhappy land, become so much a part of it that we worried about our place in the other world to which we were now returning. And from which we were now so estranged.

And then the plane lifted off, reversing its downward spiral with an upward one, flying as steeply upward into the sky as it had descended, circling the airport in wide arcs as it pulled us higher up. And as I looked down, the view never changed. We were moving higher and higher but not away; it was the same world, brown and flat and dead and hot, growing wider and wider as we turned. It was as if we weren't moving at all, it was as if we were stuck, as if the place below would never change and we would never leave.

CHAPTER 9

The Man Within

NATHAN SASSAMAN sat on the dais and walked his subjects through the first steps of democratic rule. It was a Friday morning at the Balad Youth Center, fifty miles north of Baghdad. Sassaman, an army lieutenant colonel, had gathered the newly elected members of the Balad City Council for their first meeting. He had an athlete's broad frame and he'd taken off his helmet and placed it on the table so the Iraqis could get a better look at him.

"Okay," the colonel said, glancing in the direction of an Iraqi man standing behind a card table, "could you please pick up the ballot box and show us all that it's empty?"

An Iraqi man dutifully turned over a large cardboard box and held it up high. Nothing fell out.

"And now," Sassaman told the Iraqis, "you are going to decide whether or not to extend the term of Mayor Darwash. It's a yes or no vote. It's up to you."

Sassaman looked out at the seventy Iraqis who made up the new council. He was an intelligent man, and I could almost see his eyes sparkle from my place in the audience.

"Mayor Darwash, why don't you come forward?"

A tired-looking man shuffled to the front of the room and took a seat.

With that, the newly elected members of the Balad City Council stood and walked over to the table. They filled out their ballots and dropped them into the box. Then they returned to their seats and waited for the results.

With Sassaman looking on, the Iraqi standing at the card table tallied the votes and wrote the score on a blackboard behind him. Mayor Darwash lost, 35 to 24.

"All right, that is your decision," Sassaman said. He looked at Darwash, still slumped in his chair.

"I want to take a moment to congratulate the mayor for the great job he's done, for all the effort he has made for a secure and stable environment in Balad."

Darwash stood up, and all the Iraqis clapped.

"Next week, we'll choose a new mayor," Sassaman said. And the meeting continued on its way.

Only a few weeks before, Sassaman had presided over a revolutionary event in this small, crumbling city, registering forty-five thousand Iraqis to vote in the first election that anyone could remember. The American occupation was only six months old in October 2003, and Sassaman had pushed so far ahead of his peers around the rest of the country that the civilian leadership in Baghdad had already tried to slow him down. The Iraqis weren't ready for so much democracy, the diplomats told him. Sassaman had forged ahead anyway, and his superiors in Baghdad had finally relented, telling him that he could go forward as long as he agreed to call the process a "selection" rather than an "election." So he did, and the "selection" in Balad went off without a hitch.

"It was a free election, without threats or intimidation," Ahmad Abdul Wahid, the deputy mayor, told me after the meeting broke up. "Colonel Sassaman is very patient with us. He tolerates our criticisms. I respect him. No one wants the Americans to stay, but our country is not secure yet. Six more months at least. We can live with that."

In the fall of 2003, Nathan Sassaman, then forty, was the most impressive American field commander in Iraq. He was witty, bright and relentless, the embodiment of the best that America could offer. He was the son of a Methodist minister and a graduate of West Point; as the quarterback for Army's football team, he had led the school to its first bowl victory. When I met him, Sassaman was working day and night to make the American project in Iraq succeed, inspiring the eight hundred young men under his command to do the same. He slept in his boots.

Sassaman's patch of territory, about three hundred square miles around the Tigris River, contained all the contradictions of post-Saddam Iraq. Balad, the main city, was dominated by Shiite Muslims, the majority sect that had borne the brunt of Saddam's furies. Outside Balad, the countryside was populated by Sunnis, the minority that had dominated Mesopotamia—under Saddam, under the British, under the Ottomans—for hundreds of years. Deposed by the invasion, the Sunnis had already begun to resist the American project. In the fall of 2003, the insurgency was just beginning to find its legs.

Just as the two realities, Sunni and Shia, came to define modern Iraq, they came, in the weeks and months ahead, to define the struggle for Colonel Sassaman's heart. In the Shiite areas like Balad—in halls and venues like the Balad Youth Center—the Iraqis thanked the Americans for their liberation, and their neighborhoods were largely safe and secure. Sassaman's virtues flourished there: his vision, his intelligence, his tirelessness. When I met him, in October 2003, Sassaman had already dispersed nearly $1 million to set up a new government and refurbish mosques and schools. His junior officers were studying Arabic, and Sassaman was halfway through *From Beirut to Jerusalem*, Thomas L. Friedman's book on the Middle East. Every Friday, inside a circle of armored personnel carriers, the local Iraqis and the men of Sassaman's 1-8 battalion would square off for a game of soccer.

His men loved him. "It wouldn't be anything to be out there doing a raid or doing whatever and then a Bradley would pull up behind you and it would be like, who the hell is this?" Captain Matthew Cunningham, a company commander, told me. "And you look back and it's the colonel. Whoa, whoa, whoa. It's the old man. It's Colonel Sassaman. He's out here with us."

As he drove his Humvee around Balad, Sassaman seemed to carry the hopes of the American enterprise on his shoulders. It seemed, on those good days, that it just might work, despite all the problems, because of people like him.

Yet outside Balad's city limits, the landscape changed, and Sassaman did, too. The Sunnis, disenfranchised by the American invasion, didn't see goodwill in Sassaman's promises, or in his gestures, or even in his money. They were hostile and intractable, and they were not, or at least did not appear to be, amenable to politics. In the Sunni countryside, the preacher's son saw his generosity go unrewarded, saw his good works blown up and painted with graffiti. Over time, when Sassaman went into the countryside, he began to slough off the virtues that had paid such dividends inside the Shiite city of Balad.

At first, the colonel revealed his disillusionment only briefly, usually at the end of a very long day. Once, as I was sitting in his barracks with him near midnight, Sassaman said that he and his men had come to Iraq trained to fight a big battle against a big, uniformed army, something out of World War II. They hadn't received any instruction on holding elections or setting up police departments. No one in his unit spoke more than a few words of Arabic. The men made do. One of the reservists under Sassaman's command happened to have carried with him an operations manual from the Tiverton, Rhode Island, police department, where he worked. And soon enough, the Balad police department was functioning remarkably like its New England counterpart. "We are doing a lot of missions that we didn't train for," Sassaman told me that night. "Sometimes I wish there were more people who knew more about nation building."

The struggle inside of Sassaman intensified with the insurgency itself, which, in the fall of 2003, was expanding across the Sunni Triangle, the vast area north and west of Baghdad. One night, as we sat inside a darkened chow hall eating dinner, he spoke in despair. "Sometimes I think they just want us to leave," he said. His face was invisible in the blackened tent. "I am getting tired of telling mothers and fathers that they have lost their sons."

There were ugly moments and there were hopeful ones, and they made me wonder not only what the Americans were doing to Iraq, but what Iraq was doing to the Americans. The struggle for the country was mirrored in the hearts of the men. Sassaman himself sometimes seemed like two people, the visionary American officer setting up a city council, and the warrior who took too much joy in the brutalites of his job.

"It's like Jekyll and Hyde out here," Sassaman told me after the Balad City Council meeting. "By day, we are putting on a happy face. By night, we are hunting down and killing our enemies."

At dawn the morning after the council meeting, Sassaman led his 1-8 battalion on a series of house-to-house searches in Abu Shakur, a Sunni village outside Balad. Sassaman's men had been taking mortar fire from the palm groves near the town, and the colonel was determined to stop it.

That morning, the battalion's men swept into Abu Shakur and, without warning, began to kick down doors. House after house, the soldiers poured in with their rifles ready to shoot. They rousted men from their beds and pulled them outside, many of them still in their pajamas and underwear, their wives and children looking on in horror. "Get down and don't move," one of the soldiers growled at an Iraqi man.

In a raid on a particularly large house, the soldiers dashed inside, pulling mattresses off bedframes and clothing from closets, throwing lamps and cushions onto the floor. The soldiers pulled eleven Iraqi men outside, forcing them to sit on their haunches with their hands behind their heads. As they crashed through the house, a young woman stood with three small girls, probably her daughters, each with her hands high in the air. The Americans found no weapons. The Iraqi men squatted outside for half an hour, the unhappiness etched on their faces. "I feel bad for these people, I really do," Sergeant Eric Brown said to me, standing over the Iraqi men. "It's so hard to separate the good from the bad."

By midmorning, Sassaman's battalion had searched seventy homes in Abu Shakur and questioned dozens of men, but netted not a single gun nor a single suspect. If you multiplied the raid on Abu Shakur a thousand times, it was not difficult to conclude that the war was being lost: however many Iraqis opposed them before the Americans came into the village, dozens and dozens more did by the time they left. The Americans were making enemies faster than they could kill them.

Later in the day, I drove with Sassaman into the countryside again, this time to a meeting of Sunni clerics at a mosque outside Balad. As we bounced along in the Humvee, Sassaman said he was reconsidering his policy of spending the bulk of his reconstruction money in Shiite Balad. Ramadan, the Muslim month of fasting, had begun a week before, and Sassaman had recently proposed a truce to the Sunni sheikhs: he would scale back the number of American patrols in the Sunni villages as long as his men did not come under attack. So far, the truce was holding. "There hasn't been a mortar attack in three weeks," Sassaman told me as we rolled up to a mosque. "We're going to give the people here a chance to do the right thing." I could sense the hardness in his voice.

The Sunni imams had gathered in the courtyard of the mosque, most of them seated in the grass. They smiled at Sassaman and shook his hand. Sitting before them, Sassaman asked the imams how they were faring. One by one, they aired their complaints, nearly all of them identical: young Sunni men were being roughed up and detained by American soldiers because of the misdeeds of a handful of troublemakers whose identities none of them knew.

"We are trying to calm the people down, but it is difficult," Sheikh Mushtaq Hamid told Sassaman. Hamid was dressed in a red-and-white-checked kafiya and a brown robe. "The situation is unsettled.

"From time to time some of our people are attacked by American soldiers," the sheikh went on. "They are being detained with no evidence. Sometimes the parents are not even informed of what has happened to their son."

Sassaman sat quietly. I thought of the raids in Abu Shakur a few hours before. The sheikhs were frank, but they were not angry.

"Colonel Sassaman, you must understand," Hamid said. "There is some suspicion. Before the war, the American way of life was the democratic way. Everyone knew this. And when the Americans invaded Iraq, they were not democratic with the Iraqi people. You cannot accuse innocent people."

Less than three weeks before, Hamid said, the Americans had come down his street and detained sixteen men without cause, including the sheikh himself.

"There was no evidence against me," Hamid said, pointing at himself with his fingers. "They pulled my beard. They cuffed my hands behind my back and blindfolded me."

Sassaman listened to Hamid's complaints, but he didn't address them. I wasn't surprised. The grievances being voiced by the imams were genuine. But if you happened to be an American officer presiding over an occupation, they were one-sided: the imams weren't offering Sassaman any help whatsoever.

"Who is attacking my men?" Sassaman asked.

"Foreign people," one of the imams replied. "People from the outside. People from Ramadi."

Sassaman carried on, coming to the point of his visit.

"Thank you for being peaceful of late," Sassaman said. "We have some money, and we would like to help you make some improvements on your mosques. We'd like to do some building."

The imams perked up. At last the conversation gathered speed. Sassaman and the imams began talking specifics, this mosque and that, $300 for a roof, $100 for a door. Then the subject turned to schools. Sassaman's men had paid for about 60 to be repainted so far; about 120 remained.

"We have schools, but no desks, no books," said one of the clerics, Muhata. "Also the irrigation system is destroyed. We need water for our fields. What about that?"

"Well," Sassaman said, leaning back, "if I were in charge, and I guess I am, I'd say, Water for everyone!"

The imams laughed. The climate had changed. It seemed a kind of game now: Sassaman promising and half promising, the imams indulging him with a smile. The colonel changed the subject.

"Have any of you seen Saddam Hussein?" he asked.

The imams shook their heads and smiled again.

"If you find him, I can assure you, you won't have any more problems with your schools," the colonel said. "You'll have more money than you can spend. Anything you want."

The imams laughed again; but why, exactly, was unclear. They led Sassaman to his Humvee and bid him a warm good-bye.

The next day, as I prepared to leave Balad, Sassaman told me he had been ordered to dispatch one of his companies to Samarra, a violent city twenty miles to the north. With the exception of Falluja, Samarra was the hardest, meanest city in all of Iraq. It was slipping from American control. Sassaman was excited about the mission; he invited me to go along. Come back in a couple of weeks, he said. He smiled as he spoke. His eyes were glowing.

"We are going to inflict extreme violence."

SASSAMAN WAS STANDING at a checkpoint, waving back a crowd of unhappy men. He was holding up an identification card, which he was now requiring for all the men of Abu Hishma, at the entrance to which he now stood. The Iraqis pushed and surged.

"If you have one of these cards, you can come and go," Sassaman said over the crowd. "If you don't have one of these cards, you can't."

Some of the men tried to enter the village, and they were blocked by American soldiers.

"You will not enter until you get a card," Sassaman told them. "Thank you."

Abu Hishma, a Sunni village of about seven thousand, was encased by razor wire. The wire was laid out in big, rolling hoops, one on top of the other, stretching for two miles, along the road and through the date groves and all the way to the banks of the Tigris. Along the way, signs were posted warning the locals against trying to pass through the fence.

"This fence is here for your protection," one of the signs said. "Do not approach or try to cross or you will be shot."

Sassaman was directing the Iraqis to a brick shed where his soldiers were issuing the ID cards. Inside, an American soldier stood with a camera, taking a mug shot. Before him stood an Iraqi man, holding up two pieces of paper, one in each hand, to make his ID number, 2 and 02. A line of men waited outside.

"Where is the Iraqi freedom?" Faiz Musla, forty-six, a father of eight, said as he walked out of the shack. "We are just like the people in the Gaza Strip."

A young man handed me his card. It showed his unsmiling face; his name, Mohin Hussein; his number, 284; and the make of his car, a 1981 white Toyota. "Abu Hishma Resident ID," the card said in English. Not a word was in Arabic.

Only a month had passed since I'd last been here, but both Sassaman and the surrounding area seemed different. Sassaman was a harder man, without the lightness or humor he'd shown before. The eyes that glittered were now mostly dull. The insurgency, then a simmering threat, had bloomed into a full-blown rebellion. As Sassaman had promised, he had scaled back the number of patrols in the Sunni countryside. The insurgents had used the pause to organize and step up their attacks. It was happening not just around Balad, but across the entire Sunni heartland.

Mortar fire was coming into Sassaman's base regularly. Homemade bombs were exploding under the roads, under dead animals. The IEDs were getting bigger and more sophisticated: a typical roadside bomb now consisted of a stack of antitank mines triggered by a call from a cell phone. And the insurgents had money, more than the Americans. Captain Alex Williams, the battalion's intelligence officer, told me the insurgents had put a $50,000 bounty on Sassaman's head, and smaller ones on his subordinate officers. They were paying kids $300 each to lay a roadside bomb.

The breaking point for Sassaman had come two weeks before, on November 17. A group of his soldiers was on patrol, driving a pair of Bradley personnel carriers down the two-lane road near the entrance to Abu Hishma. A group of Iraqi kids started taunting the soldiers, running their fingers across their necks. The kids knew what was coming next. A couple of seconds later, a group of insurgents fired a volley of rocket-propelled grenades. One of them pierced the front of one of the Bradleys and sailed into the chest of Dale Panchot, a twenty-six-year-old staff sergeant from Northome, Minnesota. It nearly cut him in half.

The next morning, Sassaman's men swept through the village kicking down doors, throwing Iraqis to the ground, leading young men away. In the ensuing days Sassaman called in airstrikes on houses suspected of sheltering insurgents; his tanks bulldozed others. He fired phosphorous rounds into wheat fields where insurgents had set up mortars, burning them to the ground. And they began wrapping Abu Hishma in razor wire. "We've been wreaking havoc," Captain Todd Brown told me.

I'd heard about the troubles in Abu Hishma and drove north with Ashley Gilbertson, the photographer. Still in our car, we came upon Abu Hishma, encased in razor wire. The checkpoint did indeed look like something in the West Bank. We spotted a group of American soldiers and pulled over. Sassaman was one of them. They were standing over an Iraqi man. It was an interrogation.

"If you weren't here, we would beat the shit out of this guy," one of the soldiers said.

Sassaman was looking for the men who killed Panchot and he thought he'd found one. The man was wearing a sportshirt that said "Opel" on it. The soldiers yanked it up over his head, revealing a bandaged wound on the man's back.

"Football," the man said through his upturned shirt.

"That's a bullet wound," Sassaman said, and they led the man away.

The next morning, as I watched Sassaman explain the new ID cards to the Iraqis, I slipped past the front gate and into the village itself. Abu Hishma was a drab collection of low-slung buildings, one of the innumerable farm towns that dotted the banks of the Tigris.

The streets were silent. Bulldozed houses lay in rubble. Graffiti covered the walls that were still standing. "We'll sacrifice our blood and souls for Saddam," said one. There wasn't any question that this was a stronghold for the insurgency. But there were old ladies and kids walking around, too. A group of young men watched me from inside a ruined house.

I walked over to three men sitting on a curb.

"This is absolutely humiliating," said one of them, Yasin Mustafa, a thirty-nine-year-old primary-school teacher. "We are like birds in a cage."

Sassaman and his men were sweeping Abu Hishma every night, the men said, taking away young men, sometimes all the males in a single family. They cuffed them, they put bags over their heads. The young men were disappearing into American detention camps without a word. "Even women, even children—suddenly, when the women are sleeping," one of the men said. Among those detained, the men said, were several local police officers and Fahim Mohammad, a member of the city council.

What the Iraqi men were saying mirrored the new American approach then unfolding across the Sunni Triangle. Confronted by an insurgency they had not anticipated, American commanders had ordered a crackdown across the Sunni heartland. Almost immediately the get-tough tactics brought the violence down. Prisons like Abu Ghraib swelled with new arrivals. But the tactics, even as they were restoring a measure of calm, were intensifying the hatred the Sunnis already felt for the Americans.

Now, the three Iraqi men told me, Abu Hishma was under a fifteen-hour curfew, beginning at five o'clock in the afternoon and lasting until eight o'clock the next morning. That meant none of Abu Hishma's people could go to the mosque for morning or evening prayers. And it meant they could no longer sit in their cars to buy gasoline, a daily ordeal for Iraqis that usually lasted well into the night.

I asked them about Sassaman.

"All the people know him," said Ra'ad Daoud, one of the

men. "He is a war criminal. He has killed children. He is the commander who bombed four houses in Abu Hishma. In one of those houses there were seven children; two of them were injured. He has taken our sheikhs to jail. He came into Abu Hishma and he said to us, There is no God—I am God here."

I wasn't sure how much to believe. Then an elderly man, Hamjir Thamir Rabia, spoke up: "At night, when the mothers of Abu Hishma put their boys to sleep, they tell them they had better be good. Or Colonel Sassaman will come to get them."

I walked out of the village, through the gate, to the astonishment of the American soldiers on the outside. "Those people are wild in there," Captain Brown told me, looking over my shoulder.

Sassaman was still directing traffic at the checkpoint and I pulled him aside. Most of what he was doing—bulldozing homes, calling in airstrikes, capturing families, encasing the village in razor wire—had been approved or ordered by his commanders, he said. Wrapping Abu Hishma wasn't his idea; it was his commander's. Even so, Sassaman believed he had no other choice. "I've told the people here, when they turn over the guys that killed Panchot, I'll remove the fence. Otherwise it stays."

Only eight months had passed since Saddam's regime fell, but it seemed a lifetime away. Later that day, I asked Sassaman if he wasn't alienating anyone in Abu Hishma who might have been willing to help. To the contrary, he said. "I think we are close," he said. "With a heavy dose of fear and violence, and a lot of money for projects, I think we can convince these people that we are here to help them."

I asked him if he really meant that. Fear and violence?

"The good people we can bring around," Sassaman said. "But the bad guys—they have to be convinced that there is a price to pay for opposing us."

Some of Sassaman's soldiers had begun throwing around a phrase, "the Arab mind," which they had picked up from a pseudoscientific book by the same name that was popular among American officers. One of them was Captain Brown. In the raids on Abu Shakur two months before, I had watched as Brown had stopped to give an ad hoc English lesson to a group of Iraqi schoolgirls. The girls had looked at him as if he were some great god. "You've got to understand the Arab mind," Brown told me outside the gates of Abu Hishma. "The only thing they understand is force—force, pride and saving face."

Of course, like all such generalizations, this one had some truth to it. Even with the village of Abu Hishma in full revolt, some of the locals still retained their sycophantic ways in the presence of an absolute leader. With the cars of Abu Hishma rolling through the checkpoint, an old man walked up to Sassaman and showed him his ID card. Sassaman waved him through, but the old man stayed back. He was trembling in Sassaman's presence, but he wasn't backing down.

"Colonel Sassaman, you should come and live in this village and be a sheikh," the man, Hassan Ali al-Tai, told the colonel.

Sassaman gave him a smile, and Tai looked at me.

"Colonel Sassaman is a very good man," Tai said! "If he got rid of the barbed wire and the checkpoint, everyone would love him."

SASSAMAN WALKED INTO the Starbucks in downtown Colorado Springs wearing shorts and a sweatshirt. He'd just come from running a 10K race with his ten-year-old daughter, Nicole. After so much time away, Sassaman was amazed by how fast his daughter had become, and how competitive. "You should see her," Sassaman said, beaming with a father's pride. "She really has the infantryman in her. I don't know where she got that."

He was looking for a job. Home Depot was dangling an executive position, and that paid a lot of money. But there was a clinic that trained high school football coaches that was ready to bring him in. Sassaman said he hadn't made up his mind yet, but he was leaning toward coaching, even though it paid far less. "I feel like I should give something back to society," Sassaman told me. "I know this is weird—does this sound weird? I just want to work with young kids, be able to mentor coaches. Just touch people, let them know that life is fragile, that it's fleeting. And sometimes, incredibly unfair."

Sassaman was leaving the army. His career was finished. He was lucky, all things considered, that he had stayed out of jail.

I might have guessed that something like this was coming, though I had missed the moment itself. It happened on a January night, about a month after I'd last seen him, at the foot of a bridge on the banks of the Tigris.

A group of Sassaman's men had been on patrol in Samarra when they spotted a couple of Iraqis driving around past curfew. The soldiers stopped the men, who happened to be cousins, searched their truck and found a heap of bathroom fixtures. They told the Iraqis to hurry home. Then, as the two men started to leave, the soldiers stopped them again. This time, the Americans cuffed the two Iraqis, whose names were Marwan and Zaydoon Fadil, put them in the hull of their Bradley and took them to a spot on the Tigris.

It was a dark and frigid January night. The soldiers motioned with their guns. Jump, they told them. Marwan and Zaydoon resisted, even begged. Finally they went into the water, and the Americans drove away.

"It was a dumb call," Sassaman said, nursing his coffee.

Pushing people into the Tigris at night, I now learned, was one of a number of punishments Sassaman's men had dreamed up to discipline the Iraqis who had gone completely out of control. That is, discipline the Iraqis without killing them. They called it "nonlethal force." Sassaman approved of some of the measures, disapproved of others. He claimed not to know about what his kids called "getting people wet."

Nonlethal force: it wasn't so hard to understand. By the fall of 2003, the Sunni heartland was in open revolt. It wasn't just that the insurgents were killing American soldiers. It was that the civilians were defying the Americans in every way they could. Whenever Sassaman's soldiers entered a village, children threw rocks. Adults threw rocks. People, sometimes entire villages, defied the curfew. When the Americans drove onto a street, the locals would give them the middle finger. They would drag their fingers across their necks. "If I didn't do anything when a guy flipped me off," one of Sassaman's men told me in Colorado Springs, "then the next time you drive around there, you are going to catch an RPG [rocket-propelled grenade]."

To bring the Iraqis back under control, Sassaman and his

men devised a range of "nonlethal" punishments. They thought it was cutting-edge stuff. Some of it was. When kids threw rocks at Sassaman's soldiers, he ordered his men to throw rocks back. When a kid in Abu Hishma ran his finger across his neck in front of one of Sassaman's captains, Matthew Cunningham, he chased the kid in his Bradley, plowed through a village wall and pulled the kid out of the house. When Sassaman's soldiers caught Iraqis violating curfew, they drove them miles outside of town, dropped them off and made them walk home. When they found anti-American graffiti, they bulldozed the wall it was painted on. Nothing terribly brutal—not in the beginning, anyway.

"All I was getting at was, if grown-ups throw rocks at me, we're throwing them back," Sassaman said to me. "We are not going to just wave. We are not driving by and taking it. Because a lot of the units did."

By the time he ended his tour in Iraq, the insurgents had come to fear Sassaman more than anyone else. Whenever he left Balad, even for a couple of days, the insurgents would step up their attacks. When he returned, they would back off. Once, after Sassaman returned from a mission in Samarra, insurgents fired a single mortar round into his compound, as if to welcome him back. He responded by firing twenty-eight 155-millimeter artillery shells and forty-two mortar rounds. He called in two airstrikes, one with a 500-pound bomb and the other with a 2,000-pound bomb. Later on, his men found a crater as deep as a swimming pool.

"You know what?" Sassaman told me at the Starbucks. "We just didn't get hit after that."

But for all of that, Sassaman told me, the situation in the Sunni villages kept getting worse. One day, during the middle of his tour, his commander, Major General Raymond Odierno, flew to the local HQ and gave Sassaman a direct but curiously vague order: "Increase lethality." Kill more people, the general told him. Odierno didn't tell Sassaman how; he just wanted higher body counts. So Sassaman's men started experimenting—sometimes with the colonel's approval, sometimes not.

Sassaman claimed he never knew about Iraqis being

pushed into the Tigris. In this case, the problem came when the Fadil family told the Americans that Marwan, one of the two cousins who'd been forced into the Tigris that night, had climbed out of the water, while the other, Zaydoon, had drowned.

When the American investigators arrived, Sassaman ordered his men to lie. "I told my guys to tell them about everything—everything except the water," Sassaman told me. At this point, we'd moved from the Starbucks to a Chipotle burrito restaurant, in a strip shopping center on the other side of Colorado Springs. Sassaman didn't seem especially sorry.

"I could have turned them all in and sent them to jail and gone back to the base and that would have been it," Sassaman said, echoing what he told a judge. "But I wasn't going to let the lives of my men be destroyed. Not because they pushed a couple of insurgents into a pond."

A couple of weeks after the incident at the river, an Iraqi search party found a body floating facedown in an irrigation canal off the Tigris. It was about a mile from the spot where the soldiers had made Marwan and Zaydoon jump in. Before I flew to Colorado Springs to see Sassaman, I'd watched a brief, badly lit video of a funeral. The Fadil family said it was Zaydoon's. The video showed a waterlogged cadaver covered in a shroud. The cloth was peeled back, revealing a wrinkly face. "Focus on the eyes," a voice said over the video. Zaydoon's family said they'd buried the body the day it was found.

A group of American investigators never determined whether the body was actually Zaydoon's, or whether he'd just faked his drowning to cause a stir in the United States. At the trial of one of Sassaman's soldiers, some of his comrades who witnessed the incident testified that they had watched both Zaydoon and Marwan climb out of the Tigris. Some of them said they'd seen Marwan get out—not Zaydoon. The Americans wanted to exhume and run tests on the body found floating in the Tigris, but the Fadil family was opposed, for religious reasons, they said. There was indeed some evidence to suggest that Zaydoon's drowning had been faked. An Iraqi informant, for instance, had told an American intelligence officer that Zaydoon was alive and well. But such evidence was

naturally incomplete. Sergeant Irene Cintron, an army inves-
tigator in the case, told a judge she never had any doubts that
Zaydoon had drowned. "I personally believed that the whole
chain of command was lying to me," Cintron said.

And then there was Marwan, the Iraqi survivor. I drove
him to the scene near Samarra and stood with him on the
bank of the irrigation canal. Beneath us, the water was still. It
looked like it would have been easy to jump into the water and
climb out. That is, unless it was dark and cold and you swam
in the wrong direction. In that case, the gates of the Tharthar
Dam were only thirty feet away, pulling the water in at terrifying speed.

"I felt the water dragging me," Marwan said. "I was thinking of Zaydoon. I was looking at him. The water was so cold.
My feet never touched the bottom. I tried to save Zaydoon,
but he slipped from my hands."

In the end, two of Sassaman's soldiers went to jail. Not for
drowning Zaydoon—nobody could prove that—but for pushing him and Marwan into the Tigris. For getting them wet.
The irony was not lost on Sassaman, who received a written
reprimand, effectively ending his career. "You know what's
strange?" Sassaman said at the Chipotle. "Two Iraqis out after
curfew, in a town like Samarra? They could have killed those
guys, and they would have gotten medals."

AFTER THE LUNCH with Sassaman, I drove to the other side
of Colorado Springs to meet Ralph Logan. In the sorry case
of Marwan and Zaydoon, Logan was the only American who
acted with unquestioned honor. Logan, a low-ranking special-
ist from Indian Lake, Ohio, had been in the Bradley that night
when his comrades spotted Marwan and Zaydoon driving
around after curfew. He'd helped cuff them. But when his
lieutenant ordered him to throw Marwan and Zaydoon into
the Tigris, Logan refused. Logan's commander was angry
with him, but he let him stay behind in the road. The other
soldiers walked Marwan and Zaydoon down to the riverbank.

I found Logan in the living room of his girlfriend's home.
She was at work and Logan was watching her two young chil-

dren. The floor was covered in toys and papers and uneaten food. Logan was working day and night then, building houses and tending bar. Like Sassaman, he'd left the army, too. "Basically, the guys in the unit made it clear they didn't want me around anymore," Logan said.

I asked him about the night on the Tigris. Logan spoke with the faint drawl of his rural Ohio home.

"The best way I can explain it is, it's like a new kid on the playground," Logan told me. "Say you're a fifth grader. You just moved into the school. You've got to earn the respect of the other kids. Sometimes that involves throwing down a little bit, so they know they can't push you around. Personally, the whole incident, I kind of look at it as high schoolers picking on freshmen. Us being the seniors and the Iraqis being the freshmen. We're throwing them in the river. It was like giving someone a swirly."

What's a swirly? I asked Logan. We were seated on the floor with the toys.

"When you turn the kid upside down and throw his head down in the toilet and flush it."

Logan laughed a little.

"They weren't meaning for anyone to drown."

What about Sassaman? I asked him.

"There is the white, the right way, and the black, the wrong way. And there is a large, gray middle—the gray area in the middle where most of the shit gets done," Logan said. "Sassaman liked to play in the gray. You know, Charlie-Mike. Continue Mission. Finish the mission. That was his philosophy. His company commanders did not have to call him to ask permission to do things if it was a life-or-limb situation. He left it in their hands. They are trained officers, trained soldiers. He trusted their judgment. And when they did something, he backed them up on it. Or he turned a blind eye to it."

We started talking about Iraq. Logan shook his head.

"The culture there, I just—whoa," he said. "They sat there with their hand out and saying, Help us, please help us. And then in the other hand, they are holding an M-16 behind their back, waiting for us to turn around and shoot us."

Two years later, after I returned to the United States, I decided to track Logan down. I had some difficulty at first. It turned out he had left Colorado Springs and gone back to his boyhood home in Indian Lake. His grandmother was dying, and Logan wanted to spend the last weeks with her. On the night of September 10, 2006, Logan walked into the lobby of the Comfort Inn motel and robbed the attendant at knifepoint. Then Logan drove to his mother's home. He left the $4,000 he got from the hotel in a bag in the car. He didn't try to flee. He didn't hide the money. Three days later, a police officer came to the house; he and Logan had gone to the same high school. Logan had been waiting for him. He confessed on the spot. He got two years in prison. His mother, Nancy, visits him twice a month. He is hoping to be a truck driver when he gets out, she said. She told me she'd never heard about Marwan and Zaydoon.

"I wonder every day if something happened while he was over there," she said.

CHAPTER 10

Kill Yourself

THERE WERE THESE stories going around about the suicide bombers. Just rumors, of course. One story I heard was that there were so many volunteers crossing over from Syria asking to kill themselves that there weren't enough missions to go around. A bottleneck of sorts. So the organizers were handing out numbers and sending the volunteers home—to Amman, to Damascus—and telling them to wait for a telephone call. The phone call went like this: "Number 27, it's your turn. Come." Made sense to me. So many people were blowing themselves up that it was hard to keep track. In the first five years, more than nine hundred people detonated themselves in Iraq, sometimes several in a single day. That was before you counted the car bombs, when the driver got out before it exploded. There were thousands of those. Among the insurgents, there was a large demand for the suiciders, as the Iraqis called them. In the summer of 2005, someone posted a manual on the Internet for would-be volunteers called "This Is the Road to Iraq." It gave instructions for young jihadis to get into the country and told them what to do once they got there. Go to Syria first, the manual said, and make sure you tell the immigration authorities that you are going to Turkey next. That way, they'll give you a transit visa and everyone will be sufficiently fooled. Take a bus to the Iraqi border, "wear jeans and eat donuts and use a Walkman which has a tape of any singer. Do this for Allah's

sake; war is tricks." Once you are across, the manual said, do anything your bosses tell you. "Never say that you do not do suicide work."

Another story concerned women. The young men who came across the border to join the insurgency often stopped in one of the towns on the Iraqi side of the border, Al-Qaim, say, or Husayba. While they were there, they waited for one of the jihadi groups to recruit them, or for their number to be called. And, the story went, the foreign jihadis were so popular with the locals that fathers would sometimes offer the fighters one of their daughters for marriage, or temporary marriage at least, one of Islam's loopholes for casual sex. And eventually, the jihadis would go off to war, and they'd get killed, or they'd blow themselves up, so few of them ever returned to the little Iraqi villages where they'd laid up for a while. And so, the story went, some of these Iraqi border villages contained unusually large numbers of children without fathers. And unusually large numbers of unwed mothers. It was just a story.

Once I asked an American military adviser how he thought the pipeline worked. We were sharing a Coke in the Green Zone. If you were an aspiring jihadi, how would you hook up with an insurgent group once you'd crossed the border?

"Oh," the American said, sipping his Coke, "I think it would be like wandering into a bar in Belfast and asking about the IRA." Not very difficult, in other words. The Euphrates River ran from the Syrian border all the way to Falluja, just west of Baghdad. The Americans called it the rat line.

The smoke was usually white. Not black; white. Black smoke meant other things. American bombs, for instance. But car bombs and suicide bombs sent plumes barreling into the sky that were, in my experience, nearly always white. This was useful knowledge if you were trying to figure out what was happening from a distance. Sometimes the white smoke was very white, too, even luminous. In 2004 a suicide bomber drove his car into the Lebanon Hotel. The billows of smoke shimmered in the night sky, like clouds in front of a full moon.

One autumn evening a man driving a silver Mitsubishi minivan filled with TNT drove into the cement wall that surrounded the Sheraton and Palestine hotels in Baghdad. The blast blew a breach in the wall, and before the cloud cleared, a cement mixer, also filled with TNT, drove through it. The Iraqi hotel guards had disappeared. The guy in the cement mixer made it as far as the curb outside the Sheraton's lobby when his truck, a Russian-made Kamaz, got hung up on a piece of razor wire. I watched the whole thing afterward on one of the Sheraton's closed-circuit televisions. The driver of the cement mixer, realizing he was tangled in the wire, backed up a little and drove forward again. He was aiming for the lobby, but the razor wire wouldn't give. Finally an American soldier stationed on the other side of the complex spotted the cement mixer and shot the driver, but it was too late. The blast sent up a gigantic Hiroshima cloud, a dirty white-brown mushroom twenty stories high. I was in the *Times*'s house down the street. The blast blew out nearly every window. Our three-story cement building rocked back and forth like a toy. The radiator from one of the trucks landed in the backyard, smoking and hot to the touch. For a moment I thought we'd come under attack. I went up to the roof and watched the Iraqi police shoot wildly in the chaos.

The Sheraton still stood the next morning. The lobby was in ruins; all the hotel's windows had been shattered. A pair of feet, bloodless and green, sat together on display on the side-walk. The Americans said they'd come from the driver of the cement mixer. And there was a spinal cord, unfurled on the sidewalk. And a finger, black and green.

A month later, I watched a video about the attack posted on a jihadi website. It was a slick production, "Brought to you by the media section of Al-Qaeda," a banner on the video said. First came portraits of the three suicide bombers: two of them had Saudi names and the third was Syrian. Then, remarkably, the video shifted to a briefing given by an Al-Qaeda planner to the three bombers before the attack. The Al-Qaeda leader was not shown in the video, but he could be heard speaking in a calm, dispassionate voice, with a noticeable Saudi accent. He used his electronic pointer to pick out various things on a sur-veillance video Al-Qaeda had made of the Palestine and Sher-aton complex. "This is the gas station," the Al-Qaeda man said, issuing orders to two bombers. "Brother Abu Jihan and Abu Daham will park there. They will be in the queue and no one will notice them.

"Abu Naim, pay attention," the planner said, calling to the third bomber, who was evidently present for the briefing. "You will set off your bombs right here, to destroy the blast walls around the building."

Toward the end of the video, one of the bombers offered his last will and testament. His name, he said, was Abu Daham Rahimullah, and he looked to be in his early twenties. Rahi-mullah's statement, which he read from a piece of paper, was filled with proclamations of glory. But the young man had a sullen face, and he hardly looked at the camera. "I swear to God," he said, his eyes darting, "I am the happiest I have ever been in my life."

One thing I heard a lot was how the jihadis were some-times tricked or coerced into killing themselves. Sometimes, the police would find the steering wheel of a suicide car—with the driver's hand cuffed to it. Sometimes they would find the bomber's right foot taped to the gas pedal, just in case he had second thoughts—or was shot while approaching his target. I heard something like that with respect to the bombing of the United Nations building in Baghdad in August 2003. The insurgents used a Russian-made Kamaz truck for that one, too. An American official with the CPA told me afterwards that although the cement mixer had a driver, the bomb itself might have been detonated remotely, by a radio signal. Not by a suicider. Apparently the driver had been told that his job was to park the explosive-laden truck and run, that the bomb would be detonated after he got away. It didn't happen that way, the American told me. The trigger man hit the button on the detonator before the driver could run. Boom.

The craziest thing about the suicide bombings were the heads—how the head of the bomber often remained intact after the explosion. It was the result of some weird law that only a physicist could explain: the force of the blast would detach the bomber's head and throw it up and away, too fast for the blast to destroy it. So there it would be, the head, sitting on a pile of bricks or underneath a telephone pole.

One day a man walked into the Buratha Mosque in northern Baghdad during Friday prayers and blew himself up. The explosives were hidden in his shoes. He killed eleven people and wounded twenty-five. I got there about an hour later. The walls were speckled with blood, and the workers were sweeping up the rubble. Sure enough, they'd found the head. They'd placed it on a platter, like John the Baptist's, and set it on the ground next to an interior doorway. It was in good shape, considering what it had been through. Some nicks and cuts and a thin coating of dust, which gave the skin a yellow hue. The most curious aspect of the face was the man's eyebrows: they were raised, as if in surprise. Which struck me as odd, given that he would have been the only person who knew ahead of time what was going to happen.

That day at Buratha, I pointed to the head on the plate and asked an Iraqi man where it came from. "Foreigner," he said. "Not Iraqi." The Iraqis were often adamant that the suicide bombers came from somewhere else. "Iraqis don't do this sort of thing," they'd say, like the issue was eating pork or drinking alcohol, though they did those things more than they admitted, too. Once I'd gone to the scene of a suicide bombing and the Iraqis were saying they'd found the foot of the bomber. How they knew it was the bomber's foot they didn't say. "It's not an Iraqi foot," one of them said.

The insurgents were always looking for a new and improved way to deliver a bomb. First came the car bombs, then the suicide bombers, then the car bombs driven by suicide bombers. Every time the insurgents figured out a new delivery system the Americans gave it a new acronym. Car bombs, for instance, were VBIEDs, pronounced "vee-bid," for Vehicle-Borne Improvised Explosive Device. Suicide car bombers were called SVBIEDs, for Suicide-Vehicle-Borne Improvised Explosive Device. I never heard the acronym for suicide bombers on bicycles; they rode them into weddings and funerals. The insurgents hid bombs underneath dead animals, especially dogs. No acronym for that. And then they strapped bombs to dogs. Live bombs to live dogs. That would be DBIED, or Dog-Borne IED. Also, the D could have stood for Donkey, when they tied bombs to donkeys. In the fall of 2005 some marines discovered a donkey walking around Ramadi with a suicide belt on. They didn't want to kill it, of course, but each time they tried to get close enough to remove the suicide belt, the donkey scampered away. Then they tried using a robot, one of those bomb-disposal things, which tried to waddle up to the donkey and defuse the payload, but the robot, too, kept scaring the donkey away. Finally the marines shot the donkey. It exploded.

Among the favorite targets of the suicide bombers were American ribbon cuttings—a pump station, for instance, or a new school—because of the crowds they brought. It got so bad that the Americans sometimes kept the unveilings of new projects a secret. Which kind of defeated the purpose. And the bombers sometimes got there anyway. Once a crowd of Iraqi children gathered around some American soldiers who were handing out candy at the unveiling of a pump station in Baghdad's Yarmouk neighborhood. A suicide bomber steered his car into the crowd of children and blew them up. And then came a second car, also filled with explosives, just to be sure. There were lots of dead children. You could never be sure about these things, but I figured the candy bombing was a target of opportunity: the suicide bombers were just loaded up and cruising, looking for targets. I'd hear that sometimes. A suicide bomber is driving around the neighborhood, looking for a target; look out.

They started to come in waves. Four a day. Ten a day. Twelve a day. Boom. Boom. Boom. Boom. Sometimes, all of them before breakfast. One morning, my colleague Ian Fisher was driving to Abu Ghraib to interview some Iraqi prisoners who were being released from American custody, when he came upon the scene of a suicide bombing just seconds after it had occurred. The victim had been Ezzedine Salim, the president of the Iraqi Governing Council. Ian stopped, stepped amid the bodies, did some reporting and climbed back in his car. A few more miles down the road, he came across another suicide bombing, the bomber's body in pieces on the roadside. He never made it to Abu Ghraib. "This place is crazy," he said, walking in the door.

No one wanted to stand in a crowd anymore. No one wanted to stand in line. Every morning the Iraqis who worked for the Americans in the Green Zone lined up for security checks before they were allowed inside, and the lines stretched for hundreds of yards into the streets, sometimes for hours. The same at police recruiting stations. One after the other, the car bombs flew into the lines. One after another, men wearing puffy jackets wandered into the lines, sweaty and nervous, mumbling to themselves, then exploding.

After a while, everything started to sound like a bomb. A door slamming in the house sounded like a bomb. A car backfiring sounded like a bomb. Sometimes it felt like the sounds of bombs and the call to prayer were the only sounds the country could produce, its own strange national anthem. The silence was creepy, too. One day there would be ten bombs and then the next day none. Twelve bombs and then no bombs. And I'd ask myself: Are they giving up? Or just reloading?

I think it was like porn for them. I think they got off on it. The insurgents made videos of their suicide bombings, like they were making an amateur sex tape. In the summer of 2005, one of the insurgent groups posted a "top ten" video on the Internet. It contained video snatches of their bloodiest bombings. When you watched the video, you could see that someone had arrived at the site beforehand to get a good view. It was usually someone in a car with his window rolled down, his kafiya half covering the lens. "God is great." They always said that when the bomb went off.

The videos made me wonder: What was more important to these guys, the suicide or the murder? You'd think it would be the murder, but I wasn't always so sure; there was a hint of nihilism in everything Al-Qaeda did. At the end of the Palestine-Sheraton video, Abu Musab al-Zarqawi, the head of Al-Qaeda in Mesopotamia at the time, gave a little speech. He promised victory for the Islamic world and, barring that, annihilation.

"If the enemy wins," Zarqawi promised, "we will burn everything."

I used to imagine the car bombers getting stuck in traffic jams, there were so many of them. Driving to Baghdad from Falluja, a half-hour drive. Falluja was the source. For many months the city was under the control of hardcore jihadis, who had set up something called the Council of Holy Warriors. Finally the marines went in and took the city back. I went with them. In one neighborhood, Shuhada, just about every house the marines went into was a bomb factory. Stacks of antitank mines next to stacks of cell phones next to stacks of circuit boards. Some of the marine units discovered half-built cars, too, cars with doors taken off and the back seat removed. One of the marines carried out an armful of antitank mines; he looked like a busboy carrying a stack of dinner plates.

Most of the bombs in Baghdad went off before ten in the morning. In the early days they woke me up. I'd hear the bombs and feel the walls shake and I'd jump out of bed. And I'd run up to the roof to follow the smoke, or I'd run out the door. Later on I slept through them. At first, in my ignorance, I thought there was some Islamic ritual involved, some special ceremony for suicide bombers that started before dawn and put them on the street at the same time each morning. Then I thought it was the drive from Falluja, the traffic. Then I realized: they were attacking at rush hour. There were just more people on the street then. More bodies for the blast.

MANSOUR AL-BANNA SAT at his dining room table and flipped through the snapshots of his departed son.

"Here is my son in New York City," Mr. Banna said, pushing the photo across the table. "Here, take a look."

The photograph showed a good-looking young man seated on a mountain bike, wearing sunglasses and a pale green jacket, flashing a winning smile. Downtown New York stood behind him in the distance. His name was Ra'ad, a young Jordanian lawyer on his first tour of the United States: another Middle Eastern kid who wanted to be American.

"Here is Ra'ad in California," Mr. Banna said, pushing me another photo. "That is the Santa Monica Pier."

Indeed it was, with the same exuberant young man standing in front of it. In this photo, Ra'ad was dressed in baggy knee-length shorts and a green shirt with palm trees. His hair glistened with gel.

Mr. Banna himself was a chubby, middle-aged man, dressed in a sweater and gray suit. He owned a company in Amman that made cement. He kept a cell phone on the table. His wife, daughter and other son looked on from the couch.

Mr. Banna found another photo, one of Ra'ad sitting on a Harley-Davidson.

"You see," Mr. Banna said, "my son loved America!"

And so it was especially strange when, a few nights before, the voice on the telephone had told the Bannas that Ra'ad had died while fighting the Americans across the border in Iraq. The voice said Ra'ad had been a member of a group called "The Sons of the Gulf."

"Your brother has been killed in a martyrdom operation," the caller said, employing a common euphemism to describe a suicide bombing. "Congratulations."

The day before I arrived at the Bannas, a Jordanian newspaper had reported that Ra'ad had died a suicide bomber, driving a tanker filled with gasoline into a crowded market in the city of Hilla. It was a gruesome attack even by Iraqi standards: the fireball incinerated 166 people. And then there was the puzzling obituary that had appeared in *Al-Ghad*, another local paper. It was paid for by the Bannas.

"Announcing the death of a martyr," the obituary read, "who got his martyrdom in the Iraqi land at the age of 32. Don't think that those who were killed for God are dead; quite the contrary. They are alive, and are even born again."

The Jordanian news accounts had made their way to Iraq,

and hundreds of people had rioted outside the Jordanian Embassy in Baghdad. Iraq threatened to recall its ambassador from Jordan.

We moved to the couch. Al Jazeera, the Arabic news channel, was playing an interview with the Bannas on television. The Bannas kept glancing at the TV screen and then at me.

"I had no idea he was in Iraq," Mr. Banna said. "Ra'ad told us he was going to Dubai to look for a job as an engineer."

Ra'ad never made it to Dubai. Instead, according to Jordanian records, he had headed in the other direction and crossed the border into Syria. From Syria, one could guess, he had made his way into Iraq.

The Bannas oscillated between grief and denial.

"He loved life," his mother, Bouthana, said. "He was a big spender. A big tipper—five dinars, ten dinars, even for the delivery man. This is not a boy who would become a suicide bomber. I am just waiting for him to walk through the door."

The most intriguing part of Ra'ad's story was unknowable: How did an English-speaking, American-loving, hair-gel-wearing lawyer who'd walked among the bikinis of Santa Monica come to blow himself up in Iraq?

Ra'ad had fallen in love with the United States during an eighteen-month stay in southern California from 2000 to 2002, his parents said. He'd managed to get a work permit, delivering pizza and working in a grocery store. He'd applied for a green card.

"He wanted to marry an American girl and become a U.S. citizen," Bouthana said. Her hair was wrapped neatly in a head scarf, and she freely interrupted her husband. "He wanted to marry an educated girl, not a nightclub girl."

Ra'ad had been in California during the attacks of September 11, 2001, and he told his parents they had done serious harm to the Muslims and Arabs of the United States. Ra'ad returned to Jordan when his visa expired, but soon left for Chicago, which, he believed, offered even more opportunities than Southern Cal. On landing in O'Hare, an American visa officer found a discrepancy on Ra'ad's visa application and, after questioning him, concluded that he had lied. Ra'ad was sent home.

"When he came home," Mr. Banna said, "he was crest-fallen."

It was then, Ra'ad's brother, Ahmad, told a local newspaper, that Ra'ad had begun his turn to Islam. "September 11 changed Ra'ad from a very normal to a very religious person, praying constantly in the mosque," Ahmad told *Al-Ghad.* But today, sitting across from me, Ahmad said barely a word.

In any case, whatever change overtook Ra'ad took many months. After being rejected for his visa, Ra'ad had applied to work in Amman with the United Nations, in a job handling human rights complaints. He was a good candidate, the interviewer noted, but he was turned down nonetheless.

Ra'ad's father read from Ra'ad's rejection letter: "The applicant did everything that was asked of him."

With so few prospects in Jordan, Ra'ad told his parents he would leave Jordan again, this time for the United Arab Emirates to look for a job. That was a few weeks before.

"He called only a month ago to tell me that he found a job in Dubai—a good job," Mr. Banna said. "He said he was the supervisor of an entire office."

I asked Banna about the obituary, about its celebration of Ra'ad's martyrdom. "That wasn't my idea," he said. "I was too distraught to write the thing and I gave it to my friends."

The elder Banna hardly seemed like a harborer of jihadi sympathies, or even the father of a jihadi. He seemed like a befuddled parent. He leaned forward, pleading with me to agree with him.

"The Americans are in Iraq, trying to make a new Iraq," he said. "Please tell the Americans we support them."

The members of the Banna family agreed to sit together for a photo. Christoph Bangert, the photographer who accompanied me, corralled the family on chairs. As Christoph lifted his camera, the Bannas, as if on cue, began to wail and sob. Soon, with Christoph snapping, the Bannas were rocking back and forth, cradling each other, slapping their chests and foreheads.

THE AMERICAN HELICOPTER swooped low as my car came to a halt. We were on the Syrian side of the border, a hundred yards from Iraq, across an expanse of sand known as "the forbidden area." It was a Kiowa, a two-seater, buzzing like an angry insect. A soldier holding a rifle hung out its door, searching the ground. The Kiowa had crossed into Syria. The Syrian checkpoint, which was right in front of me, was like an island; empty desert swept in every direction. I'd driven from Damascus that morning, along the green edge of the Euphrates River, which snaked like a vine through the colorless plains.

Groups of men were crowding round the border gates, pushing, moving, straining for views. Most were milling around. They didn't look like men with business to do, in Iraq or Syria. They weren't carrying suitcases or briefcases.

A pair of Syrian guards lounged inside an air-conditioned hut, smoking cigarettes. One of them spotted me. He lifted himself laboriously from his slouch and came over to my car. He was the chief, Major Ali Shamad, a thin man with a thin mustache. You will have to leave, he said, but he seemed happy to have the company. "The Americans are firing at random, firing at so many people," Major Shamad told me. The week before, two locals, one Syrian and the other Iraqi, cousins, he said, were shot dead when they tried to walk into Iraq. Two others had been wounded. "Their planes come over the border every day. It is very provocative. Very provocative."

Major Shamad sighed, in the weary manner of someone tired of having to explain his civilization to the unknowing. "The thing you need to understand," the major said, "is that people on both sides of the border are related. Syrians and Iraqis—same thing." They belonged to the same tribe, smuggled the same goods, grazed their sheep on both sides. No one had ever stopped them from doing that before. "Why don't the Americans understand these things?" he said.

I backtracked down the Euphrates to a village called Abu Kamal, where I found the father of one of the locals who had been shot. Abdul Rehman Halhoum was his name, he said, a teacher of Arabic, and he asked me inside. We sat in simple chairs on a bare tile floor without carpets or much on the walls.

Halhoum said his son, Abdul Halim, and his cousin, Same,

both twenty-five, had been shot by a sniper as they walked across the border at night. "As soon as they crossed into Iraq," he said. The family had already retrieved the bodies, Halhoum said, which the Americans had delivered to Syrian authorities. Halhoum's brother lived across the border in the Iraqi village of Al-Qaim. Another relative worked at the hospital where the two men's bodies came first, also in Iraq. "I never had a problem with the Americans," Halhoum said, "But after what they did to my son, I hate them now.

"What do they want with Arab land?" Halhoum said. "They are there only for oil. Everything is related to oil and Palestine."

We sat for a while sipping tea.

"You could say I am an Iraqi or a Palestinian or a Syrian, they are the same, it makes no difference," Halhoum said. He gestured out the window. "People here are angry enough to go and fight. They are quite ready to go and fight the Americans."

I walked into the street, and my driver, Abu Mazen, told me that a man had invited me and my Syrian interpreter, George, to lunch. I had never met the man, and neither had George or Abu Mazen. But I was desperate to talk to anyone in this desolate town, so I agreed. George and I followed Abu Mazen down a dusty street to a squat pale house where I left my boots at the door. I was led through the sitting area, where I spotted a woman darting out of the room on the far side— my only glimpse. I entered the dining room, and a man introduced himself. Sulaiman Abu Ibrahim, he said. He wore an ear-to-ear beard and a sheer white dishdasha through which a large stomach bulged.

The room was bare but for a television set and an acrylic mat spread wide with a Middle Eastern feast: two kinds of salad; hummus; a delicacy of crushed wheat stuffed with meat and onions called kibbeh; grilled chicken; a spinach dish, *mloukhieh*; and *mansaf*, a traditional Arab stew.

"For you, my American friend," Abu Ibrahim said, smiling and gesturing with his arms spread wide.

We sat down and got going on the food. Ibrahim, who seated himself next to me, began a speech about the Americans in Iraq. "Many Americans are being killed there," he said. "The American soldiers are all from Mexico and Africa, and no one really knows about them, no one cares about them. The Americans dump them into the river at night so that no one in America knows how many have been killed. They are mercenaries. Do the American people know this?"

Ibrahim picked up a plate of kebab and plunked a few pieces on my plate.

"More food, my American friend?" he asked.

Ibrahim had evidently figured out how little Arabic I understood, and after every couple of bites he turned to George and told him: "Look, now, the food will stick in the American's throat and he will start to choke."

We were nearing the end of the big meal.

"Would you mind if we watched a short video?" Ibrahim asked. And he popped it into a DVD player. On the TV screen appeared images of Arab fighters dressed in kafiyas, carrying Kalashnikovs and RPGs. There were scenes of Iraq. Words flashed on the screen: "The Battle for the Baghdad Airport." Ibrahim chuckled and sat back.

"Jihad is our oxygen," a voice on the video said, to the scenes of masked men firing guns. "Without jihad, we cannot breathe."

A camera panned a recently opened mass grave. Then it showed American soldiers entering Iraq.

"These are the things in Iraq the American people do not see," the voice on the DVD said. "Martyr yourself in Iraq in the name of Islam."

Ibrahim was nodding. The video flashed to a Caucasian man—the voice said he was an American—lying flat on his stomach. The screen showed a close-up of his face, and on the other side of him the legs and feet of other, unidentified men standing around him. A hand reached down, grabbed the Caucasian man's head and pulled it back. The hand produced a knife and began to cut the man's throat. The knife kept cutting, then sawing, and finally the head came free. The hand held it high.

Ibrahim was beside himself, rocking back and forth, running his finger across his throat.

"Ameriki," he said, dragging the finger across his neck, *"Ameriki."*

THE WALLS OF THE HOUSE swayed and the windows rattled and the bathroom door slammed on its own. I set down my coffee and spilled it over the counter. It was 8:20 a.m. The explosion was unfolding so close I could discern the intimacies of its sounds, its timbers, the cracks of the tumbling debris, the simultaneity of noise and wave. I ran out the door in my T-shirt and jeans.

It was a few blocks away. A crowd of Iraqi schoolgirls were running, mouths open, eyes wide. The bodies were spread across Al-Nidhal Street in a tableau, burned brown, blown apart, no clothes. The blast had flung a body into a metal fence, where a torso lay in the dirt. The blast had thrown a body into a brick wall, pushed the wall over and cracked the body's skull. The blast had tossed a body into someone's yard, thrown it like a dancer, and it had landed in the pose of a ballerina. A man crouched over a dirty body and looked for something to recognize in its face.

The sky blackened. The bomber had crammed his payload into an ambulance and sped down Al-Nidhal Street to his destination, the Baghdad headquarters of the International Committee of the Red Cross. Another driver in another car, a Good Samaritan, had spotted him, sped alongside to catch him and cut him off. The ambulance exploded and disappeared, and the car of the Good Samaritan lay in the street in the fire, the driver in his seat, his hands on the wheel, his head arched in a final fiery grimace. From the walls that still stood hung hunks of bleeding flesh.

The building lay in heaps and next to it a crater, and water gushed from a severed main. The street was filling, a spreading watery fire. In the smoke firemen splashed like phantoms. "Oh my God, help me, oh my God, help me," an elderly woman cried, her face and clothes spattered red, her arms extended for the young men who were leading her away. At her feet lay a severed arm.

The Americans arrived, children in the horror world.

Young in laundered uniforms, they surveyed the scene with unknowing eyes, but the order they brought was real and they did not waver. A soldier knelt with his gun next to a corpse that looked like a doll. The American's face was round and pale and his eyes were blue, and he glanced over his shoulder and bit his lower lip. Past him medics carried something on a stretcher, a lump of red and black.

A thud echoed in the distance. Then another thud.

"There have been two more bombs," an Iraqi police officer quietly said to his colleagues.

By the time we reached Shaab, a poor Shiite neighborhood a few miles away, another place had been blown up, a total of four in less than an hour. In Shaab it was a police station. When we pulled up we saw the burning building and hundreds of people gathered round. There were five of us: the driver, Waleed al-Hadithi; Warzer Jaff, the interpreter; and two photographers, Mike Kamber and Joao Silva. We drove to the edge of the crowd, stopped the car and were walking in when everyone turned and surged. Some guy put his face in my face and started screaming and I was screaming back, and people were clubbing me from other directions. Someone stripped the phone from my hand, then my notebook, and then others grabbed my arms. I began to float, as if in a riptide, dragged to the sea, not moving my legs but drifting anyway; there was nothing I could do. There was a lot of noise and a voice came through: "*Aktuluhum! Aktuluhum!*"— the voice of an old man. "Kill them! Kill them!" I wondered where my colleagues were, and then suddenly the tide reversed itself, and I lifted off the ground and started flying backwards. It was Waleed.

He put me back on my feet and pushed me toward the car as he swatted a mass of them. Jaff and I dove into the car through the driver's seat, and Joao came in behind me, but Mike was trapped outside when the bricks started coming. The windows were shattering and the crowd was yelling and a brick hit Mike in the head. He raised his hands, which turned quickly red; he crouched down and crawled into the back seat as Waleed started the car. People started leaping onto the hood. We still had our windshield, but I wasn't sure if the car would move with all the people around it but it did, it started moving and the people were falling off as the rocks kept coming and the windows kept shattering. We plowed through the crowd, gathering speed, Waleed flooring it, and we took a hard right down an alley at high speed. I saw sunlight at the other end but a kid, too, already winding up like a baseball pitcher. Vida Blue, I thought, Vida Blue, the pitcher from the 1970s. The kid had great form and Waleed gunned the engine and swerved to get him, and I was yelling, Hit him, Waleed, hit him! as the kid released his pitch and dove. The windshield shattered in our faces as Waleed swerved to run him over but the kid leaped away.

Mike was cradling his bloody head so I took off my T-shirt and we wrapped it up. We drove to the emergency room at Al-Kindi Hospital, which was filled with wailing people. We walked Mike into the lobby and then a hallway and into another room where wounded people had gathered. A doctor approached us, exhausted and jittery, and he guided Mike to a metal table to sit down. In the middle of it stood a pool of blood. Mike froze. "I don't want to do that," Mike said, looking at the blood. The doctor just laughed.

The Cloud

I WAS OUT for a run, jogging along the trail on the banks of the Tigris, heading south. I was nearing the halfway point, a defunct pump station that blocked me from running any farther. The heat was unbearable, as it usually was. I was carrying two half-liter bottles of water, one in each hand. I was about thirty yards from the pump station when I heard an explosion and the ground shook beneath my feet. I turned around and watched a white mushroom cloud rise up about a mile away. Close. They'd hit Tahrir Square again, a traffic roundabout near the Jumhuriyah Bridge. The bombers were always hitting the roundabout at Tahrir Square. They'd park their car next to one of the market stalls on the edge of the roundabout and wait for an American convoy or a bunch of contractors to come in, then they would hit the gas and fly into the roundabout and crash the middle of the convoy and explode. Happened all the time.

I stood and watched the mushroom cloud for a while. I needed the break anyway. The cloud was dissipating in the blue sky. After the blast, which was quite loud, there wasn't any sound to speak of, at least not that I could hear from so far away. The buildings along Abu Nawas Street obscured my view of the square itself. If I had tried to run back to the bureau, our guys would already have left to cover it. I stared at the remnants of the cloud for a few more minutes. I tried to imagine what was happening. I took a sip of water from my bottle. I retied my running shoes. I turned and got on with my run.

Mogadishu

THE LEGAL ADVISER walked to the front of the room, holding a sheet of paper. The marines, packed and ready, were assembled before him. The assault on Falluja was about to begin.

"Okay, guys, these are going to be the rules of engagement," the adviser, Captain Matt Nodine, said. He looked across the room. "It's going to be slightly different this time, so everybody listen up."

He glanced down at his paper. "First, you can engage the enemy wherever he engages us, or where you determine there is hostile intent," Nodine told the men.

"Your response needs to be proportional to the attack," Nodine said. "That means you use the minimum amount of force to remove the threat and continue the mission. Let me give you an example. You may come under fire from a building. If you can kill the guy with an M-16 or an M-240, do that. But don't call in an airstrike—take him out yourself. If you need a grenade launcher or a machine gun to do it, that's okay, as long as you don't cause unnecessary collateral damage. A TOW missile might be a later resort. Just remove the threat and continue the attack."

He glanced down at the paper. An enlisted man was handing out yellow note cards to the marines in the audience. "You're all going to get one of these," he said.

"There are some circumstances under which you will need specific permission to fire," Nodine told the marines. "If you are taking fire from mosques and minarets, you're going to need permission from your C.O. before you can engage. The one exception for that is if the loudspeakers are being used to call men to battle. In that case, you're free to engage. Take out the loudspeaker.

"Okay, hostile intent," Nodine said. "You can fire if you determine there is hostile intent. What's hostile intent? Let me go through some of the situations.

"If you see a guy carrying a gun," Nodine said, "that's hostile intent. It's assumed. You are free to shoot.

"If the guy drops his weapon and runs, you can engage him," Nodine said. "But if he drops the weapon and puts his hands up and indicates that he's surrendering, you cannot engage. You have to detain him."

He glanced down again at his card. Some of the men had begun looking at theirs. "If you see a guy on a cell phone—and he's talking on the phone and looking around like he's a spotter," he said, "that would be hostile intent. Use your judgment, but you can shoot.

"Okay," Nodine said, looking up, "if a guy comes out of a building with a white flag, obviously you can't shoot him. Unless he starts to run back and forth with the white flag," Nodine said. "We've had a lot of insurgents try to use white flags to maneuver. If he tries to use the flag to maneuver, that's hostile intent. You can shoot."

He glanced down at his note card again.

"Okay, ambulances," Nodine said. "You shouldn't be seeing any ambulances out there—the Red Crescent has withdrawn. But, as you know, we have had instances where enemy forces have used ambulances to transport their guns and wounded, and just to move around. So if you see an ambulance out there, fire a warning shot. If they don't stop, that's hostile intent. Use your discretion, but you can engage.

"Okay now, listen up, this is important," Nodine said. "You might find yourself in a firefight where there are civilians around. You can't indiscriminately shoot civilians, obviously. But it's also possible that you're going to see women and children acting in hostile ways—carrying ammo to the enemy, or placing themselves between you and the enemy. We've seen that. We've had cases where the enemy tries to use civilians for cover. We saw that in Mogadishu, guys hiding behind women and children to shoot at us. In those cases, use your best judgment about whether or not to engage," Nodine said.

"And, if you have women and children engaging you— exhibiting hostile intent," Nodine said, "you are going to need to prepare yourself mentally beforehand for the possibility that you might have to engage them.

"Any questions?"

CHAPTER 11

Pearland

TWILIGHT in Falluja. A yellow veil descended over the ruined city. Domes of mosques slouched in their wreckage. Apartments, split apart, surrendered their interiors. Minarets lay snapped at the stem. A handful of marines stood on the roof of a three-story building, trading shots with insurgents through the haze. A bullet whizzed past Sergeant Eric Brown and smashed a window behind him.

"God I hate this place, the way the sun sets," Brown said, wiping blood from his lip. He fired into the street.

Looking over Brown's shoulder I saw a black flag. There was no fanfare. It just appeared, a half-mile to the south, flapping from the top of a water tower. Brown's eyes were elsewhere.

"I don't see anything moving down there," he said.

Then a second black flag went up, this one over an apartment building.

"What the hell is that?" Brown said.

The black flags flapped in silence. The marines eyed each other and said nothing and started down the stairs. They gathered in a column and walked in silence down an alley. They were heading toward the flags.

It was the third day of the assault on Falluja, the jihadi safe-haven west of Baghdad. Six thousand marines and soldiers were moving into the city on foot. The unit I was with, Bravo Company, comprised 150 marines; they were at the point of

the attack, at the front and in the middle. Their goal was to sweep from the northern edge of Falluja to its southern end three miles away where it emptied into the desert. On their way the Americans could kill any insurgent they found. So far, the guerrillas were proving to be spectral beings: shooting and running, vanishing and appearing, falling back and falling back. Drawing us in.

The marines walked quietly down the alley, the only sound the clink of their gear.

A voice came over the radio.

"Enemy truck approaching your position, a white truck," the voice said.

We walked some more and the radio crackled again.

"You've got a second truck headed your way," the voice said. "Get ready."

Now at least we knew what the black flags were for. The insurgents had spotted us, and they were signaling their friends to come: Come to the fight. It's here.

A moment later the alley ahead exploded in gunfire. We leaped to the walls on each side. The radio crackled a third time.

"You've got a group of about forty insurgents coming your way," the voice said.

The radio was being handled by Captain Omohundro, the thirty-four-year-old Texas native who was Bravo's commander. In the first two days of the battle, Omohundro had moved his company through the warrens and back alleys of the city with great skill, but not without cost. Two of his men were dead.

Omohundro picked out a row of houses and Bravo Company turned. We walked into a street flooded with an inexplicable black oil and passed a burning car. Its molten upholstery popped and gasped in the fire.

"There's an attack coming," Omohundro said to one of his lieutenants.

Omohundro pointed to a house. His voice was low but he spoke quickly. When the gate refused to budge, Omohundro ordered one of his men to open it with a rocket. We poured inside and waited. Nothing. We waited in silence as the sun set. The stillness outside seemed the measure of our ignorance. The insurgents were coming, and now they were not. They were watching us.

After an hour, in the darkness, Bravo Company filed out of the house. We split into three groups; I went with Omohundro and the first platoon. I was still thinking of the black flags, now invisible in the darkness.

The column clanked and clinked in the darkness. Above us, the lights of the jets blinked and fluttered. In the first days of the battle I'd found my only peace shadowing Omohundro's every step. In the night's inky blackness, I could no longer see him; there wasn't enough light to make out his stubby form. It was an odd thing about leadership; people talked about it and CEOs wrote books about it. But there was nothing like facing death to feel it in the flesh. It was as if Omohundro wore a mask, and with that mask he gave everyone more courage than they knew they had. The trick was never showing fear. "It's not like I don't feel it," Omohundro told me in a quiet moment. "But if I ever showed it, the whole thing would fall apart."

We walked down a street that felt like a cave when gunfire and screaming rose ahead. The column froze. Then more gunfire sounded and a second man screamed. Omohundro's shadow disappeared as he ran to the front.

Word traveled quickly back. It was Private Andrew Russell, his right leg nearly severed. The bone was protruding from his leg. He was carried away screaming. Corporal Nathan Anderson was dead. He was a lanky kid from a small town in Ohio who was always taking his buddies' spare change to raise money for his sister's college tuition. A few days before, after we'd run through machine-gun fire to cross 40th Street, Anderson had braved gunfire to go back and rescue his friends. Anderson's buddies did the same here, charging into the gunfire to get him. He'd died in their arms.

Anderson and Russell had been walking point when they'd turned up an alley. Just ahead they'd spotted a group of men dressed in Iraqi National Guard uniforms, marked with the red-and-white tape the Americans had handed out before the battle had begun to set them apart. The red tape would go on the shoulder, the white on the leg. In the alley, the Americans caught the glimmer of the red and white. Anderson's point man waved. The guys in the Iraqi uniforms opened fire. Then they disappeared.

Were they insurgents? Or Iraqi soldiers? Often there was no difference. Iraqi soldiers weren't supposed to be out here, not at night. Whatever assurances were coming from Washington about Iraqis taking over the burden from the Americans, in Falluja the fiction was dispensed with. It was an American fight.

Gunfights were breaking out on both ends of the column. Bullets zipped past. I knelt against a wall, pushing on it for maximum cover, when the marine in front shoved me out of the way. I got down lower, like I was trying to hide.

A flare floated into our ranks and gunfire exploded everywhere. It was an insurgent flare—the marines had night-vision goggles—and the insurgents were using the flares to shoot at us. The flare lit the alley like it was high noon. It floated on a tiny parachute, taking its time to land, while bullets pinged off the bricks above our heads. The marines fired until the sky went black again.

With Omohundro occupied, the platoon's lieutenant, Andy Eckert, began to panic. Eckert, who was twenty-three, was tough and resourceful, but he barely reached the shoulders of some of the men in his charge. When Eckert heaped all his gear on his body, seventy pounds of it, he looked wider than he was tall.

In his panic, Eckert began leading the platoon back and forth between two houses. It made no sense. No sense at all.

"This way!" Eckert said. "Follow me." And the kids followed.

"No, this way," and the platoon turned in the darkness.

"No, here. Here!"

I couldn't see Eckert but I could sense that he was cracking. In the alley, his men began to argue.

"What the fuck are we doing?" someone asked.

"Shut the fuck up," came the answer.

"We're running around like chickens," someone else said.

I started to say something.

"You—keep your fucking mouth shut; you're not part of this unit," one of the kids said to me.

At last Omohundro returned; disorder and mutiny receded.

Omohundro stood over Eckert in the blackened alley, away from the others. Exhausted by his own exertions, Eckert was nodding and breathing hard. Omohundro spoke quietly, almost in a whisper.

"Do you want me to take over?" Omohundro said.

Eckert said nothing.

"Do you want me to take over?" Omohundro repeated.

"No, sir, I can handle it," Eckert said.

A couple of tanks came to our rescue. The M-1s were too wide to pass through most of Falluja's streets; our street was just wide enough. We tucked in behind them and moved slowly behind their clankings. As we did, rocket-propelled grenades whizzed out of the darkness, striking the M-1s and exploding but doing no harm. Whoosh-bang, like a fireworks show. Whoosh-bang.

The real weirdness was circling above. The night sky echoed with pops and pings, the invisible sounds of frantic action. Most were being made by the AC-130 gunships, whose propellers were putting out a reassuring hum. But over the droning came stranger sounds: the plane's Gatling gun let out long, deep burps at volumes that were symphonic. Its 105 mm cannon made a popping sound, the same as you would hear from a machine that served tennis balls. A pop! followed by a boom! Pop-boom. And then there was the insect buzz of the ScanEagle, the pilotless airplane that hovered above us and beamed images back to base. It was as if we were witnessing the violent struggles of an entire ecosystem, a clash of airborne nocturnal beasts we could not see.

The third platoon turned into a walled compound, which held a two-story house and a front yard with grass. After the trauma of Anderson and Russell, we were looking for a place to sleep. The guys walking point kicked down the door and went inside to clear the house. Through the windows I followed their flashlights as they moved upstairs. Then came an enormous boom, a bright flash and a scream. A grenade.

"My face! My face!" a marine yelled.

"No! No! No!"

I stood in the yard as the marines carried out the wounded on their backs. With just enough light to see, I could make out their silhouettes. One of them was Jake Knospler, a kid from Pennsylvania, and he was silent as if he were dead. Jake's cot had been next to mine in the barracks before the battle. He was the platoon's unofficial disc jockey. On a large boombox he kept next to his cot, Jake played mostly Johnny Cash, "Ring of Fire" his favorite. Jake even sort of looked like Johnny Cash, big, square jaw. Which was blown off by the grenade.

Months later, after the battle, Ashley Gilbertson and I traveled to Jacksonville, North Carolina, for a memorial service for the 1/8 battalion, which included Bravo Company. Jacksonville is a small town that lives off Camp Lejeune, a big marine base. Driving in from the airport, Ash and I stopped at a restaurant where we ate catfish and hush puppies and washed them down with sweet tea. The restaurant backed up on a pond.

I'd been expecting a ceremony and a parade and a band, with a lot of American flags and a cheering crowd. As it happened the ceremony was held inside a gymnasium on the base called the Goettge Memorial Field House. When I arrived, the gym was about a third full, mostly with members of the battalion and their girlfriends and wives. There wasn't anybody from the town, as far as I could tell, no reporters from the local paper and no band. About half of the gym's bleachers remained tucked in place against the walls. The guys from Bravo were dressed in their tan uniforms, the same ones they'd worn in Iraq, not their dress blues.

From my spot in the bleachers halfway up, I scanned Bravo's ranks. I looked first for Jake Knospler but did not see him. He survived, it turned out; doctors had begun performing the first of what would be twenty-two surgeries on his face and other parts. I spotted a guy seated in the front row. They'd put him on the floor so he wouldn't have to climb the bleachers. A metal brace encased his leg. The brace was so large and it stuck out so far that it resembled the scaffolding on a building. Or a bird-cage. It belonged to Andrew Russell, whose screams I'd heard in the alley that night. He was moving very slowly, but the leg was his.

MORNINGS WERE THE HARDEST, the combat excepted. There wasn't any electricity, of course. And there was no more water than what you could carry on your back, so of course showers and coffee were out of the question. After two hours sleeping on a cement floor and a day of combat ahead, coffee was something I thought about. Ashley was similarly needful, but most of the kids were not; their days of coffee still lay ahead of them. So they were happy to oblige us, and every morning when we woke the guys would hand over their packets of Taster's Choice from their daily prefab rations. Each morning, Ash and I would pull ourselves out of our sleeping bags on whatever rooftop we had slept on—in Falluja, we usually slept on a roof—and gathered our packets of Taster's Choice and powdered cream and sugar. We'd open our mouths and pour in all three, throw in a little water and violently shake our heads.

Writing was hard, the physical act of it. The light on my laptop would give away our position, so I was permitted to use my laptop only if I crawled into my sleeping bag and zipped it up all the way. Ashley needed more room than a zipped-up bag could offer. Many of the houses in Falluja kept an outhouse on their roof; so Ash would sit in one of those, amid the shit, and send his pictures to New York. I'd sit in the dark on the roof and I'd listen to him cursing the smell from inside the outhouse. I was obsessed by electricity, or, I should say, by the lack of it, by the fear of running out. I had my satellite phone and my laptop to consider and Ash his digital cameras. I brought all sorts of gadgetry to tap whatever source I could find, one of them being the batteries of cars. After the marines had captured the Mohammadiya Mosque, I dashed into the street with my battery clips and converter, the only human as far as I could see, and pried open the hood of a bullet-riddled car. I was worrying about snipers. The car battery was dead. I ran back inside.

Then there was the matter of going to the bathroom. This was no small thing for six thousand marines moving through a city on foot. You couldn't exactly crap in a field somewhere, even at night, as the insurgents had snipers with very good aim. The toilets didn't work because the water had been cut off. At the Grand Mosque, one of the places we stopped for a day, the marines used the storage room for the Korans, not out of disrespect for the Korans but for the privacy of the room. The marines put down a bunch of cardboard boxes in there, which were the toilets, and hauled them out when they were overflowing. Enormous, dripping cardboard boxes filled with human shit. Most days, though, traveling through the city, we just used somebody's bathroom. We'd break into their house and shit in their toilet until it overflowed and then we just used the floor. There'd be piles and piles of the stuff by the time we got going again. Shitting in the house of a person I'd never met—there were worse things that happened in Iraq every day. Still I didn't feel very good about it.

Once or twice during the battle I used a satellite phone to download my e-mail. Most of the messages came from readers wishing me well. *You've got balls the size of melons to be there,* wrote Joe from Connecticut. I liked that one. Another note came from a music critic at a newspaper in Florida asking for the name of the AC/DC song the marines had blasted that first night. Some of the readers accused me of insufficient patriotism. *Hey crap for brains. You are another reason why I canceled my subscription,* wrote someone named Andy. The most poignant notes were the ones I got from worried mothers of the marines I traveled with. I got a lot of those. This one came from Peggy Spears of Sugar Land, Texas:

Christopher is a 21 year old Texan. The son of two people that love him more than life itself. He is the LOVE OF MY LIFE. Of course most moms think that but I have the love of this young man in the core of my bones and my love for him embedded in my soul. Can love be any deeper? I think not. If you are assigned to his battalion, please find him, tell him the depth of my love for him. I want him to feel my hugs and kisses each and every moment of every day.

I read the letter and worried for Peggy Spears in the event that Christopher were killed. Then one day while riding in a seven-ton troop carrier I found myself sitting next to Christopher himself. I told him I'd heard from his mother and he shot me a funny look but he paid attention when I turned my laptop on. It had just enough juice for him to read the whole thing. Christopher tried not to smile, but his buddies razzed him and laughed.

We had a lot of downtime. Usually, if we weren't working, Ash and I would sit around and talk with the kids. At first they were suspicious; mainly, I think, because they were afraid we'd slow them down. But the wariness disappeared after the first day. We had become part of the team. I knew they would save me if I got in trouble. (And in fact they did.) "You a reporter?" one of them would ask, and we'd sit down and have a conversation. Ashley had an instant rapport, warmer than mine. They loved his Australian accent, loved the cigarettes he shared, loved the cameras he let them tinker with. I felt self-conscious of my age and my profession and my education, that they would think me an impostor who couldn't tell one end of a gun from another. Once, at the request of Staff Sergeant Brown, I called my office on the satellite phone to get the most recent NASCAR standings. I was able to tell the sergeant that Kurt Busch was in front in the Nextel Cup Series, edging out Jimmie Johnson, who held a small lead over Jeff Gordon. I got a lot of points for that.

Usually I would ask them where they were from. It was almost always some place I'd never heard of. Pearland, Texas.

Punxsutawney, Pennsylvania. Starkville, Mississippi. "Where's that?" I'd say, and they'd light up a cigarette. One afternoon I sat with Chad Ritchie, a soft-spoken intelligence officer from Keezletown, Virginia. He was twenty-two. When I asked Ritchie what the best thing about growing up in Keezletown was, he didn't hesitate: "We'd have a bonfire, and back the trucks up on it, and open up the backs, and someone would always have some speakers. We'd drink beer, tell stories."

Like many of the kids in Bravo Company, Corporal Ritchie joined the marines because he yearned for an adventure larger than Keezletown could offer.

"The guys who stayed, they're all living with their parents, making $7 an hour," Ritchie said. "I'm not going to be one of those people who gets old and says, I wish I had done this. I wish I had done that. Every once in a while, you've got to do something hard, do something you're not comfortable with. A person needs a gut check."

They might have been kids, but they were leaner and tougher than their counterparts in Manhattan and Santa Monica. Bravo Company's three platoon leaders, each responsible for the lives of fifty men, were twenty-three and twenty-four years old. Some of Bravo Company's best soldiers, like Lance Corporal Bradley Parker, were nineteen. Sometimes they wrestled over the packets of M&Ms that came in their rations. They sang together the songs they knew. One of them was "Copenhagen," a country music ditty named for a brand of chewing tobacco that they bought almost to a man at the base PX:

> *Copenhagen, what a wad of flavor*
> *Copenhagen, you can see it in my smile*
> *Copenhagen, hey do yourself a favor, dip*
> *Copenhagen, it drives the cowgirls wild.*

One night when we were camped out in an Iraqi National Guard building we came under heavy mortar fire. These were giant mortars, 120s, and the first shells fell close enough to shake the walls. Then came another and another, a ping signaling a launch, then a long silence and then a boom. The windows shattered and the ceiling caved in and the walls began to teeter. I lay on the floor and waited to die. And in the silence between the ping and the explosion I began to hear the murmur of prayers. After thirty explosions the shelling stopped.

All the guys had a story like that, at least the ones who lived. Out there, the boundary between life and death shrank so much that it was little more than a membrane, thin and clear. With hardly a step you could pass from life into death—and sometimes, it seemed, from death back to life. Anthony Silva was one of the men who dashed into 40th Street that day when all the gunfire was crisscrossing in the street. A bullet hit him in the back. Silva fell on his face, thinking of his daughter, Audrey, thinking he would die. But the bullet had hit his backpack, cut through the journal that he carried with him and broken a packet of Saltines. It stopped at his Kevlar plate. "I thought the bullet went through," Silva said. He was twenty-two.

I remembered each of them by something they carried or something they said. Corporal Romulo Jimenez, twenty-one, from Bellington, West Virginia, had flames tattooed on his arms. Jimenez talked mostly about his 1992 Ford Mustang and how he was going to take it to hot rod shows when the war was done. The day after the marines had captured the Mohammadiya Mosque, Romulo was shot in the spine. He died. Sergeant Lonny Wells was a cardplayer, Texas hold 'em his favorite, and he laughed when he took his buddies' money. He died crossing 40th Street on the first morning of the attack. "He knew all the probabilities," Corporal Gentian Marku said a few days after Wells died. Marku, an Albanian kid who came to the United States at fourteen, was shot a week later, on Thanksgiving Day. He died, too.

There wasn't any point in sentimentalizing the kids; they were trained killers, after all. They could hit a guy at five hundred yards or cut his throat from ear-to-ear. And they didn't ask a lot of questions. They had faith, they did what they were told and they killed people. Sometimes I got frustrated with them; sometimes I wished they asked more questions. But things were complicated out there in Keezletown and Punxsutawney; they were complicated in Falluja. Out there in Falluja, in the streets, I was happy they were in front of me.

One afternoon, while Bravo Company hunkered down at the Grand Mosque in downtown Falluja, I climbed into the rafters and sat with the snipers. One of them was Corporal Nick Ziolkowski. His friends called him Ski. He'd been on the roof for several hours, looking through the scope on his bolt-action M-40, waiting for guerrillas to step into his sights. The scope was big and wide, and sometimes Ski removed his helmet to get a better view. He had three kills for the day.

Tall, good-looking and gregarious, Ski was one of Bravo's most popular soldiers. Unlike most snipers, who typically learned to shoot while growing up in the countryside, Ski was raised near Baltimore, unfamiliar with guns. Though Baltimore boasted no beachfront, Ski's passion was surfing; at Camp Lejeune, Bravo Company's base, he often organized his entire day around the tides. When he got out of the Marines, he was planning on opening a surf shop.

"All I need now is a beach with some waves," Corporal Ziolkowski told me from his place in the rafters of the mosque. During the break, Ski foretold his death. The snipers, he said, were among the most hunted of Americans. In the first battle for Falluja, seven months before, American snipers had been especially lethal, and intelligence officers had warned Ski that this time he'd likely be a target himself. "They are trying to take us out," he said.

The bullet, when it came, knocked Ski backward and onto the roof. He had been sitting on the outskirts of the Shuhada neighborhood, an area controlled by insurgents, peering through his wide scope. He had taken off his helmet to get a better view. The bullet hit him in the head.

A SNIPER FIRED into Bravo Company's ranks.

Crack!

A marine fell.

Then again. Crack!

He was dead. The marines pulled his body as they ran for cover. They chose an abandoned Iraqi National Guard building that fronted Highway 10, the main road into Falluja. Twenty guys ran up to the roof. They set up their machine guns and waited. The sniper fired again. He was in the building across the street, fifty yards away, on the second floor. The flash of a shadow. The marines opened up with everything they had. Aimed, fired, raked and sprayed. Ten seconds. Three thousand shots. Bullet casings in smoking piles. The quickened pulses of young men. Smoke oozing from barrels.

"I don't see him," one of them said.

Minutes went by. Cigarettes glowed.

Crack!

A bullet zinged across the rooftop. A shadow passed by a window.

Western side of the building this time, someone said, third floor.

The marines opened fire again. They held their guns steady on the ledge of the rooftop as they let them fly: M-4s, M-16s, SAWs, 240s, M-203 grenade launchers. A blazing symphony.

The building across the street shook and smoked. A fire began on the second floor. The sniper fired. Crack, crack. A muzzle flashed.

"Goddamn you!" someone shouted as the marines fired again.

"We got one guy moving back and forth," Lieutenant Eckert, one of the platoon leaders, said calmly.

"We may have found him," another marine said, but everyone kept firing where they were firing.

Eckert stood back from the wall on the roof to get a wider view.

"The idea is, he just sits up there and eats a sandwich, and we go crazy trying to find him," he said.

The building was a sniper's heaven; it was long with dozens of windows and many points of view. Three floors. Someone had put cardboard in each of the panes, dozens of cardboard boxes, making it almost impossible to see inside.

The marines kept firing, thousands and thousands of rounds. The barrels of their machine guns glowed and sagged.

"Get me another barrel," one of the kids said.

More firing commenced.

"I don't know who he is, but he is very well trained," said Lieutenant Steven Berch, another one of the platoon leaders.

Omohundro was downstairs. He listened to the commotion and called in an airstrike. "Just blow the building to shit," he said. First a 2,000-pound bomb, then a 500-pounder flew into the building and burst. A cloud unfolded upward and revealed a gigantic fire. It rose through the ruined ceiling. Part of a wall collapsed.

Crack! Crack! Crack!

The marines ducked, cursed loudly and returned fire. No one spotted the sniper this time. The sniper fired back. The marines responded with another blast of gunfire, many thousands of rounds.

I stood with some guys at the back of the roof, behind a shed. A blue and green parakeet fluttered out of the sky and hovered in tight circles. Bullets flew past. The parakeet landed on a slumping power line. The marines stared in amazement.

"Someone's pet?" a marine said.

I ran across the top of the roof and the sniper took a shot.

Crack!

The bullet whizzed by.

An artillery barrage began. First came the 155 mm shells, each filled with fifty pounds of high explosives. One after the other the shells sailed into the building. Fire swept through the three floors. What was left of the ceiling collapsed in the smoke. Cardboard sailed out of shattered windows. Twenty shells, then thirty, each one large enough to end the world.

The shelling ceased and the shooting stopped. The building burned. Remarkably it still had a frame, and parts of its three floors still stood. Suddenly a sound rustled from a storefront on the first floor. The marines tensed. A cat sauntered out, dirty yellow, tail in the air. It walked like a runway model in front of a construction site.

"Can I shoot it, sir?" a marine asked his squad leader.

"Absolutely not," came the reply.

Crack! Crack! The sniper. More swearing and more shooting.

After some minutes two M-1 tanks arrived, clanking and smoking.

They leveled their terrible guns. Ka-boom. Ka-boom. Ten shots. The shock waves bounced off our ears.

Someone pointed and yelled.

"Look!" shouted Corporal Christopher Spears. "He's on a bike!"

A man pedaled away from the building, away from the marines, in an alley. There was no shot to take; the angle was oblique.

"He's in the road, he's in the road!" Eckert yelled. "Shoot him!"

Evening approached. The sun sagged. Six hours had passed since the sniper first fired. The ruins belched smoke and fire. Omohundro sent a squad across the street. They put out clouds of green smoke to cover their advance. No one fired. The marines entered the building, what was left of it. There was no one inside.

IT WAS 4 A.M., and Omohundro had taken some marines to a roof to survey the way ahead when a voice came over the radio. It was Bravo Company's fire-support team, called Fist, which coordinated air support and artillery. The Fist officer told Omohundro that he'd just gotten a call from Basher, the radio name of the AC-130 gunship hovering above us. He called Omohundro by his radio name, Beowulf Six.

"Beowulf Six, this is Fist," the voice said. "Basher has spotted numerous armed men on a roof next to you. Basher requests permission to fire."

Basher had been spotting insurgents all week long and killing them from the air. Sometimes the insurgents were as close as fifty yards. Or just around the corner. Basher was a fearsome thing: it had a Gatling gun that fired an astonishing 1,800 rounds a minute; hence its terrible burping sound. And it had a howitzer that could shoot as fast as a shotgun.

Omohundro told everyone to get down. Then he crept to the south side of the roof and peeked over the ledge, half expecting to draw gunfire. He didn't see anyone. The radio crackled.

"Basher has spotted numerous armed individuals moving to the west wall," the fire-support officer said.

Omohundro crept across the roof again to get a look at the building's west wall. He didn't see anyone, which wasn't, under the circumstances, all that unusual: in the dark the insurgents were sometimes very near.

"Basher is requesting permission to fire," the fire-support officer said. The Basher crew was going to use its howitzer. It was going to be a big one.

The radio crackled again. The fire-support officer gave Omohundro the coordinates of the target. Omohundro peered into his GPS, but in the darkness couldn't make out the numbers. He didn't want to light up his GPS for fear of tipping off the insurgents to his presence. Instead, he ordered one of his men to plant an infrared strobe beacon on the roof to show Basher exactly where we were. Omohundro was worried about shrapnel from a target exploding so close.

"Tell Basher they are clear to fire," Omohundro said into the radio.

About ten seconds later, the fire-support officer came back on.

"So, Basher says the insurgents have their own infrared strobe beacon," he said. "They've put it up on the roof. Basher is preparing to fire."

Omohundro screamed into the radio.

"Basher, Basher, this is Beowulf! Abort! Abort! Abort god-damnit! Friendlies on the roof! Abort! Abort! Hold your fire! I say again, friendlies on the roof! Abort! Over?"

There was a pause on the radio. It was one of Basher's crew.

"Roger, aborting firing sequence," the voice said. "Sorry about that."

Another pause. Omohundro shook his head.

"Five more seconds and we were goners," Omohundro said.

The radio crackled again. It was the fire-support officer.

"Sorry about that, Beowulf Six."

THE GEESE CAME IN from the north, flying in a slightly broken V, as the fighting of southern Falluja unfolded below. As the birds approached, they appeared unable to alter their course. They kept flying until they were directly over the fighting. There was machine-gun fire, then an explosion.

Then the formation of geese began to break apart. The V dissolved into a tangle of confused circles, the birds veering past each other in the sky, seemingly trapped above the apocalypse below. They flew in circles, some large, some smaller. It was as if their internal gyroscopes, ancient and delicate, had been knocked awry. It was quiet where I stood, but I watched the fighting a few blocks away, directly below the geese. A building exploded, sending up a tunnel of flame.

After several minutes, the geese began to gather themselves and re-form into their broken V. Then they turned to the southwest and continued on their way.

WORD CAME OVER the radio that one of the patrols had discovered a tunnel network used by the insurgents. I was excited; I wanted to see it. That's where all the insurgents were, I thought. "Ash, we gotta go!" Ash said no way, too risky. Ash was usually the one who wanted to go, but this time it was me. He thought it was stupid. No way. We'd have to cross that open field again. Snipers are everywhere. We don't have an escort. We don't know the streets.

"We're going," I told Ash. We always went together, even when it was stupid. Omohundro radioed ahead and told the patrol that we were coming. We dashed into the open field, the two of us, Ash swearing the whole way. "Fuck you," he shouted in his Aussie accent as we ran. "Fuck you. We're going to die." We couldn't run fast because we didn't have uniforms, and we were afraid the marines might think we were insurgents. "This is bullshit," Ash screamed. "Fuck. Fuck. You're a fucking asshole."

We turned on what we guessed was the correct street and saw a hand come out of a metal gate and wave us in. We ran at top speed, hit the gate and fell into the courtyard. "You guys are crazy," one of the marines said. It turned out the tunnel was only a sewage pipe. The insurgents weren't using it for anything. Nothing but an ocean of shit. So we turned back and ran again.

"Fuck you," Ash shouted, running across the field. "You're a fucking asshole."

I don't remember any of it. Not the tunnels, not the shit,

not even Ash swearing at the top of his lungs. My notebook is blank.

"It totally happened," Ash said. "One hundred percent."

IT STARTED WITH a face. Black, possibly an Arab from North Africa, covered by a thin layer of dust. Rubble around the head. Lips parted slightly. No blood. The marines had found him at the top of the minaret in the southern part of town, at the top of a winding set of stairs, and snapped a photo. It had been in the evening, and the face had a bluish cast. From the start, the guerrillas had used the minarets: to shoot, to spot, to signal one another. When they first came into Falluja the marines weren't allowed to shoot into the mosques without permission; after a few hours the marines threw the rule away.

We knew there were a lot of dead guerrillas; we weren't seeing them. By then, a week into the thing, nearly a quarter of Bravo was wounded or dead: Romulo, Nick, Nathan, Lonny. Bradley Parker, nineteen, from Marion, West Virginia. Jake, the mouthless mangled face; he was still alive. There were others. But we had gone forward anyway, rolling, absorbing the blows, moving forward through the streets. They were shooting at us, the marines and me and Ash, but we were moving and now we were at the city limits, where the streets opened onto a big, flat plain of brush and trash, abruptly, just like a movie set. End of town. So where did the insurgents go? They were dead, under the rubble, that's where they were. Buried. Vaporized. Ground to dust. "Have you ever seen what a 2,000-pound bomb does to a person?" an American officer asked me once, not really bragging because in this case the victims had been American soldiers. Friendly fire, Afghanistan, five guys. "We put the remains in a sandwich bag," he said.

Still, it was a curiosity that we had seen so few bodies. The generals were reporting hundreds of dead, thousands even, we knew that from the radio, but we weren't seeing many. You'd think by then we would have seen an arm. A head. Like in the suicide bombings in Baghdad. So I'd been rolling it over, the lack of bodies, considering the explanations: the Muslims bury their dead very quickly; it's a religious thing. That was one. The insurgents never leave their dead behind. That was another. They're fucking invisible, with their own passage-ways out of the city. How was that?

The face. We were on top of this building on the edge of town, staring out at the big plain that swept out of the south-ern edge of the city when one of the marines, Lance Corporal Alex Saxby, came over and showed Ashley the picture. He tilted up his point-and-shoot camera to show us. Saxby had brought us the photo because he knew we needed one, a photo of a dead insurgent. "I got two dead friends," he said. Alex's glasses had broken at his nose, and he was holding them together with a wad of first-aid tape. The photo of the dead jihadi seemed to be all he had left in the world. "It's my birth-day today," he said.

I remembered when the marines killed the insurgent; it had been a couple of days before. We had come to this open spot in the city, a kind of Falluja Central Park, with trash and junk strewn about it, and there was a long row of buildings on the other side. Filled with bad guys, or so they said, and they seemed to know well enough. They'd send up the ScanEagle, the model airplane with cameras, the one you could hear at night buzzing around like a big fly. They had sent the tanks in front of us, and they had blasted the shit out of those build-ings, blowing giant holes in them, so we could advance across the junk field. They blasted a minaret, too. Two shots, two large holes in the tower and then silence. The marines went up later, up the winding stairs, and found the guy. In the rub-ble. Saxby snapped a photo. A face in bluish hue.

And so with the fighting over it seemed like the thing to do. Ashley needed a corpse for the newspaper. So he asked Omohundro, and he gave us a dozen guys. They liked us now; we'd been through hell with them, seen their buddies die. They wanted to help us. So we walked back up the street we had come down the day before. By then, you hardly noticed the wreckage, there was so much of it. Long piles of white rocks and dead wires and sliced-up cars, some of them still smoking. A ruined world. Nothing like the way we had found it coming in, when it looked more or less like a normal city. The marines had blasted everything: every building, every car, even if there was no one in it, every fucking person, even the ones hidden in the shadows. It was like a party. Now the town was quiet. Nobody said much. It had been many days since I'd heard my own footsteps. It was only then that I thought something might be wrong.

We came to the door of the minaret. Ashley stepped to go inside. When Ash needed a photo, he had no fear. He'd go anywhere for a picture, right into death if he had to, snap and click. A few days before he'd run right into machine gun fire, right into it. I'd stayed crouched behind the wall. I didn't much feel like following him into the minaret. It was a picture, after all. There wasn't much I could do with a corpse. I wanted to leave. I followed him anyway. So Ash and I stepped to go through the door when a pair of marines stepped in front of us. We'll go first, they said. The first marine put his hand out. I didn't get a look at them, maybe a sidelong glance of the first guy, and they bounded up the stairs. Ashley with his camera fell in behind them and I was behind Ashley.

The stairs squeaked as we went up. It was a narrow staircase, winding, just wide enough for your body. A nautilus, maybe a hundred feet high. Not very stable. Dark, too, but for the holes shot by the tank. I could see beams of light above. I slowed my step. The shot was loud inside the staircase, and I couldn't see much, because the second marine was falling backwards, falling onto Ashley, who fell onto me. Warm liquid spattered on my face. Three of us tumbled backwards out the doorway.

The first marine was stuck, maybe three-quarters of the way up the stairway. The shot had come from farther up the stairs. A very loud shot. Then tumbling and screaming and quiet. The guy who had fired was in the minaret, at the top of the stairs, sitting up there.

"Miller!" the marines shouted.

"Miller!"

No answer.

I tried to imagine him up there, Miller, foot stuck in the stairwell in some odd way that prevented him from falling like the rest of us. Unable, for some reason, to speak.

Ashley was sitting on the stoop beside the entrance to the minaret mumbling to himself. His back was turned to the tower, and his helmet was on crooked so he looked especially vulnerable. His shoulders were heaving. My fault, he was saying, my fault. There was blood and bits of white flesh on his face and on his flak jacket and on his camera lens. My fault.

"Miller!" The marines were screaming now.

They started to run into the tower. It was crazy, but they ran into the tower, heedless and headlong, the way you would charge a machine-gun nest. Young and determined, up the winding stairs. They ran up the stairs and there were more shots, I couldn't tell whose, there was fighting and yelling. Then the marines came out empty-handed. Alive but empty. Fuck, the first one shouted.

That was Goggin. Michael Goggin, Irish kid, Weymouth, Massachusetts, heavy accent, nineteen. Face covered in dust. Like the dust in the photo, looking like a ghost. "I can't get to him," he said.

Again and again they went up, Goggin and the others, and there were more shots and more dust and more loud fucks. I wondered how many people were going to die to save Miller, who was shot for a picture. The insurgents didn't leave their dead behind, and neither did the marines. Miller was trapped and an insurgent was up there, in a perfect spot, with perfect lines of fire. You could see the marines, too; it was in their eyes. Obsessed and burning. Maybe the whole platoon would die, I thought.

"Miller!"

Silence.

"Miller!"

Our leader that day was First Sergeant Sam Williams, a twenty-six-year-old from northern Michigan. Sam pointed to the top of the tower and told his men to fire. And so they did, guns singing, grenades launching, machine guns blasting, boom-boom-boom-boom. Fucking horrendous. Unbelievably loud.

What if Miller is still alive? I thought. There was so much firing and so much crap flying, bricks, shrapnel, bullets. Two marines were wounded. One of them was Demarkus Brown, a kid from Martinsville, Virginia, twenty-two. The marines were raking the minaret, Demarkus was, too, and then he dropped his rifle and grabbed his right cheek. "I'm hit! I'm hit!" he said, panic in his eyes, real panic like he was going to die. But the wound was small and Demarkus was so young, he seemed like one of those kids on the playground who gets hurt every time. He seemed so frightened. He was killed four days later.

The firing stopped. Smoking rifles. Two more marines went up, and the minaret began to come apart. Bricks falling, dust and rocks, the tower swaying. Gunfire started to come into the mosque from the houses nearby. The insurgents had found us.

Ashley was still seated on the stoop, helmet crooked, mumbling to himself like a child. My fault.

Miller appeared. Two marines had pulled him out, Goggin one of them, choking and coughing. Black lung, they called it later. Miller was on his back; he'd come out head first. His face was opened in a large V, split like meat, fish maybe, with the two sides jiggling.

"Please tell me he's not dead," Ash said. "Please tell me."

"He's dead," I said.

I felt it then. Darting, out of reach. You go into these places and they are overrated, they are not nearly as dangerous as people say. Keep your head, keep the gunfire in front of you. You get close and come out unscathed every time, your face as youthful and as untroubled as before. The life of the reporter: always someone else's pain. A woman in an Iraqi hospital cradles her son newly blinded, and a single tear rolls down her cheek. The cheek is so dry and the tear moves so slowly that you focus on it for a while, the tear traveling across the wide desert plain. Your photographer needed a corpse for the newspaper, so you and a bunch of marines went out to get one. Then suddenly it's there, the warm liquid on your face, the death you've always avoided, smiling back at you like it knew all along. Your fault.

A troop carrier, one of the old marine jobs, had come for Miller. Bullets were bouncing off it as it rolled up. It was going to head straight for the hospital, as if there were a chance for him. The marines lifted Miller onto a gurney, arms flapping, face flapping.

The escape was left to Sam. Ashley got up finally and we moved inside the main body of the mosque next to the minaret. Gunfire everywhere, so loud. The insurgents were closing in. One of the marines was holding a rifle covered in blood and he looked at Ashley and figured, I think, that he'd best not give him a gun right now. So he shoved the M-16 into my hands; sticky and warm. The marines don't leave their guns behind either. When I was in high school I shot a duck with my friend's gun, barrel out the window of his parents' station wagon. The duck swam in circles for a while and then he died. Take this, asshole. I didn't actually hear him say that. It was too loud to hear.

Sam held up three fingers and counted them down. Three-two-one and we were off, out the door and into the street, me carrying Miller's blood-soaked gun, a pair of machine guns to our east opening up as we ran. Legs like jelly, legs like wings, we were all flying together. Bullets zinging past, hitting the bricks. "I want to die," I heard Ashley say. "I hope they shoot me." We jumped a final fallen tree and turned a corner down an alley and we were safe.

"I know you guys are thinking you got Miller killed," Sam said back at the house with the rest of the platoon. He was pulling on a cigarette, seated against a wall on the second floor. He seemed a wise old man sitting there, not a line on his face, and we the children. "It's a war," he said slowly, like a man as old as time. "That's what happens in war."

Lieutenant Eckert walked in. He hadn't gone with us.

"We take full responsibility for what happened out there," Ashley said to Eckert. I said it, too.

"Yeah, it was your fault," he said.

A jet came later and dropped two 500-pound bombs. It seemed an angry gesture: two big bombs for one shooter at the top of a tower. The marines went back the next day—they didn't bring us this time—to make sure everyone was dead. They found two bodies. Sometimes I imagine the live insurgent with the gun and the dead one we wanted to photograph, powder on his face, together at the top of the minaret in the moments before we arrived. What was he doing up there, the live insurgent? Cradling his buddy, weeping for him? Had they come from Saudi Arabia together to fight the jihad, riding together on a decrepit bus to the Syrian border? Or had the live one come to retrieve the dead one on orders from his commander, only to be interrupted by Miller coming up the stairs?

Lance Corporal William L. Miller, twenty-two, Pearland, Texas. The town made me think of pearls. A necklace. Miller's official portrait shows a boyish cadet with a long, thin face untroubled by thoughts of the future. Rummaging through Ash's photos, I found a photograph, taken at another mosque a few blocks back—the Grand Mosque, the center of town. The marines had fought hard for that building; the photo shows Miller and four of his buddies taking a break during a quiet moment, sprawled in a perfect row, illuminated by a ray of light that entered through a nearby window. Miller's head is tilted to the right. He's asleep.

A few months later, at the memorial service in the gymnasium in North Carolina, I spotted Miller's parents, Susie and Lewis. Billy's helmet and rifle and boots and dog tag were out there on the gym floor, arranged in a tombstonelike structure along with those of the other marines who had died there in Iraq. The graves were splayed out in a large V on the gym floor. Billy's memorial was the fourth from the bottom on the right-hand side.

I wasn't sure if I could face the Millers but I felt like I needed to say something. They'd no doubt read the marines' after-action report, which, for all its jargon, had laid out in detail what had happened that day. "First platoon was given the order to escort two reporters to a mosque at the 883 northing on the west side of PL Frank, so they could get a picture of a dead enemy in the mosque minaret."

I walked up to the Millers with some hesitation and they saw me. I was carrying a notebook. I figured the Millers would say something cutting, something full of despair, maybe even lunge at me. The father of a woman who'd been murdered in Palm Bay, Florida, did that to me once, in the waiting room of the local hospital. "You bastard," he said. I hadn't even asked him a question. I hadn't gotten his daughter killed.

"We're so grateful to you," Lewis said to me when the service was over, down on the gym floor. "If it weren't for you, we would never have known how our son died."

I wanted to tell the Millers what had happened. Hadn't they read the after-action report? My eyes met theirs; their eyes looked tired. Exhausted. When I was a kid I had a friend who shot himself, Pat Galloway, and I went to the viewing, and his mother and father, Bob and Natalie, had the same exhausted eyes. All cried out. After he died the Galloways put Pat's high school graduation photo on the mantel in their living room. I imagined a photo like that of Billy on the mantel in the Millers' home.

I asked them about Pearland.

"Pear-land," Lewis said to me, "Pear-land. We're known for our pears."

Habibi

In the summer of 2005, the American military spent $1.5 million to renovate a fifty-yard-wide strip of earth between Abu Nawas Street and the banks of the Tigris. They called it Tigris River Park. They cleared away the old cars and the animal carcasses. They sodded the fields with green grass. They installed a sprinkler system and swing sets for children, erected a "community center" for barbecues and weddings. The soldiers even built a winding sidewalk which one of the American commanders referred to as a "lovers' lane." The project seemed out of place in Baghdad, which every day was slipping deeper into anarchy. But in its own way Tigris River Park was a symbol of American goodwill.

The American engineers also laid a heavy, paved road along the bank of the Tigris, thick enough to hold tanks and troop carriers. It ran for a couple of miles, north to the Jumhuriyah Bridge. Until the American engineers came, the banks of the Tigris had been spooky—for the carcasses and the old cars, for the corpses and the wild dogs. The wild dogs yipped and howled from their hiding places in the reeds—dozens of them, hundreds of them—and they harassed anyone who approached. One day, some of the security guards who protected a nearby hotel came out and, with their M-4s and Kalashnikovs, shot most of them. They mowed them down; I listened to the shooting from my bedroom. I was never certain whether the shooting was part of the American-backed project, or whether the security guards were just bored.

Yet for all the effort to improve Tigris River Park, the Iraqis didn't show much interest. On most afternoons, most of the park was empty. An American Humvee sometimes planted itself in the middle of the sodded fields, the soldiers seated inside as motionless as blue herons. The Humvee didn't exactly help attract the locals. But what really chased the Iraqis away was the park itself: before the renovation, the Iraqis would gather for soccer in the late afternoon, with three or four games starting up amid the dirt and junk. When the Americans renovated the park, they laid down a curvy, S-shaped sidewalk—the lovers' lane—that snaked its way from one end of the park to the other. The sidewalk cut right through the old soccer fields. Now, instead of three or four games, there was usually just one, in a small corner of the park that had been left untouched. By sundown, the park was more often than not abandoned, the lovers' lane and the swings desolate, intensifying, rather than diminishing, the sense of despair that pervaded the city.

Personally, I couldn't complain. Tigris River Park was great for me. In the afternoons, I could take off running along the river, cruising atop the smooth heavy blacktop. It was hot, but I could run all the way to the Jumhuriyah Bridge. If I closed my eyes, it felt like Phoenix.

One day, returning from a trip, I headed out and ran less than a mile before I approached a checkpoint manned by Iraqi army soldiers. It had gone up when I was away. It was a long cement wall with sandbags and watchtowers that cut the park in half. The soldiers were half-asleep in the heat, wilting under the sun. As I approached, they perked up, looking on with fascination. I stopped, sweating and panting in my shorts, and one of the soldiers recoiled a little and waved me through. "*Shukran*," I said to him. "*Shukran jazeelan.*" Thanks, thanks very much. And then I slipped through the gate and ran to the bridge. I passed the soldiers on the way back and thanked them again.

For the next several weeks, I followed the same route, the same routine. As the sun began to set, I'd come running up the Tigris, usually offering a few Arabic words to ease my way through. "*Shlounik, habibi*," I'd say, "How are you, my friend?" Or "*Kulish hara*"—"Very hot." The Iraqis marveled at my willingness to run in the furnace that enveloped the city. I'd approach, and one of them would come down and look at me, sweating and faint, and say: "*Laish? Laish, habibi?*" "Why? Why, my friend?" And he would always wave me through.

Over time I realized that I was the highlight of the Iraqis' day. I was the only thing that happened. The soldiers would sit in their checkpoint for hours at a stretch, enduring the heat, without so much as a fender bender to keep them awake. Then I would come running and the soldiers would brighten, come out and greet me. They'd offer me water; sometimes I'd take it. Sometimes I'd offer them a swig from the bottle I carried with me. A few times, as I passed through the checkpoint, a wild dog plunged out of the reeds to menace me. The dog population had made a comeback. It would bare its teeth and snap at me as the Iraqis looked on. And then a few days later as I ran through the checkpoint I noticed the dog was gone. The Iraqi soldiers were smiling proudly. "Boom-boom, mistah!" one of the soldiers said, mimicking a shot with his rifle.

The one thing that bothered the Iraqis was my shorts. Whenever I approached the checkpoint, the soldiers stared at my legs. They looked at them in horror, as if I were naked and deranged. But they never complained. They were too polite. I knew what I was doing was rude—showing one's bare legs is considered offensive across the Arab world. But after much deliberation I decided I was going to keep my shorts. It was the heat—the piercing, suffocating heat. Even if I took off in the early evening before sundown, at 7 p.m., the temperature would still be around 120 or 130 in the sun. It took everything I had to run at all. Staying inside—not running—didn't seem like an option, either. Running in Iraq was dangerous, it was reckless, it was arrogant. If I were kidnapped, the whole American army would be dispatched to look for me. But as Baghdad slipped deeper into chaos, the more cooped up my colleagues and I had to be. The dissonance was jarring: a war was unfolding outside, the war we'd come to write about, and yet more and more we had to seal ourselves off from it, there in the middle of it. I could hear the bombs from my bedroom and I couldn't chase them. I could climb on the roof and see the Iraqis in the street and I couldn't talk to them. I needed an outlet, something to do. I needed to run like a wild horse. The little road along the Tigris was probably the only place in all of Iraq an American could run and have a reasonable expectation of surviving, outside the Green Zone or a military base or Kurdistan. And by chance I happened to live right next to it. I thought it was worth the risk, come what may. My legs—the Iraqis were going to have to put up with my legs.

One day, late in the summer, as I ran toward the checkpoint, one of the Iraqi guards stepped out and put his hand up for me to stop. I was panting and delirious. The Iraqi soldiers gathered round. The soldier was holding something and he offered it to me with both hands. It was a gift: a uniform of the Iraqi national soccer team, white with green trim, with the red, white and black Iraqi flag sewn into the chest. I was deeply touched. The Iraqis were crazy about soccer; I couldn't imagine a more heartfelt gesture. I thanked them and shook their hands. The uniform contained shorts, too, which, I could not help but notice, plunged far below the knee. Later that night, as I was trying on the shorts, it occurred to me that the Iraqi guards were, in their subtle way, trying to persuade me to cover my legs.

The next day I hit the trail and ran north toward the Jumhuriyah Bridge. I'd tried the shorts on, and they were ridiculous: clingy and polyester and too small, which meant that they would cook my legs like a pair of rubber pants. I put them on and took them off and put them on and took them off. I left them behind. I did put on the Iraqi top. The top, too, was made of polyester, and as I approached the checkpoint, I was near collapse; it was like I was wearing a plastic bag. The chief walked out and gave me an affectionate but disappointed look, like a father would his wayward son.

"*Laish, habibi,*" he said, reaching down and tugging on his pants. "Why, my friend?"

CHAPTER 12

The Vanishing World

JAFF AND I were riding in a taxi on Highway 1 outside of Bayji, at the tip of the Sunni Triangle, when we pulled into a roadside kebab joint for lunch. It was November 2003. The kebab place was big and loud, maybe fifty tables, and the driver told us he'd be waiting outside. We were about fifteen minutes into our kebabs when the driver walked back in, leaned over and spoke in a quiet voice. "Be calm," he said. "Please stop eating, get up and leave immediately." And we got up just like that. I don't remember if we paid. We walked quickly to the car and climbed in and the driver hit the gas and sped off. "Some people in the parking lot were talking about killing you," he said.

That was one of the first signs. A month later, Jaff and I drove to Ad-Dawr, a village on the Tigris near the spider hole where Saddam Hussein had been captured a few days before. Saddam, I was told, had been attending Friday prayers at the mosque in Ad-Dawr during his months on the run. We stopped and asked some kids where the mosque was, the one where Saddam prayed, and the kids pointed us around the corner. So we rounded the corner, and the mosque was right there, and so were a group of men with wrapped faces who started shooting at us. At the moment, I was on a satellite phone with the antenna stuck up against the rear window. "Jesus, they're shooting at us!" I yelled to a colleague. We were moving pretty fast and they missed, and we rounded the corner. As we drove out, I saw men with wrapped faces everywhere, standing on the rooftops, looking down on us.

My colleagues were coming back with similar stories. Ashley and his driver, Tariq, had been driving around Samarra in Tariq's Toyota when three insurgents pulled up next to them with Kalashnikovs and opened fire. The bullets missed and Tariq sped off. In traffic, Tariq put some distance between his Toyota and the BMW carrying the insurgents. Then, on the open road, Tariq hit a patch of broken glass and one of his tires went flat. The BMW was approaching fast. Just then, out of the sky, appeared an Apache helicopter. Ash figured afterwards that the Apache pilot must have thought that Ash and Tariq fixing their flat were insurgents laying IEDs. The Apache circled a couple of times to check them out. The BMW turned away.

Joao, the photographer, was asleep in his car in Falluja when his driver, Qais, noticed a car behind them with four guys with faces covered by kafiyas. Wrapped faces: that was a bad sign. Qais gunned his old BMW to 140 mph. The car behind them, an Opel, pulled alongside them but couldn't keep up. Qais had to buy a new car after that, his engine was ruined, but they got away. Ian Fisher was just sitting in traffic one day, also in Falluja, when a man came over and stood in front of his car, flipped the switch on his Kalashnikov to fully automatic and fired the whole clip. The guy shot the bullets out and away from Ian but he stared at him the whole time. When the clip was empty, the guy walked away.

Falluja was always the worst. In early 2004, I went to see the police chief—Falluja still had a police chief then—and Jaff and my driver, Waleed, and I noticed that a car was trailing us. I wasn't sure but Jaff and Waleed seemed certain; the Iraqis always knew. We drove out of town and pulled into Camp Falluja, the American base. About an hour later we drove toward Baghdad for a couple of miles, and the car appeared again. Whoever it was had been waiting for us to come out. We had a BMW that day, and I was grateful for that. We sped up and left them behind.

It was the spring of 2004 when we lost the country—as a place to go, I mean. For a month Iraq was engulfed by upris-

ings, Sunni and Shia, full-blown rebellions in every city outside of Kurdistan. Iraq disappeared for us then, and it never
came back. I was in Falluja a couple of days before the uprising. The Marines had just arrived in Iraq, all pumped up and
determined to take over for the Army, and they'd gotten into
a firefight on their first day. They'd killed some civilians
and shot up a neighborhood called Al-Askari. Jaff and I had
spent the day trying to figure out what had happened, and at
lunchtime we drove into the downtown and pulled into Hajji
Hussein's, Falluja's best kebab house. The place was jammed,
a hundred tables, all the clamor of lunchtime, when I stepped
through the door, and all the noise stopped. It was like a scene
from one of those westerns when the sheriff walks into the
saloon through the swinging doors and everyone stops talking. "Be calm," Jaff said under his breath. Jaff, a former guerrilla fighter, was always cool. We sat down. We were careful
not to show any fear. It took a few minutes before everybody
started carrying on again. I never went back to Hajji Hussein's
after that. Never went back to Falluja after that, except with
the invading marines.

A few days after that, a group of four American security
guards, Blackwater guys, were attacked and killed. A crowd of
frenzied Fallujans dragged their bodies through the streets
and hung two of the black and toasted carcasses from the city's
main bridge over the Euphrates. The images were beamed
around the world. The seven-month-long siege of Falluja
began. A few months later, Hajji Hussein's kebab house was
destroyed in an airstrike. The Americans said it was a terrorist
"safehouse," from which "innocent civilians knowingly stayed
away," but I always wondered about that.

In August 2004, the Mahdi Army had taken over the Imam
Ali shrine in Najaf, the Shiite holy city, and the American
Army was going in to flush them out. A huge battle was
unfolding. Najaf lay at the southern end of a string of Sunni
cities south of Baghdad that had slipped from American control. I knew it was going to be a bad drive. We hung dark
screens in the car windows, and I lay in the back seat for most
of the drive. Along the way, whenever I peeked out the back
window, I spied an apocalyptic landscape of shot-up cars and

abandoned trucks. No government, no army, no police. Out-side of Mahmudiya, south of Baghdad, an ambulance from the Red Crescent sat in the middle of the road, smoking. Only a couple of days before, an Italian reporter named Enzo Bal-doni had traveled to Najaf in a similar convoy and been kid-napped by insurgents as he passed through the town of Mahmudiya. We drove through Mahmudiya as well, down its narrow main street, which was so glutted with traffic that the locals were peeking inside our car. I lay down in the back seat and pulled the bulletproof vest over my face. A few days later, Baldoni was murdered.

It didn't take a lot of energy to imagine what would happen if they got you. All you had to do was watch one of the videos the insurgents were putting up on the web. One of the first showed a pale young man with a thin beard sitting cross-legged on the floor. He was dressed in an orange jumpsuit. The orange jumpsuit: you knew right away that stood for Abu Ghraib, the place where the American soldiers had humiliated the Iraqi prisoners and taken photos for souvenirs. You knew right then the video wasn't going to end well. But in the video, the young man seemed remarkably calm; as if he hadn't imag-ined what was coming. Five men stood behind him, each wearing a mask and black clothing. The pale-skinned young man introduced himself. "My name is Nicholas Berg, from West Chester, Pennsylvania." The masked man in the middle began reading from a script. He had a hoarse, guttural voice, not the voice of a gentle man. "Where is the sense of honor, where is the rage?" the masked man asked. "Where is the anger for God's religion?"

Then, with a little flip of his hand, the man with the hoarse voice handed his script to a man on his left. It was a nonchalant gesture, the kind an executive would make when he wanted his personal assistant to take his briefcase. Just a little flip. And then he pulled out a large knife. The masked man grabbed Berg's hair and pushed him to the ground and Berg screamed, realizing what was next. The masked man pulled Berg's head back and went to work with his knife. When the masked man finished, he held up Berg's head for the camera. Berg was found a couple of days later near an overpass in Baghdad.

It was one of the truisms in Iraq that it would be better to be captured by Shiite guerrillas than Sunni ones. The Mahdi Army guys could be violent, and a lot of them were uneducated, but they seemed to lack the hollow-eyed bloodlust of their Sunni counterparts. Whatever else they were going to do, the Mahdi Army wasn't going to put you in an orange jumpsuit and make a video. During the summer of 2004, my colleague Ed Wong ventured into Sadr City and spent the night with some Mahdi Army fighters. At the time, AC-130s gunships were pounding the Mahdi Army's strongholds; you could hear the cannons going all night. Ed came back the next morning, and everyone asked him how it was. Ed said it went fine. "They spent most of the night trying to figure out how to get the porn channel on their satellite television," he said. We all got a kick out of that.

WE'D HAVE THESE conversations, usually over dinner. What would happen, someone would say; if the bad guys got inside the compound? What would we do then? We'd knock that around a little. Then someone would say, What if they actually got inside the house? Would it be better, for instance, to use a pistol, which was more easily controlled, or a Kalashnikov, with its greater accuracy and power? A discussion would follow. All the Westerners in Baghdad were having the same conversations. Some of us had already been kidnapped. Some had been killed. There was a story going round about a reporter for the *Los Angeles Times* who had ordered his Iraqi guards to shoot him if any kidnappers managed to pull him from his car. Just kill me, he said. I don't want to end up in an orange jumpsuit.

What if the compound were overrun? For a time, we had a trapdoor built into the brick wall at the back. It led to the outside world, toward the Palestine Hotel, only a few hundred yards away, which housed a company of American soldiers. Then one day the Americans departed. So we talked about what it might take to land a helicopter inside the compound— not enough room for that. Then we started talking about Zodiac boats, inflatable rafts we could drag down to the

Tigris, fifty yards away. Paddle them over to the Green Zone. There was a lot to consider. Assuming, for instance, that space in the boats was limited, which Iraqis were we going to take with us and which would we leave behind? And how were we going to make sure the Americans protecting the Green Zone wouldn't mistake us for insurgents, out there in the river?

The bureau became a fortress, a high-walled castle from another century. We blocked off Abu Nawas Street, one of the city's main thoroughfares, which ran along the front of the house. We brought in a crane to erect concrete blast walls, a foot thick and twenty feet high. We strung coils of razor wire across the top. We hired armed guards, twenty of them, then thirty, then forty. After a time, armed guards became our single largest expense. We gave each of them a Kalashnikov, and some of them kept grenades in their lockers in the basement. We put searchlights on the roof, then machine-guns, 7.62 mm, belt-fed. The French Embassy was around the corner, and we determined at one point that the bullets from our machine guns intersected with the bullets of the French guns in the area behind our houses. We liked that, the interlocking fields of fire.

We hired a security adviser, a former soldier, for near $1,000 a day, making him the highest-paid member of our staff. We bought three armored cars, including a BMW once owned by the German diplomatic service, for $250,000. Not long afterward, the BMW stopped a Kalashnikov bullet fired into its roof. Then there was the life insurance the newspaper took out for us, about $14,000 per month each, an amount we figured indicated that the insurance company had determined that at least one of us was not going to live. The electricity in Baghdad usually lasted for only about four hours, so we generated most of our own. For $60,000, we imported a generator the size of a toolshed from the United Kingdom. We trucked it overland across Europe and then through Turkey and across the Iraqi border. Some of the Iraqis working for us went up to the border to bring it down, and on the way south they were stopped by insurgents.

"For the Americans?" the masked men kept asking.

"No, no," our guys said. "Not for the Americans."

Then they waved them through.

I trusted the Iraqis who worked for us. And if I hadn't trusted them, they would have proved me wrong. The Iraqis who worked for us could have done us in so many times. They liked the money we paid them, of course, but it was more than that, I think. Living through all that together, we wanted to help each other survive. Waleed, whom I always drove with— he pulled me out of the crowd that day. Jaff saved me I don't know how many times.

Plus, the Iraqis who worked with us were getting killed. We Americans might have been cowering behind the blast walls, but our Iraqi employees had to go home at night. Fakher Haider, our stringer in Basra, was a man of few words and a large mustache. He'd fought against Saddam in the uprising in 1991, and in Basra's murky byways he could still make out the good guys from the bad. One night, a group of armed men who said they were police officers came to his house and took him away. Fakher told his wife not to worry, that he'd be back soon. He was found a few hours later in a deserted area outside the city, with his hands bound behind him and a bag over his head. There were bruises on his body and a bullet in his head. Fakher had been reporting a story about the infiltration of Basra's security forces by sectarian militias. He was our first, but not our last.

I never asked about loyalties. In July 2004, when Saddam Hussein was arraigned, the Iraqis on our staff sat riveted in front of the television in the newsroom. On seeing Saddam in the dock—reduced, haggard, dressed in a cheap suit—one of our translators began to weep. Jaff, who'd fought against Saddam, laughed out loud at the sight of him. On hearing Jaff, one of our Sunni translators, Basim, stormed away.

"How dare you make fun of our president that way!" he said.

Iraq was so complex, its ways so labyrinthine, that trust, in the end, was all we had. If we had tried to understand what was really going on outside, if we had tried to understand the pressures the Iraqis were working under, we would have left the country. In November 2005, one of our drivers, Emad al-Samarrai, told us that he'd received a series of telephone calls from a man claiming to be an insurgent. Emad was one of several members of the Samarrai family who worked for *The New York Times:* his father, Abu Ziad, and his brother, Uday, worked for us, too. They were Sunnis from Samarra, and I presumed they knew insurgents. Most of our Sunni employees did.

Emad was so petrified that, with the help of some of the other Iraqis on our staff, he made a transcript of the threatening calls. It was impossible to know where the truth began and where it ended, but Emad was a delicate, sensitive man, and the fear in his eyes seemed real when he told us the story. Assuming the record of the conversations was accurate, it opened a window onto the world we never saw.

> Caller: Emad, for how long have you and your father
> and brother been walking in this dark way?
> Emad: Which way do you mean?
> Caller: Which way? You know which way I mean.
> Emad: You mean journalism?
> Caller: Journalism, Emad? Emad, listen to me carefully.
> We have accurate information from trusted sources
> regarding your work, and your location near the
> Ishtar Sheraton. We know all the Iraqi staff, and we
> will work on killing them one by one.
> Emad: Why?
> Caller: Because we know you are not press, we know
> what goes on with you . . .

The next day, the anonymous caller dialed again:

> Caller: We have someone who works with you, who
> supplies specific information about you, we are
> tracing you and we know the nature of your work.
> You are not press but CIA, and the one who sits
> behind you in the car is CIA.
> Emad: The CIA?
> Caller: Don't act surprised. The one who sits with you
> in the car, the one with the gray shirt, is a senior
> official with the CIA. He destroyed Iraq.

The caller went on to tell Emad that the only way he could save himself was to bring one of the Western reporters to him. That is, to the insurgents. If Emad refused, the caller said, he and his cohorts would kill him and his family.

That's when Emad came to us. Should we have believed him? We didn't have much choice. We decided to give Emad and his family two months off, and they left the country. When they returned, the threat had evidently passed, but after a time Emad and his brother left Iraq and did not return.

Incidents like the one with Emad made me wonder: Why do the insurgents let us stay in Baghdad? Out there in the wide open, driving around? Some of them had started killing reporters, and, sure enough, over time, most of the Western reporters left the country. Those of us who stayed kept on working. Sure we were crazy, but it was also true that the insurgents knew where to find us. They knew who we were. If they had wanted us dead, then we would have been dead. So why did they let us live? I assumed they had decided that we were useful to them. That was not a comforting thought, even if it meant they would let us survive.

ONE DAY in the summer of 2004, Jaff and I were driving through the string of unfriendly towns north of Baghdad. We were hungry, and as we entered the town of Tuz Khurmatu Jaff ordered the driver to stop. Tuz was an ethnically mixed place—split between Arabs, Kurds and Turcomen—and one of extreme tension. Jaff picked out a kebab house which, he said, was owned by local Kurds and so relatively safe. We walked in and Jaff said something to the owner, and then we headed toward the back and sat down. And everyone in the restaurant was staring at us. No one was saying anything, just looking. It was like the scene at Hajji Hussein's a few months before. Under my breath, I suggested to Jaff that perhaps we ought to leave. Jaff didn't say a word, but reached down and unstrapped his Browning 9 mm pistol and laid it on the table in front of him. Then he ordered his kebab, as if there was nothing amiss. Within a few minutes, everyone got back to minding their own business.

Jaff was always a step in front of me. That day when we drove to the mosque in Ad-Dawr where Saddam had been praying, my jaw fell open as I saw all the masked insurgents standing on the rooftops. I muttered something to Jaff and then I looked: he had already pulled his Browning out and was pointing it at one of the insurgents through the car window, as if to say, Don't even think about it. Jaff was tall and good-looking, with a taciturn air he picked up as a member of the peshmerga, fighting the Baathists. He looked like Clint Eastwood and carried himself like Harry Callaghan, Eastwood's famous cop. Jaff was shrewd and calm, and, like Dirty Harry, he gave off the hint that he was enjoying himself.

As an American—as someone who could leave Iraq anytime I wanted—I sometimes found myself taking cheap thrills from my brushes with death. Most of the Iraqis I worked with had had enough of those. At times, Jaff, too, seemed like he was living off his adrenaline, seeing Iraq not as his home but as a great adventure. During the battle of Najaf in August 2004, Jaff and I waded into a demonstration of Iraqi pilgrims who had come, they said, to protect the Shrine of Imam Ali from an American attack. The crowd surged, and the Iraqi police panicked and opened fire. With gunfire ringing out and demonstrators dropping around us, Jaff and I took off running. Then, three hundred yards down the road, he stopped.

"I forgot my sunglasses," he said.

So Jaff ran back, against the massive human tide, into the gunfire. I hid behind a telephone pole. He came running up a few minutes later, his $200 Ray-Bans in hand. They were a gift.

"Christine would have killed me," he said, referring to the reporter who'd given him the glasses. We resumed our running. We were laughing, too.

Yet for all of Jaff's coolness, he'd known hardship as well. He'd survived many close calls as a guerrilla fighter, including street-to-street fighting with the Baathists in Sulaimaniya after the first Gulf War. Jaff's father was a prince in his tribe, the largest in Kurdistan, and in the poison gas attack on the village of Halabja in 1988, Jaff lost thirty-four members of his family.

Jaff was always listening, even when I didn't realize. Once I told him I'd spent a summer working on a natural gas pipeline in the Gulf of Mexico, and that my coworkers had been mostly rednecks from Louisiana. Their not-very-playful nickname for me was "college boy," which, I hardly needed to explain to Jaff, was short for "sissy." I was taunted mercilessly, I told him.

Some weeks later, Jaff and some of his friends found themselves at an American checkpoint in Adamiyah, a dangerous Sunni neighborhood in northern Baghdad. They'd gone out for late-night kebabs. It was a spooky part of town, and probably not a good idea to be out at all. The American soldiers weren't quite sure what to make of Jaff. They checked his pistol and they checked his weapons permit, and they handed them back. The Americans were friendly but they were intimidating just the same. One of them spotted his Thuraya satellite phone, with which, courtesy of *The New York Times*, Jaff could call anywhere in the world.

"Hey, let me see that," one of the soldiers said.

Jaff handed it over.

"You mind if I use this to call my mom?" the soldier asked in a cocky way.

"Forget it, college boy," Jaff said, and all the soldiers burst out laughing at their comrade.

"Where'd you learn that?" the embarrassed soldier demanded. "Where'd you learn that?"

BY THE SUMMER OF 2006, the Green Zone had come to resemble one of those medieval fortifications designed by Vauban, the French engineer of castles. With every possibility of attack accounted for, the fortifications grew into gothic, improbable shapes, triangles and diamonds and mazes, ends in themselves. Concrete blast walls formed a perimeter around the vast compound and then turned outward, reaching hundreds of yards into the city. There were walled lanes for American soldiers to enter the Green Zone, walled lanes for VIPs and walled lanes for the Iraqis, each one topped and crisscrossed by coils of barbed wire. Inside each concrete lane stood an interior wall that could be sealed off, offering perfect lines of fire without escape, in case things got out of hand. Kill-zones, they called them. They looked like the chutes in a slaughterhouse.

The first checkpoints were manned by untrained Iraqi cops, cannon fodder for the bombers. The Iraqi cops let almost everyone through, which was part of the problem, of course. Closer in stood a layer of Iraqi soldiers, young Shiites in their first jobs. They were getting bombed all the time. Behind them stood the first handful of Americans, kids on a tank. The Iraqi soldiers, perhaps because they were always new, perhaps because they had resigned themselves to dying, were friendly and good-natured. The Americans were pulled as tightly as wires.

Most Iraqis weren't allowed to drive into the Green Zone—they had to approach on foot. Each morning, hundreds of Iraqis lined up to go inside the Green Zone to their jobs, and the lines stretched into the street. The lines moved at a glacial pace, stalling because of the searches; and the suicide bombers feasted on them. In the beginning, the Americans just pushed the lines farther out into the street, presumably because it was the Green Zone itself they wanted to protect. So the bombers struck the Iraqis there. It took many months for the Americans to finally secure the Iraqi employees, but even then the bombers kept coming. I never witnessed a bombing at the entrance to the Green Zone, but often, as I walked in, I stepped through heaps of glass and metal.

Once you got through those first lines of defense, you could expect to be searched six or seven times before you got into the Green Zone itself, and more if you were going to see an American or an Iraqi official (as opposed to attending a press conference). The people along the way who were conducting the searches were usually soldiers from one of the smaller countries that had joined the American coalition. For a long time, it was soldiers from Georgia, in the former Soviet Union, who checked IDs. Most of them couldn't speak any English or any Arabic, so there were a lot of problems. The same with the Gurkhas, armed guards from Nepal, who were well trained but usually unable to communicate.

Once you got through the searches and ID checks, you'd walk through a barbed-wire path to the bus stop in front of the Rashid Hotel. The Rashid was an old Baathist place that still functioned even though it was inside the Green Zone. And after a time, a bus would come, and it would take you to the Republican Palace, where the American embassy was. And here, met by an escort, you'd go through a bulletproof door and into an alcove where you would drop off your ID and passport and head inside the embassy itself. And then, perhaps ninety minutes after you'd left your office, you'd be ushered in to see an American diplomat who would proceed to tell you what was happening outside.

Most of the diplomats were serious, dedicated and capable people, and they were brave, too. But they couldn't resist the tide that was pulling them deeper and deeper into their fortified bunkers, farther and farther away from Iraq. In the summer of 2006, I went to the embassy to meet a new diplomat, a political-military officer. He was new to the country. I'd gone to talk to him about Iranian influence in the Mahdi Army. "They pay people to pay Iraqis to do stuff," he said. That was it. A blank look. I pressed the diplomat for a few details, but all I got was the blank look. In 2003 and 2004, when I saw that look on the face of an American official, I presumed it was because he was holding something back, something secret. And now, in the wilted, dying summer of 2006, I realized that the diplomats weren't telling me anything because they didn't have anything to say.

One night, after I'd flown into Camp Victory, the American military headquarters adjacent to the Green Zone, some soldiers agreed to drive me to the front gate where I could meet my ride home. As a captain drove his SUV toward the edge of the secure area, his hands began to tremble on the steering wheel. "We don't like doing this at night," he said. It was as if he were driving me to the edge of the known world, a place of children's dreams. The soldiers dropped me off and sped away, kicking up sand in the parking lot, before my ride showed up.

It was in the Green Zone that I would think the war was lost. I didn't think about losing when I was outside—when I was in Iraq. There was too much reality pressing in, too many things changing, too much in play. No: it was when I was waiting for the bus outside the Rashid Hotel, watching the overweight American contractors, making more money than they'd ever dreamed of, saunter into the restaurant for dinner at 5 p.m. It was when one of the American generals in charge of Baghdad, in his office in Camp Victory, pronounced the name of the Iraqi prime minister three different ways in a half an hour, "Molokai," "Maleeki," "Malaaki," each time as if he were speaking of some sort of exotic plant.

One night George Packer, a writer for *The New Yorker*, and I stayed late in the Green Zone talking to an Iraqi intelligence officer. It was dark when we left his office, and I called ahead for Waleed to come and get us. The Iraqi official had left it to us to walk out through the maze of gates and blast walls, perhaps a mile in all. When we got to the last checkpoint at the main entrance, all that remained for us was to walk through a final gauntlet of concrete. A group of Chilean guards tried to stop us. They seemed genuinely alarmed for us. "*No se puede ir afuera en la zona roja*," one of them said, looking at us as if we were mistaken. You can't go out into the Red Zone. "*Peligroso demasiado. Muy, muy peligroso.*" Too dangerous. Very, very dangerous. A few days before, the Chilean told us, a reporter had walked outside from this very spot and been shot at by a sniper in the building across the road as she made the half-mile walk to her car. "*Vivimos en la zona roja*," I told the guards, resurrecting my Spanish. We live in the Red Zone. Out there. The Chileans, stunned, looked at each other and looked at us. George and I walked into the street.

IN EARLY 2006, as I sat with a Sunni sheikh in the lobby of the Babylon Hotel, I noticed an American security guard walk in. He was as large as an NFL lineman, with a crewcut, a tight shirt and a microphone in his ear. He was carrying an M-4 rifle. Definitely a man from Blackwater, the American security firm that protected VIPs.

"What is this?" Sheikh Akbar said, sitting up in his chair, a look of fear coming over his face.

The Babylon Hotel, which sat on the east bank of the Tigris, would have been at home in the old Soviet Union. It was a massive, brutalist thing, with marble floors and monstrous, sequined chandeliers. The lobby's news shop sold out-of-date Arabic newspapers and rusty cans of Right Guard.

A second American appeared in the lobby, also with a gun, and then a third. Outside the lobby window, a pair of snipers had taken up positions nearby. A helicopter hovered overhead.

Soon my answer appeared. A phalanx of Blackwater gunmen stepped into the lobby, and behind them, nearly invisible in the pack, was Robert Ford, the American embassy's chief political officer. Ford spoke perfect Arabic and was the best American diplomat in Iraq, and he was always friendly. Surrounded by the gunmen, he was almost invisible. The phalanx moved our way, guns pointing. I stood up.

"Hi, Robert," I said, as calmly as I could, daring the Blackwater guys to shoot me.

"Hi," Robert said. He was wearing a bulletproof vest.

Sheikh Akbar sat in petrified silence. The phalanx moved by, gliding toward the corner of the lobby, toward a small table like mine. And then I saw him: Wamid Nadmi, the leader of something called the National Patriotic Movement. He was a Baathist to the core, an apologist for Saddam. I'd listened to his lectures at his home in Adamiyah.

Ford and Nadmi sat down. It was a routine meeting between an American diplomat and a Sunni political leader. Nothing more, nothing less. Ford stayed for a while, and then got up, disappearing inside the phalanx, disappearing inside his Humvee, disappearing into the Green Zone.

ONE DAY, IN the summer of 2005, with the temperature hovering at 122, I drove across town to see Ahmad Chalabi, the deputy prime minister. Unlike most of the senior Iraqi officials, who by then had retreated into the Green Zone for protection, Chalabi was still living in his own home. Along with the car I rode in, I deployed a "chase car," a second vehicle, filled with armed guards, to follow behind me and come to my aid if we came under attack.

To get there, I drove to the outskirts of Chalabi's neighborhood, Mansour, passing through a series of checkpoints and concrete chicanes manned by Iraqi gunmen without uniforms. At the entrance to Chalabi's street, there was another checkpoint, made of cement and barbed wire, and more armed guards. I realized why he didn't live in the Green Zone: he had one of his own. In front of Chalabi's house, stood another blast wall. Next to the wall stood a bank of generators, guzzling gasoline and coughing smoke.

In his sitting room, Chalabi and I drank tea and talked about Iraq. As usual, he had a raft of plans and diagrams spread out before him. We talked about electricity. We talked about corruption. Then Chalabi began describing his efforts to broker a cease-fire in Tal Afar, a city that had imploded in bloodletting. It was 250 miles away.

"I had all the sheikhs here with me," Chalabi said. "Right here in this room."

Chalabi walked me outside. About a dozen bodyguards walked with him.

On my way home, I noticed that a car was following me. Three times, the mysterious car accelerated to get close. Two men were inside: a young man, maybe in his thirties, and a bald man behind the wheel. As the car drew close, my chase car—that second vehicle, filled with guards—cut the men off in traffic. I sped away.

Communiqués (1)

1.

Total number of attacks on Americans and Iraqis, for the
week ending October 7, 2005: 743.
Average number of attacks per day, for the week ending
October 7, 2005: 106.

—Press briefing
Major General Rick Lynch, spokesman
Multi-National Forces–Iraq
October 13, 2005

2.

The mujahideen stayed in the area for nine days and nine
nights, waiting for the American forces. The Marines came. A
patrol of nine came on foot to ambush our mujahideen while
they were firing their mortars, but their ambush became a
mujahideen ambush. The mujahideen surrounded the
Americans—their aim was to capture them—but the
Americans started shooting, so the mujahideen fired back with
machine guns supported by their brothers with mortars. They
killed some of the Americans and cut the throats of whoever
was still alive. All of them were dead except for one. He was
injured and asked the mujahideen for help. The mujahideen
captured him before the American helicopters arrived. They
carried away the captured soldier and also the gear of the dead
Crusaders. No one was hurt, thanks unto Allah.

Allah is great; glory to Allah, His messenger, and the believers.

—News Release
Bashir al-Sunnah, spokesman
The Military Corps of Ansar al-Sunnah Army
August 3, 2005

3.

Insurgent groups claiming responsibility for attacks on Americans and Iraqis in Iraq, May to October 2005:

1. *Al-Qaʾeda of Mesopotamia*
2. *Ansar al-Sunnah*
3. *Khalid bin al-Walid Military Column*
4. *Fatma Group*
5. *Ali bin al-Hussein Group*
6. *Jaʾafar bin Mohammed Group*
7. *Zein al-Abedin Group*
8. *Mohammed bin Musailam Brigade*
9. *Mohammed al-Fateh Brigade*
10. *The Martyrs Brigade*
11. *Military Brigades of the Abu Anas al-Shami*
12. *Abu Imam al-Iraqi Brigade*
13. *Military Column of the Martyrs*
14. *Abd al-Rahman Company*
15. *Omar Hadid Brigade*
16. *Abu al-Yamani Brigade*
17. *Abdul Aziz al-Moqren Brigade*
18. *Al-Fatʾh Brigade*
19. *Al-Farouq Brigade*
20. *Mohammed al-Qassem Brigade*
21. *Abu Osman Brigade*
22. *Mohammed Jasem al-Issawi Brigade*
23. *Al-Baraʾa bin Malik Suicide Brigade*
24. *Abi Suleiman Khaled ibn al-Walid Brigade*
25. *Snipers' Brigade*

26. *Al-Waqas Group of the Seif al-Haq Brigade*
27. *Abu Bakr of Seif al-Haq*
28. *Abdul Aziz al-Muqrin Brigade*
29. *Al-Hoda Brigade*
30. *Martyrs Brigade of Abdul Ghaffar*
31. *Tawheed Group of Seif al-Haq Brigade*
32. *Ansar Suicide Brigade*
33. *Al-Qa'aqa'a Brigade*
34. *Om al-Momenein Brigade*
35. *Abu al-Walid al-Ansari Group*
36. *Al-Zobeir ibn al-Awam Brigade*
37. *Islamic al-Ghadab Brigade*
38. *Mohammed ibn Salma Brigade*
39. *Al-Moqren Brigade*
40. *Assassination Brigade*
41. *Brigade of al-Falluja Martyrs*
42. *Sattar al-Hadid Brigade*
43. *Abu Sifyan Hasan al-Zaedi Brigade*
44. *Ali bin Abu Talib Brigade*
45. *Al-Waqas of al-Tawhid Brigade*
46. *Al-Tawheed Brigade*
47. *Abu Bakr Brigade*
48. *Omar ibn al-Khattab's "May Allah Be Pleased with Him" Brigade*
49. *Abu Yaman al-Madaenini Brigade*
50. *Rocket Brigade*
51. *Attack Brigade*
52. *Al-Shohada'a Brigade*
53. *Thi al-Nooraine Brigade*
54. *Mohammed Allah Messengers Brigade*
55. *Forqan Brigade*
56. *Ibn Taimiya Brigade*
57. *Tawheed Lions of Sharhabil bin Hosna*
58. *Men's Faith Brigade*
59. *Tawheed Lions of Abdullah ibn al-Zobeir*
60. *Al-Mustafa Brigade*
61. *Othman bin Afan*
62. *Al-Muqdad bin al-Aswad*
63. *Abu Bakr al-Siddeeq*

64. *Martyrs Brigade of Ansar al-Sunnah*
65. *Al-Miqdad Brigades Group*
66. *Mohammed Brigade of Thi al-Nouren Brigade*
67. *Al-Qa'aqa'a Brigade of Ansar al-Sunnah*
68. *Air Defense Brigade*
69. *Engineering Section of Thi al-Noorain*
70. *Knights' Brigade of the Al-Qa'aqa'a Brigade*
71. *Muslim Youth Brigade*
72. *The Mujahideen of Othman bin Affan*
73. *Assassination Brigade of the Men of Faith Battalion*
74. *Al-Furqan Battalion*
75. *Snipers' Brigade of Ansar al-Sunnah*
76. *The Assassination Brigade of Ansar al-Sunnah*
77. *Usoud al-Tawheed*
78. *Al-Forsan Brigade*
79. *Sharhail bin Hosna*
80. *The Jihad Information Brigade*
81. *The Islamic Army of Iraq*
82. *The Victorious Army Group*
83. *Saraiya al-Hamza*
84. *Huthaifa ibn al-Yaman Brigades*
85. *Saria al-Baraa Brigades*
86. *Al-Jihad Brigade of the Victorious Army Group*
87. *Al-Farouq Brigade of the Victorious Army Group*
88. *Twentieth of July Revolution Brigade*
89. *Saad bin Maaz Brigade*
90. *Abdullah bin al-Mubarak Brigade*
91. *Al-Zalazel Brigade*
92. *Al-Hassan Brigade*
93. *Islamic Front of the Iraqi Resistance*
94. *Imam al-Hussein Brigades*
95. *Al-Rashideen Army*
96. *Imam Brigade*
97. *Abu Obeida Aymer bin al-Jarrah*
98. *Army of the Mujahideen*
99. *Al-Miqdad Brigade*
100. *Hassan al-Basri Brigades*
101. *Army Squad of the Companions of the Prophets of Mohammed*

102. *Al-Raa'd Brigades*
103. *Supporters of the Sunni People*

4.

*The growing number of mujahideen groups, which
multiplied when the people realized their value, is causing
confusion about which group is speaking for which. We are
asking people to reject any statement signed by the Sajeel
Battalion of the Islamic Army that does not carry their
slogan or seal.*

—Leaflet, found on the streets of Ramadi
Islamic Army of Iraq
October 2005

CHAPTER 13

Just Talking

T HE WORKERS at the General Factory for Vegetable Oil took their seats in the fifth-floor meeting hall to listen to the speech. The election was two weeks away, and the violence had driven the campaigning indoors. More than 7,400 Iraqis were running for office. But they weren't really running: there were almost no rallies, no parades, no public gatherings. A number of candidates had been murdered; the ones who remained flitted about like ghosts, appearing briefly and disappearing as fast.

A man stood first to warm up the crowd. He had written a poem for the occasion.

"Iraq, my soul, my wounds are still not healed," he said. "What a pity that in this land where we were masters, we have now become the slaves."

He sat down, and two men walked to the front of the factory hall. They were surrounded by men with machine guns. The first man introduced himself as Abu Muntaher al-Naqid and the second as Hussein Ali. They said they wanted to talk to the workers about the United Iraqi Alliance (UIA), the big Shiite coalition that was expected to sweep the election. The moment, indeed, belonged to the Shiites; they had been the majority in Iraq since its birth but had never held power. Through the unlikely events of the American invasion, it was finally in their grasp.

"We Iraqis are not used to this democracy," Naqid told the workers "we don't know what this election is."

Naqid's credibility came from his face, which was gaunt and battered. He wore a plain set of clothes.

"The people—that is you—need someone to tell you what democracy is—what a constitution is, what freedom is, and why you need to respect the opinions of others," Naqid said. "The UIA can do this if you give them a chance."

The vegetable oil workers listened intently, even with fascination. The men from the UIA were asking for their support. No one who had ever sought power in Iraq had ever done such a thing.

"We are prepared to take your questions," Naqid said.

The workers seemed a little stunned—there was a long pause—then one of the workers called out from his plastic chair.

"I'm worried about Israel," he said. "Israel's influence and secret operations inside Iraq."

Ali was ready with an answer.

"We stand in solidarity with the people of Palestine," he said. "And, God willing, we will help to liberate them."

The crowd started to get the hang of it. Another man raised his voice.

"How can I be sure that the UIA is supported by Ayatollah Sistani? This is very important to me."

Grand Ayatollah Ali al-Sistani's gaunt, humorless face adorned every UIA election placard. He was the Shiite God-king.

"If you like, you can go to Najaf and ask him yourself," Ali snapped.

Everyone laughed. One of the workers, Adnan Khazel, a young man, leaned over and whispered: "If this party has been approved by Sistani, then I will support it. There is really nothing else."

One of the workers raised his hand and asked what seemed like a silly question. "How can we be sure that you yourselves are candidates?" he asked. "Are you on the list yourself?"

Naqid and Ali both froze.

"It's a secret," Ali said. "It's too dangerous for us to say who the candidates are. Too dangerous."

The staff of the General Factory for Vegetable Oil looked

on in silence. Naqid and Ali turned on their heels and, with their bodyguards in tow, left the room.

Later that day, an election worker handed me a UIA flier. Sistani's unhappy face looked out from the top. The poster listed the names of thirty-seven candidates, including the coalition leaders, like Abdul Aziz Hakim and Adel Abdul Mahdi. The 188 other names, the flier said, could not be published.

"Our apologies for not mentioning the names of all the candidates," the flier said. "But the security situation is bad, and we have to keep them alive."

. . .

This is a final warning to all of those who plan to participate in the election. We vow to wash the streets of Baghdad with the voters' blood. To those of you who think you can vote and then run away, we will shadow you and catch you, and we will cut off your heads and the heads of your children.

—Leaflet tossed from a black sedan in Mashtal, a neighborhood in eastern Baghdad, in the days before the nationwide election on January 30, 2005

. . .

DAWN BROKE OVER empty streets. Soldiers and police stood behind their barricades, bracing themselves against the chill. On foot, I set out for the closest polling place, the Marjayoon Primary School, a mile away. The first Iraqis looked tense: a man and his son, not smiling, not waving back.

The night before, sitting around the dinner table, we'd set up an office pool to award the person who most closely predicted the day's voter turnout. Everyone had put in fifty dollars. We talked about the situation—the violence, unrelenting, and the Sunnis, unforgiving. Eighteen percent? someone suggested. The Sunnis would boycott, but what of everyone else? Twenty-two? Public life was dead. The fish restaurants along the Tigris stood empty. Fifteen percent? Twenty-four?

As I walked into Karada, a mostly Shiite neighborhood, the streets were starting to fill. The Iraqis came with mixtures of pride and defiance on their faces. Husbands and wives and children were walking together, some of the men in coats and ties. Mortar shells were exploding nearby. An American armored car, as ungainly as a dinosaur, turned a corner.

I turned off the main drag in Karada toward the Marjayoon Primary School. People were waiting in silence in long lines between coils of barbed wire. They were shuffling inside, without a sound, as bombs exploded a block away.

An old man rolled up in a wheelchair. Then a group of women appeared, falling into line in their long black abayas. A pair of women walked out, one of them talking into her cell phone. "It's okay, it's okay," she was saying into her phone.

Inside the school, a one-story, carpetless cement building, it was as quiet as a library. People were busy. Some signed their names to ledgers. Others stood inside one of the cardboard voting booths lined up against the wall, lost in concentration. Others were dipping their fingers in vials of purple ink.

A bomb exploded somewhere outside and the school vibrated. The Iraqis didn't look up.

I spotted a young woman with eyes so bright they seemed to beam out of her head scarf. Her name was Batool al-Musawi. She was a physical therapist and a newlywed. Her parents stood by.

"I woke up this morning at 7 a.m., and I could hear the explosions outside," Musawi told me. "And I threw the covers back over my head. I did not want to come. I was too afraid. It is so bad now. And then, hearing those explosions, it occurred to me—the insurgents are weak, they are afraid of democracy, they are losing. So I got my husband, and I got my parents, and we all came out and voted together."

Outside, Ehab al-Bahir, a captain in the Iraqi army, commanded a group of soldiers guarding the school. He'd been there all night, fortifying the place against insurgent attacks. The mortar shells had arrived, as he had anticipated, and so did the voters, which he had not.

"I never expected so many people," Captain Bahir said, looking down a line of voters outside the school. "I'm in charge of thirty polling places, and they are all saying the same thing. Hundreds of people are coming out to vote. One place said that there are already up to a thousand."

As he spoke, Rashid Majid, age eighty, pushed his way past the guards and stepped through the schoolhouse doors. He was wearing a coat and tie, and his silvery hair was combed to perfection.

"Get out of my way," Majid said, hurrying by. "I want to vote."

I stepped outside. A group of children had started a game of pickup soccer, with their parents looking on. It was a scene I had not witnessed in many months. Up a little farther, I saw Adel Abdul Mahdi, the finance minister, walking, shaking hands—another astonishing sight. "Peace be upon you," a man called to him.

I stepped inside Lebanon High School, another polling place. It was filled and it was quiet. The explosions were thundering outside. A middle-aged man looked up from a ledger, a finger pointed to the ceiling.

"Do you hear that, do you hear the bombs?" Hassan Jawad said, calling out to me over the thud of a shell. "We don't care. Do you understand? We don't care."

"We all have to die," Jawad said. "To die for this, well, at least I will be dying for something."

And then he got back to work, guiding an Iraqi woman's hand to the ballot box.

A FEW MILES AWAY, a woman stepped from the voting booth at Yarmouk Elementary School, named for the largely Sunni neighborhood where it was located. Yarmouk was slipping fast, but some of the Sunnis were still coming out to vote. Her name was Bushra Saadi. Like Batool al-Musawi, the young Shiite woman, Saadi covered her hair with a scarf tightly wrapped. But she was older than Musawi and carried herself with greater dignity. Her face was drawn, and her eyes looked as hard as little diamonds. Her neighbors shuffled past her to go inside.

Why vote at all? I asked Saadi. Why not just stay home?

She shot me a withering look.

"I voted in order to prevent my country from being destroyed by its enemies," she said. She spoke English without an accent.

What enemies? I asked Saadi. What enemies are you referring to?

She began to tremble.

"You—you destroyed our country," Saadi said. "The Americans, the British. I am sorry to be impolite. But you destroyed our country, and you called it democracy."

"Democracy," she said. "It is just talking."

CHAPTER 14

The Mahdi

T HE MEN WOULD gather at the Mohsin Mosque, ten
thousand of them even in the heat of summer. They
were the downtrodden of Sadr City, the Shiite slum
that took up most of eastern Baghdad. At the edges of the
crowd, confident young men with guns but no uniforms
searched those coming in. Among the supplicants, each carried his own prayer mat to cushion his knees from the street.
The sermon was outdoors. The imam would exit the mosque
and climb a ladder to a raised wooden platform and look out
on the assembled men on their knees. The imam would place
his hands at his side to signal the beginning of the prayer:
There is no God but God and Mohammed is his prophet.
Then someone in the crowd would call out, then a second
man, and the rest of the men would join in. Raising their arms
and shouting. In a few moments the mass of men would be
throbbing and contracting like a beating heart.

> *Wa ajal faraja'hou.*
> May God speed his appearance.
> *Wa ala'an adouwahou.*
> May God curse his enemies.
> *Wa'ansur waladahou.*
> May God make his son triumphant.
> *Muqtada!*
> *Muqtada!*
> *Muqtada!*

I went to the Mohsin Mosque to remind myself of what I didn't know. As the months wore on I went there more and more. I'd stand at the front of the crowd, at the foot of the platform, underneath the imam, just to take it in, to feel the power. The Mohsin Mosque was a corrective: I'd gotten caught up in the trappings and the pronouncements of officialdom, Iraqi and American. I'd believed there was a center. I'd thought the maneuverings of the Iraqi leaders, the exiles from the West, had been unfolding toward some greater purpose. Perhaps in the beginning they had been: Allawi, Chalabi, Hakim, Jafaari—men who'd lived their adulthoods in London and Tehran. They'd taken me in, served me tea in their drawing rooms and showed me the black-and-white photos of their childhoods. They wore suits and spoke English. Some of them were serious. They worked hard, worked until they were red in the eyes.

In the beginning, the American-backed political project had a plausible structure. It had a coherence, even if it was a shaky coherence. Grand Ayatollah al-Sistani, the supreme Shiite religious authority, sat at the center. He was the man who would deliver the Shiite majority to the dominance in Iraq that it had been so long denied. To do this, Sistani had endorsed the American-backed project—never explicitly, but just enough so that Iraq's exiles could feel secure in joining in. In the new structure, Sistani was like a sun, with the exiles orbiting round him like planets, sustaining themselves on his nurturing rays. Meet with Sistani. Speak of Sistani. Echo Sistani. Agree with Sistani. It was in this way the exiles would become legitimate, become real Iraqis again. And it was in this way that they would win elections and take hold of the broken country.

Then came Muqtada al-Sadr. He was the antithesis of the pampered exile: black-eyed and glowering, a man of the streets, with a black beard and turban. He'd never left Iraq. He was only in his early thirties. Muqtada rarely showed his face, but when he did, he gave wild sermons about the Shia messiah, the Mahdi, revealing himself to a world torn by war. The prevailing wisdom was that Muqtada was a nuisance, that he was cashing in on the reputation of his father, the ayatollah

for whom Sadr City had been named. He'd been murdered by Saddam in 1999, and his face still adorned tea shops throughout the Shiite slums.

In the beginning, Muqtada had flirted with the exiles, hinting that he might like to join them at their table inside the Green Zone. But the exiles had balked, and the Americans had balked with them. So Muqtada was out of the American-backed project, and he returned to the streets. From then on, the exiles and the Americans thought it best not to think about Muqtada, convincing themselves that the political process was representative without him.

Then it happened: almost a year to the day after the Americans arrived, Muqtada called for an uprising to throw the occupiers out. With that, the Shiite underclass that he commanded seized Sadr City and provincial capitals across southern Iraq. They took the holy shrines in Najaf and Karbala, too. The Iraqi police and the army, trained and armed by the Americans—the very backbone of the new Iraqi state—melted away. The Americans and the British had to shoot their way back in so the exiles could have their chairs back. And Muqtada skittered back into the shadows.

The exiles had been exposed. They and Muqtada may have

been Shiites, but now they would be fighting each other. "They want him dead," one of the Shiite exiles, a senior Iraqi official, told me. At one of the cabinet meetings, they had even drafted Muqtada's obituary, typed it up for immediate release. But by then the exiles couldn't decide what to do. No one could decide if Muqtada would be better alive or dead.

At the Mohsin Mosque, the sermons went on. At the end, the crowd would be delirious, the men jabbing their fists and yelling. I could almost feel the waves of sound coming off the crowd.

Kala, kala, Amrika
No, no, to America
Kala, kala, Isra'il
No, no, to Israel
Kala, kala, Lilshaytan
No, no, to the devil
A'ash, A'ash, Al-Sadr, Muqtada Lil Jana Jisir!
Long live, long live, al-Sadr. Muqtada is the bridge to
    heaven!

THE SHIITE FIGHTERS stepped into the darkened alley. They put down their rifles and sat down and exhaled. The gunfire was coming down the street, but here they were safe. The alley ran through the old city directly to the Shrine of Imam Ali, fifty yards away. Its giant wooden doors were visible through the far end. The alley seemed like a tunnel; even in the white heat of August, it was so high and so narrow that it was bathed in shadows. A jet roared above us and there was a terrible crash. For a second, the alley seemed to turn on its side. One of the men lit a cigarette.

The Mahdi Army, the name Muqtada had given his militia, had seized the Shrine of Imam Ali earlier in the year. The shrine was named for one of the great icons of the Shia faith. Muqtada had rallied his men by declaring that the shrine was under attack, but in fact he was just outmaneuvering his rivals. The Iraqi government, led by Prime Minister Ayad Allawi, had given the Americans the green light to come in here and route Muqtada's militia. His only condition was that the shrine and its glorious golden dome be spared. The first American soldiers had entered the old city the night before. The Mahdi Army fighters had fallen back to this tiny perimeter around the shrine. From the air, the Americans had begun destroying the perimeter, too.

"God is with you—you are heroes," a hoarse voice called into a loudspeaker from the shrine. "Fight, fight, fight!"

Jaff and I had walked for hours to get here. We'd tried to cut through the old city but snipers were killing so many people that we backed out and walked into the desert at the edge of town, called the Sea of Najaf. We walked out into the sand and across the old lakebed until we spotted a passageway near the shrine. We walked back in and snaked our way through the back streets until we made it to this alley just off the shrine. We arrived as the Americans were moving in for the kill.

A pair of Mahdi fighters entered the alley, carrying a bleeding comrade. "No pictures, no pictures!" one of them cried, dragging their comrade past. His black tunic was soaked in blood. "You are a hero," one of them whispered to the wounded man. "A hero." The fighters carried him through the alley and into the open space between the alley and the shrine. Someone had built a barricade across this last bit of open space, and the Mahdi fighters scampered to the entrance and lay the wounded man down. They pounded on the twenty-foot-high doors. "Open! Open!" they cried. The door cracked, a head appearing, and the great doors swung wide. The fighters pulled the bleeding man inside and the giant doors closed. An Apache swooped in low, its rotors turning and dipping over the rooftops.

Jaff and I sat down in the alley next to the fighter who was smoking. I asked him where the Americans were.

"Thirty meters," he said, exhaling smoke. "This is the last line."

I asked his name. Walid Shakir, he said. Thirty-four, a driver from Nasiriya, a husband and father. He'd come as soon as Muqtada had put out the word that the Americans were attacking. Shakir wore a fake Casio watch with a heavy metal band and a yellow checked shirt. He was barefoot. Between his legs lay a Dragonoff rifle.

"Perhaps there will be an agreement to end the fighting soon," he said. "Where is Sistani?"

He's on his way from London, I told him. I asked him about Muqtada.

"We are all under his command," Shakir said. "He is our leader. We are his soldiers. We act together, like fingers on one hand."

Gunfire sounded behind us, in the area between the alley and the shrine. The barricade splintered and blew apart. Shakir glanced at it for a second and turned back to me.

"If the Americans do not agree, then we will not give up," he said.

His bare feet were enormous, like pontoons. How can you walk in the heat without shoes? Jaff asked him.

Shakir flipped his feet up and revealed their leathery bottoms.

"I've been walking in my bare feet all my life," he shrugged. "They're like flip-flops now."

A pair of fighters appeared in the alley, hunched over, like the men carrying the wounded. They'd come from the shrine. They were carrying a container as large as a steamer trunk. It was a vat of rice and vegetables, stirred together, warm and greasy. Shakir got up and dug his hand into it and began to eat.

There was more gunfire, more explosions. The alley shook again.

He finished eating and wiped his palms on his pants. He looked at Jaff.

"Is that a camera?" Shakir said.

It is, Jaff said.

And so, to the sound of bombs and gunfire, we sat together, Shakir and I and three other Mahdi Army fighters, while Jaff snapped a picture of us on a bench in the alley by the shrine. The alley shook again. There wasn't much time. Jaff and I dashed out, back into the sunlight.

A ROW OF BUILDINGS lay crumbled and blown to dust, along a street that marked the entrance to the old city. Wires snaked through boulders and smashed cars. An American tank sat in the intersection. Gunfire came from the ruins. It was pinging off the tank's shell.

The tank sat there for a time, absorbing the gunfire like some large animal still asleep. It was an M-1. Bullets flew out of the rubble, plinking its impenetrable coat. Finally the turret began to turn, like it was waking up, swiveling toward the rubble. More gunfire. The tank looked at the rubble for a while and lowered its gun and fired. The gun exhaled a terrible sound. The rubble bounced. It was silent.

I started walking up the street, toward the M-1 but keeping my distance. Trudging in the rubble. Avoiding the wires. The tank sat quietly.

Then there was a noise, and the hatch swung open.

A young man appeared, a tiny head with a large helmet and goggles. He was waving his arms. His voice was very high.

"Get out of here!" he said in a boy's voice, waving me out of the road. "Go on, get out of here!"

It was a boy's voice, the voice of a child before it changes.

"Get out of here!" he said.

Then he lowered himself into the tank and closed the hatch.

I WAS SITTING in my hotel, The Sea of Najaf, waiting out the battle, when the Iraqi police pulled up, shouting into their bullhorns. It was near midnight.

"Attention, attention," the police shouted. "There is an agreement to end the fighting!"

A press conference was being held at the home of one of the ayatollahs, they said. Sistani had brokered a cease-fire. The police escorted us through the town with the same bullhorns and flashing lights.

When I arrived, I stepped inside the front courtyard of the ayatollah's house. Hamed Khafaf, an aide to Sistani, stood on a raised platform before a crowd of reporters. His face shone in the lights of the TV cameras. He was flanked by several of Sistani's clerics. They looked exhausted.

Then, out of the corner of my eye, I saw him: Muqtada

scuttling out a side door. He had an aide on each arm. He headed for his car as Khafaf started to speak. It all happened too fast; by the time I realized it was him, he was gone. Muqtada: he'd wrecked the city and thrown the country into crisis. And now he was leaving it to the grown-ups, and the grown-ups were letting him get away.

AT DAWN, the tall wooden doors of the shrine swung open and the fighters began filing out. They were dirty and bedraggled and some of them limped. They walked over to a donkey cart and threw their Kalashnikovs and RPGs into a pile and walked into the streets. A voice on a loudspeaker was telling them to drop their guns and go home.

"The Americans could not enter the shrine," one of the fighters, Mohammed Abid Qasim, told me as he walked out. He was filthy and tired. "That's the important thing."

The fighters disappeared. There was no surrender. There was no handover. There were no American soldiers; they had pulled back. There were no Iraqi policemen, no Iraqi soldiers. The Mahdi Army was being allowed to slip away, like Muqtada himself. That was the deal. They would live to fight again.

A pair of clerics stood at the wooden doors as the guerrillas filed out. Their white turbans said they were from Sistani's office. They both wore scowls on their faces. "We are taking over the shrine," one of them said.

Jaff and I were pestering some of the fighters to talk with us when a couple of gunmen stopped us. They put their hands on our arms.

"You're under arrest," one of them said.

Jaff started to speak.

"Shut up," one of them said.

They wore black baggy pants and black tunics and black dirty turbans. They had ammo belts slung over their shoulders. Their eyes were hollow and red.

Jaff spoke again, saying we had met one of Muqtada's aides, Ali Smesim, a couple of days before. We were well received, he said.

"That is shit," one of the Mahdi guys said. "I am going to take you to the sharia court. They'll decide."

The men motioned with the guns. We walked away from the shrine, into the back alleys of the old city. The men were jittery, like they hadn't slept. One of them turned to me.

"You are the second American spy I have captured today," he said.

We arrived at a small storefront. Inside was a cleric with a black turban and a beard. He was sitting behind a table covered with a dark gray blanket. He didn't get up.

Jaff started explaining, slowly and carefully. Jaff was great that way: always calm. It was only afterwards that he told me how close it was. Jaff didn't lie—he said, Yes, he is American, and yes, we are journalists.

"We met Ali Smesim, an aide to Seyyed Muqtada," Jaff said.

The two Mahdi Army guys stood behind me and Jaff. Waiting for the word.

Jaff finished talking. The cleric stayed in his chair for several minutes. A blank face, not friendly at all.

The Mahdi Army guys waited.

"Get out of here and don't come back," the cleric said.

The Mahdi fighters slumped in disappointment.

A couple of days later, after the Mahdi Army had cleared out of the old city, Jaff went to the militia's sharia court and found the bodies of executed people in the courtyard, bloated and decomposed. About sixty in all, he said.

CHAPTER 15

Proteus

THE CONVOY streamed south out of Baghdad. Twenty cars, mostly men with guns. The gunmen hung out the windows, pointing their Kalashnikovs at the terrified drivers. Get out of the way or we shoot, and maybe we shoot anyway—that was the message. The convoy moved quickly, weaving, south in the southbound, south in the northbound. Very fast. Unbelievably fast. Drivers veered and careered. We went wherever we wanted.

Ahmad Chalabi, the luminous Iraqi exile, rode in an armored car near the front. Two years before, Chalabi had helped persuade the American government to go to war to topple Saddam. Then he'd returned to Iraq, and the superweapons Chalabi assured the United States were there never turned up. Then Iraq imploded. The Americans had shoved him away; they had even, some months before, sent intelligence officers to raid his Baghdad compound, accusing him of passing secrets to the Iranians.

And so here was Chalabi, driving south in a convoy full of guns. After forty-five years in exile, he had come home to a strange land. In the West, he was a famous man, and now a notorious one as well. He was a banker and a millionaire and a mathematics professor trained at MIT and the University of Chicago. He owned homes in London and Washington. But in Iraq, his roots had withered and died. And so now, in January 2005, Chalabi was reinventing himself as an authentic Iraqi. He was running for a seat in the new Iraqi parliament.

The convoy was low on fuel, and a gas station beckoned. Since the American invasion, Iraqis waited hours—even days—for gasoline at the pumps. Lack of refining capacity, smuggling, stealing, insurgent attacks: it was complicated. On the road south of Baghdad, the line was perhaps three hundred cars deep.

The Chalabi convoy cut straight to the front of the line. No one protested. It was the guns. Chalabi's effrontery brought not even a peep. We got our gas and we sped away, guns out the windows. Very fast.

An hour later, we arrived at our destination, a Shiite town called Mushkhab. It was friendly country—to Chalabi, and still, then, to Americans. Chalabi got out of the car and walked forward. All the men of the town gathered round. They were wearing dishdashas and kafiyas. Chalabi stood in the center, dressed in a gray Western suit.

The Iraqis clapped and read poetry; some of it they sang. It was a tradition in Iraq, a serenade to the honored guest.

"Hey, listen, Bush, we are Iraqis," one of the Iraqis called out, and everyone started clapping. "We never bow our heads to anyone, and we won't do it for you. We have tough guys like Chalabi on our side—be careful."

Everyone laughed.

We moved inside a *mudhif,* a long, fantastic structure woven of dried river reeds, a kind of pavilion of rattan. The room was laid with handwoven carpets, and the walls were hung with framed yellowed photographs of the leaders of the tribe, Al-Fatla, meeting with their British overlords many years before. A pair of loudspeakers sat at the front. Chalabi took the microphone in his hand.

"My Iraqi brothers, the Americans pushed out Saddam, but they did not liberate our country," Chalabi told them. "We are asking you to participate in this election so that we can have an independent country. This is not just words. The Iraqi people will liberate the country."

Chalabi went on a little more, warming to the men in the room.

"On my way here, I saw a huge line of people waiting for gasoline," Chalabi said. "Some of them were there for two nights, carrying blankets with them. It makes me very sad to see my brothers wait for days to get gas at the station."

Chalabi, the artful dodger. He could dissemble and dance and deflect, and he would never have to pay.

Lunch was served: a long table heaped with rice and roast lamb. Everyone stood, dozens of us, and we dug in with our fingers. After a time, we prepared to leave. The table and the ground around it were littered with rice and lamb bones. We re-formed into a convoy and sped toward the holy city of Najaf.

It was dark when we arrived. Only a few months before the fighting between American soldiers and the Mahdi Army guerrillas had destroyed the city, but on this night, Najaf was remarkably calm. The pilgrim hotels lay in ruins, but the golden dome of the Shrine of Imam Ali shimmered under a January moon.

Chalabi exited his SUV and strode through the twenty-foot-high wooden doors. A clutch of Sunni leaders, whom Chalabi had agreed to show around, trailed in step. The curiosities intersected: The shrine was one of the holiest of Shiite places, the tomb of the son-in-law of the Prophet and the very heart of the Shiite faith. A civil war was brewing, but the Sunnis were allowed to pass. As a non-Muslim, I waited outside the shrine. Across the street, a group of Iraqis gathered to stare.

Chalabi had entered his Islamist phase. It was another dance, another reinvention. In his speeches, Chalabi, the Western-educated mathematician, had begun to speak reverently of Islam and the Prophet. In Baghdad, he had begun forming alliances with Islamist leaders, most notably, most remarkably, with Muqtada himself.

It wasn't terribly convincing. Chalabi did not wear a turban. He had no beard. He did not pray. He did not, really, even pretend. But as a practical politician—as an exile come home to a strange land growing stranger by the day—Chalabi had needed to do something.

After ten minutes inside the shrine, Chalabi reemerged.

He climbed into his SUV and sped away, back to Baghdad. His goal had been accomplished. By morning, all of Najaf would know that Chalabi had come to pay homage to Ali at the shrine. I pressed him on this bit of opportunism, but he would not give the game away. "It's bad for me to do this," Chalabi said, cutting me off. "It defeats the purpose."

Gamesman, exile, idealist, fraud: Chalabi was someone whom I never missed a chance to follow around. It wasn't just that he was brilliant, or nimble, or ruthless, or fun. When I looked into Chalabi's eyes and saw the doors and mirrors opening and closing, I knew that I was seeing not just the essence of the man but of the country to which he'd returned. *L'état c'est lui.* Chalabi was Iraq.

It was 11 p.m. when I reached Chalabi's house. It was only then, usually, that I could get in to see him, when the rest of the work was done. I walked past the armed guards and the rattling generators and up the stairs to his study. He was perched in a chair, sitting in a dishdasha, starched and brilliant. This was an oddity. For all of Chalabi's posings as an Islamist, it was the only time I'd ever seen him dressed this way. As an Iraqi, that is. I'd come with a colleague, Jim Glanz, who had a doctorate in physics from Princeton. Chalabi and Jim regarded each other as fellow scientists. Sometimes the two of them would begin a conversation about a mathematical riddle or a scientific imperative, and I would be left to doodle in my notebook.

We sat down. Chalabi put on a Vivaldi concerto, and an attendant appeared with bowls of mango ice cream. Even in Baghdad, surrounded by armed guards, blast walls and generators, there were few pleasures that Chalabi denied himself. The Vivaldi floated out from a pair of sleek, expensive speakers. The chairs, tall and slim, were Frank Lloyd Wright, modeled after those in the architect's well-preserved house on the University of Chicago campus, Chalabi's alma mater.

No Iraqi leader worked harder than Chalabi. Many of them worked for a few hours in the morning and slept away the afternoons. Many of them, as the chaos deepened, returned to exile. Whenever I went to Chalabi's house, night or day, I found him working, often on the most mundane aspects of public administration. One day, he had spread before him the charts of Baghdad's antiquated electrical grid, then coughing and sputtering only four hours of electricity a day. Another time, Chalabi was examining the Jordanian bank records of fellow Iraqi officials who he believed had stolen public money. In addition to being deputy prime minister, Chalabi also served as minister of oil, and he often had oil production figures on the table before him.

I asked Chalabi about the negotiations on the Iraqi constitution. It was the summer of 2005 and the deadline was near. The Sunnis, Shiites and Kurds were at a standstill. Chalabi was intimately involved in every aspect of the negotiations. He spoke perfect English and perfect Arabic and his energy and intelligence were limitless.

Even so, I had to be careful whenever I chose to rely on him. Chalabi always had his own agenda, usually several of them, which he worked on different levels, like a game of three-dimensional chess. Chalabi wanted a unified Iraq, but he was a friend of the Kurds, who wanted autonomy. He was an entirely secular man, but he had pulled close to Muqtada, who wanted an Islamic state. He wore suits and he wore dishdashas. Who was he this time? I felt like any member of the American government must have felt in dealing with Chalabi: was I getting more out of Chalabi than he was getting out of me? Or was I being conned and charmed into submission?

"We are on the brink of an agreement," Chalabi said. "Everything has been settled."

I took out my notebook. This was news. Chalabi's face was blank. What was settled, exactly? I asked.

"Oil," Chalabi said, spooning some ice cream. "There is an agreement on how to share the oil."

Oil lay at the heart of everything in Iraq.

How?

"It's settled," Chalabi said, face still blank. "The central government will control the oil and gas extracted from existing fields, and the regional governments will be allowed to control fields that are not currently being exploited."

We talked details, about which Chalabi was distressingly vague. What's left to be settled? I asked.

Well, Chalabi said, there is no agreement yet on the role of Islam in family disputes.

This was a delicate issue. The Shiite Islamists had been pushing to give clerics a role in the new Iraqi state. The proposed language would allow ordinary Iraqis to go to a cleric to settle domestic disputes. That would have marked a departure from the secular, progressive law that Iraqis had enjoyed for decades, and which the Americans were pushing now.

"Whether to allow clerics on the Supreme Court has not been decided," Chalabi said, taking in another spoonful of ice cream.

I sighed. There wasn't much point in asking Chalabi where he stood on all these issues. I knew him too well for that; he would not have answered.

"It's the same old story," I told Chalabi. "You call it progress, you say you are near an agreement, but at each session you resolve maybe half of your differences. And the next day you resolve half of what is left. But it never ends."

"Yes," Chalabi said crisply, glancing in Jim's direction. "Zeno's Paradox."

Jim nodded knowingly.

"An infinite converging series," Chalabi said.

"It's called Zeno's Paradox," Jim said, jumping in, with Chalabi looking on. "You add an infinite number of smaller and smaller numbers together and get a finite sum. In other words, an infinite number of meetings and you get to the constitutional agreement in a finite time."

"Yes, exactly," Chalabi said with a smile.

"So you'll never get there," I said, trying to pick up on the metaphor, whatever it was, "because it's infinite."

"No," Chalabi said, smiling blankly. "That's not right."

Jim laughed. I tried to change the subject.

"Okay," I said to Chalabi, "you seem to be backpedaling on women's rights. You say you are secular, but if you let

Islamic courts get involved in family disputes, then you are inserting Islam into the state. You are doing the Islamists' bidding."

Chalabi put down his spoon. "Absolutely false," he said.

"But how can you square being secular with allowing imams to settle divorces and inheritance?" I asked.

Chalabi shifted in his chair and smiled warmly.

"Have you heard the joke about the rabbi and the priest on the airplane?"

How could I refuse? I didn't know the joke.

"A priest and a rabbi are riding on a plane," Chalabi said, leaning back. "After a while, the priest turns to the rabbi and asks, 'Is it still a requirement of your faith that you not eat pork?'

"The rabbi says, 'Yes, that is still one of our beliefs.' "

Jim and I had put our pens down.

"So the priest asks, 'Have you ever tasted pork?'

"To which the rabbi replies, 'Yes, on one occasion I did succumb to temptation and tasted pork.' "

Chalabi was grinning widely.

"The priest nodded and went on with his reading," Chalabi said. "A while later, the rabbi asked the priest, 'Father, is it still a requirement of your church that you remain celibate?'

"The priest replied, 'Yes, that is still very much a part of our faith.'

"Then the rabbi asked him, 'Father, have you ever succumbed to the temptations of the flesh?'

"The priest replied, 'Yes, Rabbi, on one occasion I was weak and broke with my faith.'

"The rabbi nodded understandingly for a moment and then said, 'A lot better than pork, isn't it?' "

Chalabi beamed at his joke, and Jim and I laughed. After a few more minutes it was time to go. Past curfew. The streets of Mansour were dangerous in the fall of 2005. Kidnappers and insurgents were everywhere, even in Baghdad's best neighborhoods. Chalabi uttered something to an attendant, and we said goodbye. As we drove from the compound, a row of Iraqi police cars appeared, their blue lights flashing, getting in line to escort us back across town.

. . .

A COUPLE OF MONTHS later, Chalabi returned to Washington, for the first time since the start of the war. This was no small thing. Only a year before, American intelligence agents had claimed Chalabi had passed secrets to the Iranian government. The break seemed final.

But the wheel was turning again. Iraq was imploding, and in the fall of 2005, the men and women inside the Bush administration were scrambling for any friend they could find. So here was Chalabi, riding in a limo, making the rounds at the Pentagon and the Old Executive Office Building. Just like the old days. After that, he took a detour to DuPont Circle and the American Enterprise Institute, one of the think tanks that had backed him and the war. Dressed in a dark gray suit and red necktie, Chalabi told a gathering of people in a twelfth-floor conference room that Iraq, now freed from Saddam, was making its way toward democracy and the rule of law. Then he asked for questions. A hand went up.

"Mr. Chalabi," a man said from the back. "Did you deliberately mislead the American people about weapons of mass destruction?"

Chalabi smiled as if he'd been waiting for the question.

"This is an urban myth," he said.

The audience gasped.

The meeting broke up a few moments later. I walked outside, past the protesters on the sidewalk, to my hotel a few blocks away. I was pondering the mystery of Chalabi. I called Robert Baer, a former operative for the CIA. I'd never met Baer but people told me he was the man to talk to. He'd worked with Chalabi in the 1990s in Kurdish-controlled Iraq, when the CIA was trying to cause trouble for Saddam. Back then, the CIA loved Chalabi; he seemed willing to go anywhere, do anything. He'd cobbled together a band of guerrillas that was harassing the Iraqi army, just what the CIA wanted. Then things got out of hand; it turned out Chalabi was serious, even if the CIA was not. Chalabi wanted to topple Saddam, and he'd turned his guerrillas loose on one of Saddam's divisions. He'd almost started a war. Back in Langley,

CIA officials were furious. They claimed to be stunned. After that, the CIA pushed Chalabi away. It was only later, when he was adopted by neoconservatives in other parts of the American government, that Chalabi began to rise again.

Baer was at his home in Colorado.

"Chalabi?" Baer said on the other end. "Smarter than the collective IQ of everyone in Washington. So fast. And he reads. And he figures out relationships. He read me like an open book."

How did things get so out of control out there, way back then? I asked.

"It was a paper-flow problem," Baer said of Chalabi's mini-invasion. In other words, Baer said, Chalabi made his plans clear to his handlers in the CIA, but for bureaucratic reasons, people in the upper reaches of the American government had not been informed.

"Let me just say, everything Chalabi said he was going to do, he did," Baer told me. "This was not some rogue Chalabi coup. They knew about it back in Langley. I understand that the division chief at the CIA never thought Chalabi would do it. I still have the cables."

I asked why the CIA came to loathe Chalabi.

"Chalabi was as true to me as the day is long," Baer said. "The thing with Chalabi is, he is Levantine. In order to get anywhere with him, you've got to conspire with him, enter his world. Manipulate people. Do people in. Like when he tried to introduce me to Iranian intelligence in Salah al-Din."

Iranian intelligence? I said.

"Yeah," Baer said. "Chalabi said to me, Look, I need these guys. I need to make sure the Iranians are not going to cause trouble for me. Would you like to meet them?"

Baer explained how, as an American, even as an American spy, he was prohibited from meeting representatives of the Iranian government. At the time, the Iranians were sitting at the other end of the hotel lobby from Baer. They were wearing turbans.

"This is where the gray area comes in," Baer said. "The whole time we were there, Chalabi was traveling in and out of northern Iraq and in and out of Tehran. If you asked Chalabi, he would say, I have to deal with the Iranians. In our terms, in American terms, that would make him an Iranian asset. All of his CIA connections—he wouldn't get away with that sort of thing with the Iranians unless he had proved his worth to them. He's basically beholden to the Iranians to stay viable. If he got out of hand, they would kill him.

"He's not our guy," Baer said.

WE DROVE EAST out of Baghdad, in a convoy as menacing as the one we had ridden south to Mushkhab on the campaign trip earlier that year. After three hours of weaving and careering, we reached the end of the plains of eastern Iraq, and the terrain turned sharply upward into a ridge of arid mountains. We had come to the border, one of history's great fault lines, the ancient boundary between the Ottoman and Persian empires. To our right lay the abandoned fortifications and rusting hulks of the Iran-Iraq war.

I rode with Aras Habib, Chalabi's chief of intelligence and one of the targets of the CIA raid the year before. The Americans were not so interested in Aras anymore. He seemed a character from an Eric Ambler novel—of uncertain origins, of uncertain ends. In Baghdad, the word was that Aras had used the Baathist files he and his men had seized after the fall of the regime in 2003 to hunt down and kill many of its senior members. With Aras, there wasn't any way to know for sure. Talking to him was like trying to get a quote from a monk. Aras was a Feyli, a Shia Kurd, and as we approached the Iranian border he pointed to a cluster of houses off the main road. "My grandfather's father is from this town." Then we crossed over into Iran itself, and the ruins of Iraq gave way to swept streets and a tidy border post with shiny bathrooms. A different world.

Chalabi got out of his SUV as an Iranian cleric approached. The cleric wore a turban and a robe, Chalabi a camouflage T-shirt and slacks. They shook hands. Then the cleric said something strange: "We are disappointed to hear that you won't be staying in the Shiite alliance," he said to Chalabi. "We were really hoping you'd stay." I considered the irony: an

Iranian cleric expressing regret that Chalabi had left an Iraqi political alliance. For the moment, the border between Iran and Iraq had disappeared.

Chalabi ducked into a bathroom and reappeared in a well-tailored suit and tie. Then we drove to Ilam, a nearby city, where an eleven-seat Fokker jet was idling on the runway of the local airport. We took off for Tehran, flying over a dramatic landscape of canyons and ravines. We landed in Iran's smoggy capital, and within a couple of hours Chalabi was meeting with the highest officials of the Iranian government. One of them was Ali Larijani, the national security adviser.

I met Larijani the next morning. Chalabi arranged it. "Our relationship with Mr. Chalabi does not have anything to do with his relationship with the neocons," Larijani told me. His red-rimmed eyes, when I met him at 7 a.m., betrayed a sleepless night. "He is a very constructive and influential figure," Larijiani said of Chalabi. "He is a very wise man and a very useful person for the future of Iraq."

Useful to whom? I wondered. The Iranians were deeply involved in Iraq, pumping in guns, pumping in money. I asked Larijani about reports that a few months before, the Iranian government had brokered a deal among Iraqi Shiite leaders to choose a prime minister. At the time, Chalabi had been one of the contenders. Larijani was happy to have me believe it. "America should consider this power as legitimate. They should not fight it."

A couple of hours later came a meeting with Mahmoud Ahmadinejad, the Iranian president. I was with a handful of Iranian reporters who were led into a finely appointed room just outside the president's office. First came Chalabi, dressed in another perfect suit, beaming. Then came Ahmadinejad, wearing a face of childlike bewilderment. He wore a pair of imitation leather shoes and bulky white athletic socks, and a suit that looked as if it had come from a Soviet department store. Only a few days before, Ahmadinejad had publicly called for the destruction of Israel. He and Chalabi, several inches taller, stood together for photos, then retired to a private room.

Chalabi wanted to be prime minister; of that there was no doubt. Was he telling the Iranians that he was running? Or was he asking for their permission? Was he carrying a note from the Americans? Or taking one back? The possibilities were endless.

When the meeting ended, Ahmadinejad asked Chalabi if there was anything he could do to make his stay more comfortable. Chalabi said, Why, yes, in fact, there was: would he mind if he, Chalabi, took a tour of the Museum of Contemporary Art?

In a few moments, we were there, in the middle of a country still in the throes of an Islamic revolution, strolling past one of the finest collections of Western modern art outside Europe and the United States: Matisse, Kandinsky, Rothko, Gauguin, Pollock, Klee, van Gogh, five Warhols, seven Picassos, much more, and a sprawling garden of sculpture outside. The collection had been assembled by Queen Farah, the shah's wife, with the monarchy's vast oil wealth. On this day, the gallery was all but empty. We had the museum's enthusiastic English-speaking tour guide all to ourselves.

"Thank you, thank you, for coming!" Noreen Motamed exclaimed, clapping her hands.

We walked the empty halls. Chalabi moved deliberately, nodding his head, pausing at a Degas and a Pissarro.

"Wow," Chalabi said before Jesús Rafael Soto's painting *Canada*. "Look at that."

A retinue of turbaned Iranian officials walked with us, unmoved by the splendor. Ahmadinejad had stayed behind.

For all of the furies that emanated from its halls, the Iranian government had taken fine care of Queen Farah's collection. The only clue that we were in Tehran, and not New York or London, was the absence of the middle panel from Francis Bacon's triptych, *Two Figures Lying on a Bed with Attendant*, which depicts two naked men.

"It is in the basement, covered," Motamed said with a disappointed expression.

Finally, we came across a pair of paintings by Marc Chagall, the twentieth-century modernist and painter of Jewish life. The display contained no mention of this fact.

Chalabi gazed at the Chagalls for a time. Then, with a rueful smile, he turned, to no one in particular, and said loudly: "Imagine that. They have two paintings by Marc Chagall in the middle of a museum in Tehran."

The Iranian officials seemed not to hear.

Your Name

I WAS RUNNING along the Tigris toward the Iraqi check-point when I noticed a different group of guards. Not un-friendly, but no one from the old crowd was there. As I approached, one of them told me to stop and he asked me for an I.D., which he pronounced slowly and loudly "Eye-Dee." Of course I didn't have one with me. I started haggling with the new guards: I let them talk, I talked myself, I huffed and sighed, the usual things that worked. I moved through the checkpoint and got on with my run. After only a few steps I heard a heavily accented South African voice yelling "Stop!" I looked toward the Baghdad Hotel and saw one of the South African guards. Big and bald, dressed like Rambo. I ignored him and kept running. He raised his rifle and took aim. "I'll shoot," he said. He was running, scurrying actually because he was so fat and so loaded down with gear. "Restricted area," he said. Not a trace of humor or warmth. The Iraqis looked on, obedient and oblivious. That was the end of that. I turned around and started running back.

The Tigris River Park was in a shambles. The Humvees were gone and the Americans had left. The grass, so green only a few months before, was dead and brown or departed. In a few places it was overgrown. The sprinkler heads had all been stolen; here and there a single pipe sprouted from the ground and gurgled water. Someone had put up another con-crete wall in what was left of the open space, and coils of barbed wire had been strung across the lovers' lane.

I spotted a group of children. They saw me and came run-ning. They were brothers and sisters, the children of our next-door neighbor, a friend. They lined up in a row, as if for inspection, to say hello: Bilal, Shahla, Sukaina and one of their playmates. It had been some time since I'd seen them and there had been a change: Shahla, only nine, had begun covering her hair. She wore a bright white hejab. She looked like a tiny imitation of her mother.

I ran as far as I could to the other end, where the usual soccer game was unfolding. I stopped for a minute to rest. A couple of our Iraqi guards had joined in; they seemed strange outside of their usual American world. A young Iraqi boy came over and stood at the chain-link fence and stared at me for a while. "What is your name?" he said to me in loud English. I told him but it didn't seem to reigster. He kept looking at me. "What is your name?" he said again, and I told him again. I rested some more then resumed my running, back toward the checkpoint for another lap. The Iraqi boy ran with me on the other side of the fence, repeating the question again and again. A look of desperation came over his face.

"What is your name?" he said, running along.

"What is your name?"

Communiqués (2)

I.

There is no doubt that the Americans' losses are very heavy because they are deployed across a wide area and among the people, and because it is easy to procure weapons, all of which makes them easy and mouthwatering targets for the believers. But America did not come to leave, and it will not leave no matter how numerous its wounds become and how much of its blood is spilled. . . .

The Shia—these in our opinion are the key to change. I mean that targeting and hitting them in their religious, political, and military depth will provoke them to show the Sunnis their rabies . . . and bare the teeth of the hidden rancor working in their breasts. If we succeed in dragging them into the arena of sectarian war, it will become possible to awaken the inattentive Sunnis as they feel imminent danger and annihilating death. . . .

The solution that we see, and God the Exalted knows better, is for us to drag the Shia into the battle because this is the only way to prolong the fighting between us and the infidels.

—Letter, said to have been written by Abu Musab al-Zarqawi, head of Al-Qaeda in Iraq, to the leadership of Al-Qaeda in Afghanistan and Pakistan. Obtained by Kurdish forces in January 2004.

2.

We the group of Al-Sahaba Soldiers of Iraq claim responsibility for an explosion of a Shia temple in Saydia, on the commercial street. Thanks be unto Allah they were victorious, and a number of the unbelievers were killed—those friendly with the Americans, the oppressors and the killers in Iraq.

—News Release
Al-Sahaba Soldiers
May 20, 2005

3.

A Tahwid lion, Abu Leith al-Nagdi, from the Ali Daggana al-Ansari Suicidal Brigade, drove his car bomb on the morning of Monday, Moharam 1, 1427, to attack one of the barracks of the apostates of the governorate of Al-Nasariya. It was a blessed operation. Many of them were killed or injured—not less than thirty apostates. Some of them were high-ranking officers. Thanks unto Allah.

   Allah is great, Glory to Allah, His messenger and the mujahideen.

—News Release
Information Department
The Mujahideen Shura of Iraq*
January 31, 2006

4.

The lions of the Al-Bara'a bin Malik Suicidal Brigade made a new attack on a volunteer center of the apostate

---

*The Mujahideen Shura Council, formed in early 2006, was made up of Al-Qaeda and a number of other militant groups.

National Guard in the area of Moshahada, north of Baghdad. The lions chose the time when hundreds of apostates were gathered at the site. The lions burst into the center with light and medium weapons and harvested many heads. All whose feet could not carry them away fell in their own blood. All who were in the center were killed. Their dead bodies were all over the place. Thanks unto Allah.

Allah is great, Glory to Allah, His messenger and the mujahideen.

—News Release
Information Department
The Mujahideen Shura of Iraq
January 18, 2006

CHAPTER 16

The Revolution
Devours Its Own

THE MAN WHO called himself Abu Marwa sat in the half-light of a Baghdad house, his face shrouded by the shadows of a room without electricity. The capital was nearly always without power now, and the curtains were shut to the outside world to hide the men inside. Abu Marwa grumbled about having to come to Baghdad, which was teeming with American soldiers. After much deliberation, he agreed to make the drive from Yusufiya, twenty miles to the south.

Abu Marwa's three comrades were arrayed in the couches and chairs around him. Like the man himself, they were members of the Islamic Army in Iraq, one of the busiest insurgent groups in the country. They wore checked kafiyas and white dishdashas. Their faces were crisscrossed and dry, and they talked with hoarse voices through their own cigarette smoke. It wasn't hard to imagine them triggering a bomb beneath an American Humvee. Abu Marwa stood slightly apart: he was thirty-two years old, wore blue jeans and a yellow button-down shirt. His face was clean-shaven, and it had the unlined look of a student's. He'd been a captain in the Iraqi army.

Abu Marwa had not come to talk about the Americans. There was something else. With a nod of his head, he got down to his story.

"According to our Iraqi tribal traditions and beliefs, each tribe must take revenge for the death of one of its members," he said. "This is a solemn obligation, even if it means you must kill a member of Al-Qaeda."

Everyone agreed about the need to kill Americans, Abu Marwa said. There was no argument about that. The trouble, he said, was that Al-Qaeda was killing not just Americans but Iraqis, too. Al-Qaeda was bombing Shiite mosques, public markets, murdering Iraqi civilians by the thousands. Al-Qaeda's war, he said, had nothing to do with his own.

"You have to differentiate between the real resistance and Al-Qaeda," Abu Marwa said, sitting in the shadows at the corner of the room. "We want to liberate our country. We want to rid our country of the Americans. We are the real resistance.

"Al-Qaeda attacks even though many Iraqis are around their targets," he said. "They have done this repeatedly.

"Sunni, Shia—this means nothing to us," he said.

AMERICAN AND IRAQI officials had been trying for months to exploit the fissures between the Sunni insurgents. On one side stood the Iraqi nationalist groups like the Islamic Army, of which Abu Marwa was a member, whose goal was to drive the Americans out of Iraq. On the other stood the ultraviolent Islamists of Al-Qaeda and Ansar al-Sunnah, who wanted to resurrect the Islamic caliphate of bygone days. These groups were fanatically pro-Sunni, and they were murdering Shiite civilians. The Americans believed that the nationalists like Abu Marwa could be placated, and perhaps even turned against the Islamists. But so far there had been scant evidence of any such shift.

It was finally happening. Ordinary Iraqis were turning against Al-Qaeda. I had been hearing about clashes between nationalist insurgents and Al-Qaeda terrorists taking place across the Sunni Triangle. A civil war of sorts was breaking out inside the insurgency itself.

"Al-Qaeda killed two people from our group," one of the insurgents said from his place on the couch. "They repeatedly kill our people."

The man who spoke was Abu Lil. He smoked Marlboros and spoke in a gravelly voice, and he'd sunk so far into the couch that he had to tilt his head upward to speak. "We confronted Al-Qaeda about this, fifteen months ago," he said. "In a farmhouse outside of Mosul. Five of us and about twenty-five men from Al-Qaeda. They were mostly foreigners. Pakistanis and people from—I am not sure—Indonesia. These men didn't speak Arabic. They required a translator."

That two insurgent groups would meet with one another was not unusual; the groups often shared expertise and talent, and combined forces for big operations, Abu Lil said. This was different. Abu Lil and the others at the meeting told the Al-Qaeda fighters they were unhappy about the murder of Iraqi civilians. A few days before, Abu Lil said, an Al-Qaeda attack in Baghdad had killed two American soldiers and several Iraqis who happened to be standing nearby. The incident prompted Abu Lil and the others to ask for the meeting. The Al-Qaeda fighters were unmoved.

"They said, 'Jihad needs its victims,'" Abu Lil said. "'Iraqis should be willing to pay the price.'

"We said, 'That is very expensive.'"

After seven hours, the meeting ended, he said. Abu Lil and his comrades walked out feeling powerless and angry.

"I wished I had a nuclear bomb to attack them," he said. "We told them, 'You are not Iraqis. Who gave you the power to do this?'"

Let me give you another example, Abu Marwa said. He was seated in the far side of the living room, in a chair in the corner. Only a few months before, he said, Al-Qaeda gunmen kidnapped his uncle, Abu Taha—who, like Abu Marwa's mother, was a Shiite. Abu Marwa, like all the other insurgents in the room, was a Sunni. Groups like Al-Qaeda and the Islamic Army were overwhelmingly Sunni. But Abu Marwa's case was common; many of Iraq's Sunnis had, through marriage, Shiite relatives. Intermarriage—and relations between Sunni and Shiite—lay at the heart of Abu Marwa's fight with Al-Qaeda. When he discovered his uncle had been kidnapped, Abu Marwa began a frantic search through the villages and towns south of Baghdad.

At the time, Abu Marwa said, each of the Sunni villages in the area around Yusufiya, where his own family lived, was under the exclusive control of one or another insurgent group, which competed for territory. Each village was like a fief in a gang war. When the insurgents wanted to travel into a village their group did not control, they needed permission to enter from the dominant group.

And so Abu Marwa began to scour the lush farmlands around Yusufiya, walking the orchards at night, often under escort. He would reach the end of territory controlled by Mohammad's Army, he said, and then a fighter from that group would introduce him to a fighter of Ansar al-Sunnah, where its fief began.

After three days, Abu Marwa said, he made it to the outskirts of Karagol, a village about ten miles from Yusufiya. According to the locals, his uncle had been taken there.

"Karagol is an Al-Qaeda village," Abu Marwa said. "When the American patrols come through Karagol, they have no idea of this. They just drive through, and Al-Qaeda just watches them."

One of the escorts, he said, finally took him into Karagol, and then to the house of a local man said to be one of Al-Qaeda's executioners. Before departing, the escort told Abu Marwa to beware, that the executioner was a brutal, psychotic man, who kept, among other things, the heads of his victims as souvenirs. Abu Marwa walked the final steps to the house alone, he said, and Al-Qaeda's hired killer asked him inside. "The executioner examined a ledger with a long list of names, and Abu Taha was not there," he said.

I winced in disbelief at this fantastic turn of the tale.

"By God's name it is true!" Abu Marwa said. "He was the man who did the beheading for Al-Qaeda. So many beheadings."

The other insurgents looked on impassively. A cloud of cigarette smoke hung in the air.

This was one of those moments in Iraq, not the first, when I felt like I had drifted far from the world I thought I knew. The whole tale, of course, might have been a concoction. Abu Marwa himself might have been a fake. And that was the thing about Iraq: you were untethered, floating free, figuring out the truth by a different set of standards. But Abu Marwa felt real; I could feel that in my gut. And as fantastic as his tale was, it rang true. Al-Qaeda suspects had told Iraqi interrogators on other occasions that they had collected skulls and skeletons and kept lists of their victims, in order to gain plaudits from their superiors. In 2005, for instance, an Iraqi man confessed at his trial to cutting the eyes out of a police officer he had killed and putting them in his pocket so he could bring them to the sheikh who wanted the officer dead.

Failing to find his uncle, Abu Marwa said, he continued into the center of Karagol, where another local warned him to stay away. " 'I advise you, if you know he's with Al-Qaeda, don't go there,' " Abu Marwa recalled the man saying.

Abu Marwa found his uncle in the local morgue a few days later. His legs had been drilled by electric power tools. His jaw had slid to one side of his head, and his nose had been broken. Burn marks peppered his body. His knees were raw, as if he had been dragged. "I was totally crazy," Abu Marwa said. "A mad man was more rational than me."

Abu Marwa called a meeting of his local group, Thunder, a cell loyal to the Islamic Army. After several days, he said, the group's intelligence network had determined that two Syrian members of Al-Qaeda were responsible for the killing, Abu Ghassan and Abu Wadhah, jihadis from Aleppo. "After many meetings, we decided to terminate the men from Al-Qaeda," he said.

Abu Marwa said he realized that by taking on Al-Qaeda he would be putting himself and his comrades in the Islamic Army in exceptional danger. "It's more than crazy when you want to hit Al-Qaeda," Abu Marwa said. "Even the entire net-work of the resistance couldn't think of doing such an act."

Within days, Abu Marwa and his buddies in the Thunder cell had tracked down the Syrian gunmen. Within a couple of weeks, they devised an intricate ambush. In their beige Opel sedan, the Syrians regularly drove a desolate stretch of road. There, on the roadside, four of Abu Marwa's comrades parked in a BMW. When the Syrians approached, the insurgents, ap-pearing to be troubled travelers with a flat tire, flagged them down. "They pretended they didn't have a jack," Abu Marwa said. As soon as the Syrians pulled over, the insurgents shot them dead.

"When my uncle was killed, I promised my aunt that I would avenge his death," he said. She had answered, Abu Marwa said, by repeating an Arabic saying that is often invoked and rarely acted on: *Ashrab min Damhum*, I will drink their blood.

After they killed the Syrians, Abu Marwa took their kafiyas and brought them to his aunt, proof that revenge had been taken. She accepted them with gratitude. And then Abu Marwa presented her with a vial of the killers' blood.

"She drank the blood of the Syrians," Abu Marwa said, still seated in the couch, in the darkness. "You see. We were for revenge. She was filled with rage."

As I stood up to leave, the electricity returned and the house brightened suddenly, giving the room the feeling of a theater at movie's end. I left the house first, and Abu Marwa and his three comrades stayed behind.

The Normal

IT WAS 9 P.M. in June and the heat lingered heavy in the dark. Joao, my colleague and photographer, and I were waiting for a chopper to Anbar Province. We were in the Green Zone, at Landing Zone Washington, where the helicopters flew in and flew away. We had no choice but to fly at night; we were going with the marines. The army guys could fly whenever they wanted with their Black Hawks, which raced and weaved like sports cars over the flat Iraqi landscape. But the marines, with their lumbering Sea Stallions leftover from Vietnam, did not have such luxury. When they flew during the day they got shot down.

It was 120 Fahrenheit, so we sat inside the air-conditioned trailer next to the LZ. There was a refrigerator with all the shelves removed and filled with liter-size bottles of cold water. We drank those for a while and watched television with the soldiers. They had it tuned to a station that was showing music videos, and we watched Depeche Mode sing "John the Revelator." The video showed President Bush speaking about Iraq and each time he did a graphic flashed on the screen that said, "Lie, Lie, Lie." The soldiers watched the screen with blank faces. The guy at the desk told us it would be three hours until the next chopper came. Joao and I walked over to the Green Bean Café, next to the American embassy and Saddam's former swimming pool. The café was closed, but a couple of Iraqi janitors pointed us up the road. "Kebab," one of them said, nodding into the blackness. A kebab stand inside the American zone: it was not so far-fetched. There was an entire Iraqi neighborhood inside the Green Zone called Tashreeya, which had been sandwiched inside the protected area when the Americans put the walls up in 2003. About five thousand Iraqis were said to be living there, but the Americans didn't let anyone near it.

Joao and I walked alongside the Green Zone's main highway, our way illuminated by the passing cars. It was illegal to do what we were doing—walking around the Green Zone unescorted. If we were caught, the embassy guards would kick us out. In that way, as in so many others, the Green Zone felt like high school—a tiny world filled with jocks, nerds and hall monitors who ratted out their classmates who broke the rules.

Joao and I walked along the road for about twenty minutes, until sure enough, in the distance, we spotted a glow. A kebab stand! We walked faster. The Iraqi kebab man was just closing, pulling shut the aluminum shutters on his stand. "Kebab?" we asked. "All finished," he said with a wave. He apologized, appearing genuinely sorry that he could not serve us. He nodded up the road. Joao walked some more, spotting another glow. A grocery store! We practically ran. It was still open; the owner was sweeping up for the night. Joao and I were so hungry we bought a couple of cans of Pepsi and a pack of cookies. When we asked about kebab, the owner motioned down a side street.

Joao and I turned right and walked into Tashreeya. It was as if we had stepped into a dream: nine o'clock and the streets were alive, teeming with people. A group of kids kicked a soccer ball while their parents looked on. A middle-aged couple walked past and waved. Women walked with unfurled hair; they wore dresses with their calves exposed. Outside of the Green Zone, in Baghdad—in so much of the rest of Iraq—there had not been a scene like this in many years. Outside, the streets of Iraq were dead. Here in Tashreeya, the chaos had never come.

We stopped one of the kids in the street and asked him about a restaurant. He motioned for us to follow. We turned a corner and there it was: an outdoor kebab restaurant open at night, something unseen in Baghdad in three years. Iraqis—mostly men—sat around plastic tables, picking at their food. The faint murmur of Arabic music wafted in the air: there was even electricity at night. The embers from the grill glowed in the dark.

Joao and I sat down. I worried that we might unsettle the Iraqis—because Americans were not allowed in. Before the war, Tashreeya, given its proximity to Saddam's palace, had been filled with Tikritis, members of Saddam's very tribe. Now the area had been taken over by Shiites. The Iraqis looked over at us, looked us up and down. But they turned back to their food. They didn't seem to mind. I felt indifference, perhaps even warmth: more relics from 2003. It was just shy of 11 p.m. when our plates came. Kebabs and pita bread and hummus and green peppers. Marvelous.

It was then that the Iraqis started getting up from their tables. Quietly and without fanfare, they all got up, nearly in unison, and walked away. I was stunned. There was no curfew here, as in the rest of Iraq. Perhaps I had misread them; perhaps it was not friendliness I had felt. With my white polo shirt and my blue jeans, I could have passed for a CIA agent. "Maybe they think there is going to be a raid," Joao said.

And then we remembered. It was June 25: the second round of the 2006 World Cup was coming on at 11 p.m., as it had every night over the past two weeks. Tonight, Portugal was playing the Netherlands, via satellite from a stadium in Luxembourg. The Iraqis had televisions and electricity and were leaving to indulge their national passion. As Joao and I walked out of Tashreeya and back toward the landing zone, we saw in the windows of the Iraqis' apartments a long succession of glowing blue lights.

CHAPTER 17

The Labyrinth

THE TIP WAS THAT Jill Carroll, an American reporter, was being held in a stable at a horse-racing track in western Baghdad. Carroll, a freelancer, had been kidnapped less than twenty-four hours before, in the middle of the day, in the middle of the street. Her translator, Allan Enwiyah, an Iraqi Christian, had been shot dead.

The tip was plausible enough. The Amiriya racetrack was under the control of insurgents; most of Amiriya was. The Americans didn't go inside the racetrack. The Americans didn't go to a lot of places in Baghdad anymore. Baghdad was a city very near total anarchy, with thirty or forty Iraqis being kidnapped each day. Often the victims were children; often they were killed. Iraqi parents were keeping their kids indoors, even out of school. More and more Iraqis were spending their life savings to rescue their relatives from the armed gangs that controlled the city. It was a nightmarish world.

I'd only met Carroll once before, at a press conference. She seemed young and a bit wide-eyed, but, unlike a lot of freelancers who came through Iraq, she had made it work for her and stayed. I threw myself into trying to help her. I knew Baghdad as well as anyone, and I had Iraqi sources across the city. I hoped she would have done the same for me in similar circumstances.

"Sir, Jill is being held at the racetrack in Amiriya," said Ahmad, my Iraqi fixer. "I am talking directly to one of the kidnappers. He is criminal. He is resistance. One hundred percent."

"I am talking directly to the kidnappers"—that was Ahmad's style: self-dramatizing and, in the end, as clear as a muddy river. Ahmad was a freelancer I hired when I couldn't get information any other way. As Baghdad grew more dangerous, and Western reporters were moving around less and less, stories became harder to find. People became harder to reach. That is where Ahmad came in: he lived in the middle of the anarchy; he understood it and used it to his advantage. Ahmad could find people and get to places like no other Iraqi I knew.

Ahmad, a Shiite, lived in one of Baghdad's mixed neighborhoods. He was a character: he wore black leather jackets and carried two cell phones into which he whispered and shouted almost continuously. He had a pair of eyebrows that seemed perpetually arched, as if in wonder. His laugh was a madman's cackle. "Sir!" Ahmad would say, "I have a story for you—a great story!" Almost always he did.

The thing that made me worry about Ahmad was what made him so necessary. He patrolled the Iraqi underworld, talking to marginal people—creeps, hustlers, gunmen—people whom most Americans, and most Iraqis, avoided. Ahmad introduced me to death squad leaders and insurgents. It was Ahmad who led me to the group of Iraqi insurgents who were fighting Al-Qaeda. No one else I knew could have managed that.

Usually I met these seedy people at Ahmad's house, which was more often than not dark from lack of electricity. It was surreal, talking with a person who might kill me, in a room so full of shadows I could hardly see the face. Ahmad kept a flock of sheep on the roof of his home. "For eating, sir!" he said. There were about twenty-five of them in all, scurrying from one part of the roof to another, leaving their waste in trails behind them. Sometimes, as I sat in Ahmad's darkened house talking to some marginal figure, I would hear the sounds of hooves trampling across the ceiling.

By the very nature of the people Ahmad was bringing to me, I sometimes got the troubling feeling that I was being lied to. It wasn't that the folks he brought me were unreliable—

their stories always checked out. It was Ahmad himself. It's an axiom of journalism that the best sources are often people of marginal repute—not necessarily people you would invite to your home for dinner. How would an ordinary voter know about the bribes being paid to city commissioners? How would a person of upstanding character know about shady zoning deals? Ahmad seemed slightly shady, but it was his very shadiness that made him so valuable.

Some of my hesitation about Ahmad rose from his manifest joy at making money. His eyebrows never rose higher than when I counted hundred dollar bills into his hand. (Usually he charged $250 a day.) Part of my hesitation was due to Ahmad's style: I rarely had any idea what he was doing until he was finished doing it. I'd tell him I wanted to talk to the leader of a police commando unit, and a week later he would call and say: "It is ready." And some of my doubts came from the circular, nonlinear way that Ahmad spoke. Often when I asked Ahmad a question, the answer I got back seemed to be only tangentially related to my query. "Sir," Ahmad said to me more than once, "it is very complicated."

Waleed, my driver, who rarely offered a bad word about anyone, told me to stay away. "Not good man," Waleed said to me. "Not honest man." Other Iraqis I trusted told me the same.

So, when Ahmad called me about Carroll, all these misgivings weighed heavily. "Jill is at the racetrack." Under the circumstances, I decided to take him seriously. If any Iraqi could find Jill Carroll, it was Ahmad. And if it turned out Ahmad didn't know anything—that he was just bluffing me, or if other, sleazier Iraqis were bluffing him—I would only be out a few hundred bucks. The important thing was to do everything we could to try to get Carroll released.

Ahmad described in detail what he'd learned about Carroll's whereabouts. He said the kidnapper he'd spoken to was apparently willing to betray his cohorts for a hefty reward. He relayed a description of Jill to me: a brunette with a streak of pink dye in her hair, which was correct, even though, at this point, Carroll's kidnapping had not been publicly announced.

"Sir, she is there, 100 percent," Ahmad said.

He told me he had met Jill once before, which could have accounted for his accurate description. But I asked myself: What did Ahmad have to gain by sending me or the American embassy on a wild goose chase? Money, to be sure. I told Ahmad I needed to tell the Americans at the embassy what he was telling me. I asked him if he wanted to come with me, to tell them in person. Ahmad looked at me in horror.

"The Green Zone?" he said, shaking his head. He might have said Devil's Island. "No."

By the winter of 2006, so many Westerners had been kidnapped in Iraq that the embassy had set up an entire team to solve the cases. It was headed by a man named Erik Rye. I drove across the Tigris and went into the Green Zone, where I waited for Erik to pick me up. Erik told me they didn't have much on Jill. "The whole embassy is working on it," he said. I told him what I knew, but told him I wasn't sure. "Take it or leave it," I said, and I went home.

And it was then that things began to get strange. A few hours later, after nightfall, my phone rang. It was Erik.

"I need you to come back over and meet someone," Erik said. "There are some people who would be very interested in talking to you."

I didn't go out at night much anymore—the streets were too dangerous. But this time I made an exception. I got in our armored car and drove back across the Tigris to the Green Zone. I met Erik again at the entrance to the Rashid Hotel. I tried to get him to tell me what was up, but he wouldn't say.

"You'll see," he said.

We stopped in the embassy parking lot, and I figured we were going inside. Instead, we climbed into a golf cart. It was a cold January night and I had not worn a jacket. We drove for several minutes, turning corners and hopping over median strips, going into areas of the Green Zone I had never seen before. I shivered the whole way. Finally we arrived at the gates of a walled compound. The Green Zone, of course, was a walled compound itself. Whatever it was I was going into amounted to a walled compound inside of a walled compound—an inner sanctum.

Erik spoke into a radio and a pair of heavy doors opened. He punched the electric motor on the golf cart and glided down a narrow street flanked by white trailers. At the end of the street stood a large man with a goatee and a vest; he looked like a Hell's Angel. Next to him was a more normal-size guy, in a windbreaker and jeans. A lawyer on his day off. The guy in the windbreaker asked me to follow him into one of the trailers. Erik stayed behind. Inside was a single room with two plastic chairs. Just the two of us. The carpet was green, like at a miniature golf course. A small refrigerator stood against the wall.

"You want a Coke or something?" the man asked.

"You've probably figured out where you are," he said. I said nothing. "You're inside the CIA compound. I'm the deputy director for Iraq. You can call me Mike."

Mike, if that was his name, looked exhausted, his face haggard and his eyes rimmed with red.

"We've been working day and night," Mike said. "I haven't slept since she was kidnapped. None of us have. When an American is kidnapped, we put all of our operations on hold—everything we're doing. You cannot believe the effort we are putting in to find this woman."

I told Mike everything Ahmad had told me. Mike agreed that the story made sense. The Amiriya racetrack, he said, was a well-known transit point for kidnappers, who often used the place to buy and sell their victims. Kidnapping auctions: that was something to think about. There was a road that led straight from the Amiriya racetrack to Garma, an insurgent-controlled town outside of Baghdad. Kidnapping victims were often taken there.

Mike knew a lot about Iraq, every tribe and subtribe. I didn't have to explain how all the pieces fit together. I could tell by how jaded he looked that he'd been in Iraq a long time. Probably too long. He reminded me of myself. I looked at his haggard face and I wondered why he'd stayed so long, which was the same question my friends asked me.

When I tried to tell Mike how difficult it had been for me to follow Ahmad's story, he interrupted.

"Yeah, I know," he said. "Their minds work differently. Totally nonlinear. No straight lines. No beginning, no end."

He started moving his finger in wide circles. "Believe me, I know," he said.

As I talked, I noticed that Mike wasn't writing anything down. I asked him if our conversation was being recorded.

"We don't record anything," he said.

I thought he was joking but he didn't smile.

Then Mike asked for Ahmad's phone number. I asked him if he wanted to call Ahmad; I could do that for him. No. Did he want to meet him? No. Mike told me that if he had Ahmad's phone number, he could listen to his conversations and trace his calls and get a good idea whom Ahmad was talking to. I didn't ask him, but I assumed that the CIA had the ability to geographically pinpoint a particular cell phone by its number.

"It could take us back to the kidnappers," Mike said.

"I can't do that," I said.

"What you've told us is the best information we have," Mike said. "It's all we have."

I told him I would be betraying Ahmad, who trusted me.

"Every minute counts," Mike said. "The first twenty-four hours are the most important. If she is still in Baghdad—if she is still at the racetrack—she will not be there for long.

"After that," Mike said. "we might as well forget her. Once a kidnap victim is taken out of Baghdad, chances are we will never find them. They'll put her on a farm somewhere and we'll never find her.

"Not long ago," Mike said, "some of our guys were searching one of the farms in Anbar. Middle of nowhere. And they came across this guy who'd been kidnapped months before. They found him in a crawl space. It was as big as a closet." He held his hand about three feet from the floor. "We had no idea he was there. No idea."

"I need to think it over," I told Mike. "Not tonight. Not now."

Mike was bearing in, trying to lay a guilt trip on me. And yet at the same time, everything he said was true. Carroll was in the hands of a group of very bad people—they'd already murdered her translator. Her chances were not good. I wasn't sure if my information was any good, but how could I sit on it?

"Imagine where she is right now, surrounded by those hairy guys," Mike said, bearing in. "They smell. They're breathing on her. Every minute."

It didn't take me long to decide. That night, I called my editors in New York and talked it over with them. The next day, I called Ahmad and told him his phone was being tapped. I didn't give him details but I told him to be careful whom he spoke to. I realized that by telling Ahmad this I was probably defeating the entire purpose of the tap, but it was the only way I could do it and live with myself. After sundown I called Erik and told him I needed to come back over. And before long I was back in the trailer with the green carpet. I told Mike that before I would give him Ahmad's telephone number, I needed him to promise me that he would not harm Ahmad in any way. I told Mike that if anything happened to Ahmad, I would write a story about the entire episode—about Mike and the compound and everything else. It wasn't much, but it was something.

"We won't touch him," Mike said. "Whatever you may think, we take care of our sources. We have to, or we would never get any information. Our jobs are very similar that way."

I told Mike the phone number—I had not even written it down, suspecting that if I had refused he would have taken it from me anyway. Mike listened and then stood up—he hadn't written it down either. I didn't feel good about any of it. I was betraying Ahmad. I was putting him at risk. But I felt that, given the assurances I had, and given the danger that Carroll was in, I didn't have much choice. I was deep inside the labyrinth.

Ahmad called three days later. He spoke in an agitated voice. "Sir, there is big problem," he said. I asked what was the matter and he told me he couldn't talk on the phone. I drove to his home across town.

When I got there, Ahmad told me that one of the people he'd been talking to was Abu Marwa, the insurgent leader from Yusufiya whom I'd interviewed a few weeks before. Talking to Abu Marwa made sense: Ahmad might have had links to the Iraqi underworld, but Abu Marwa was the underworld itself. Abu Marwa, he said, had been helping him look for the kidnappers.

"He knows everyone in the area—he knows everything," Ahmad said. "Naturally I call him. He can find out anything. He could find Jill in twenty-four hours."

According to Ahmad, the night before—only three days after I handed over his phone number to Mike—a helicopter full of American commandos, dressed in black and wearing masks, had dropped into a hover above Abu Marwa's house. The commandos slid down on ropes and kicked down his door.

"They hung him up from the ceiling!" Ahmad said, nearly hysterical. "They beat him. They hold up picture of Jill Carroll and they shout at him, 'Do you know this woman? Do you know this woman?' "

Then the Americans took Abu Marwa away.

"Sir," Ahmad said, "American helicopter come right after I talk on the phone with him."

Ahmad's brow wrinkled with worry. I didn't doubt him for a second—not on something like this, where his own welfare was concerned.

I was furious. I called Erik the moment I left Ahmad's house. It took me more than a day to get back to the trailer with the green carpet.

"You have really complicated my life," I told Mike, thinking he might care about me if not about some random Iraqi. I was waiting for some acknowledgment of their screwup.

Mike didn't blink.

"We promised not to touch your friend, and we didn't," he said. "Your friend is talking to some bad people. The guy we captured—he's a very bad guy. We were having a lot of problems in that area and we think he was behind a lot of it."

He gave me a hard look.

"He's a bad guy," Mike said. "A very bad guy."

I asked how he expected to catch Jill Carroll's kidnappers if he apprehended the one link that we had.

"Your friend was being lied to by his friend," he said. Abu Marwa, he said, "was talking to a lot of people, but not with the kidnappers. He was just making up a lot of crap to your friend."

I didn't know what to say.

"In this country, everyone is lying to everyone else. You know that. They are all doing each other in."

When I'd interviewed Abu Marwa, he had refused to talk

about attacking American soldiers. Mike was obviously suggesting that Abu Marwa had killed a lot of Americans, or possibly Iraqi soldiers and police. In that case I couldn't be all that angry that Abu Marwa was off the streets. But I was angry because Mike had interpreted our agreement the way a slick lawyer would—adhering to its letter while violating its spirit. And, of course, I was disgusted with myself for being a fool, for being dumb enough to trust the CIA. I felt dirty and compromised; I'd betrayed Ahmad to help free Carroll and gotten nothing but trouble in return.

"You've put me in a very difficult situation," I said.

Mike shrugged.

"I'm here to kill terrorists," he said.

As I walked out, I couldn't help but feel cynical about the CIA in Iraq. It was hard to believe they were so bereft of intelligence that they had been forced to rely on a newspaper reporter to help them with the whereabouts of a kidnapped American. And it was even harder to believe that they were so ignorant of Iraq that, when given a single phone to tap, they'd discovered an Iraqi whom they wanted to take out of circulation. They had acted, of course, without concern for who or what they might upset in the process.

And the information I had given them on Carroll's whereabouts? For all of Mike's expressions of urgency, he told me that he had waited two full nights before he had sent a team into the racetrack.

"She wasn't there," Mike said.

ABOUT A WEEK LATER, Ahmad called to say that Abu Marwa's father had accused him of conspiring to hand over his son to the Americans. The father had no evidence, but he knew that Ahmad had been working with American reporters like me. And he knew that Ahmad had been asking Abu Marwa to help him find Carroll. The American commandos had landed on his roof, the father said, only minutes after Ahmad and Abu Marwa had finished their last telephone call. Abu Marwa's father was raising the issue of *al-sulh al-ashaeri*, the Arab tradition of paying money to compensate for a wrong. This was, suddenly, a grave matter. If Ahmad refused to pay, Abu Marwa's family would be obliged, under the same tribal traditions, to kill him. That was called *thar.*

I found Ahmad very down. He had stopped joking altogether. He said he would have to make the compensation payment, called a *fasal,* to Abu Marwa's family, even though he had had nothing to do with his capture.

I hadn't told Ahmad everything I knew about what had transpired. I was afraid now, afraid of everything I didn't know. I was afraid of Ahmad's reaction when I told him I was the source of his problem. I was afraid he would tell Abu Marwa's family what I had done. And where I lived. That family was, after all, part of the insurgency.

Things grew stranger still. Ahmad claimed that Abu Marwa's family was demanding a $35,000 *fasal.* According to the tribal tradition, the payment would erase forever any claims Abu Marwa's family held against Ahmad—even if, for instance, the Americans or the Iraqi government sentenced Abu Marwa to death. If Ahmad did not pay, Abu Marwa's family might choose to kill him. Ahmad said he was preparing to sell his cars and his wife's jewelry.

"I am not comfortable," Ahmad told me. "My father is angry. We must settle the issue."

Even so, for all of Ahmad's worries, I had serious doubts about the $35,000 figure. Iraqis didn't have that kind of money. I didn't doubt that Abu Marwa's family had invoked the tradition of *al-sulh al-ashaeri,* but I began to suspect that Ahmad was trying to profit from his problem. The Iraqis at *The New York Times* bureau shared my suspicions. With so much killing in Iraq, the tradition of *al-sulh al-ashaeri* was being invoked all the time. According to the Iraqis who worked for the *Times,* a typical *fasal* payment in Baghdad was about $3,000—and that was when the person was dead. Abu Marwa was alive.

It was possible, of course, that Ahmad was telling me the whole truth. Totally possible. After much deliberation, a colleague who also worked with him and I decided to pay Ahmad $6,000, twice the average *fasal,* and out of our own pockets. Ahmad accepted the $6,000 wholeheartedly, in hundred-

dollar bills. He thanked us and called us to say that the families had gathered and resolved their differences.

"Everything is settled now," Ahmad said, looking relieved.
"I am feeling much better."

The crisis seemed to pass. Over the next several days I continued to pay Ahmad to help me look for Carroll. The business with Abu Marwa never came up again. One day, though,
Ahmad called excitedly, saying he had found a Sunni sheikh
from Anbar Province, named Akbar, who he was certain could
spring Carroll.

"He is in contact with the kidnappers," he said.

The doubts I had about Ahmad began to grow again. But
Carroll was still missing, and I thought it worth one more try
to see what Akbar thought he had. So, after laborious negotiations, Ahmad and I met Sheikh Akbar in the lobby of the
Babylon Hotel.

It was a surreal conversation. Akbar spoke no English.
Ahmad did not translate. They spoke to each other, in sub-
dued voices. They spoke to each other like old friends. They
might as well have been talking about the price of tea, for all I
knew. The meeting broke up without a conclusion, except
that, according to Ahmad, Sheikh Akbar had agreed to give
him a phone number for the kidnappers.

Later that night, Ahmad met Sheikh Akbar again, and
Ahmad did indeed return with a phone number. But, as ever,
with Ahmad, there was a curious but important twist. During
their meeting, Ahmad said, Sheikh Akbar had called the kidnappers and spoken to them. And then, after he'd hung up, he
had refused to give Ahmad the number, after all. And so
Ahmad said he had waited for Sheikh Akbar to go to the bathroom, and then grabbed his cell phone, which he had left
behind on the table, and taken the number he'd dialed directly
from the phone.

My dealings with Ahmad, I concluded, had sunk to the
level of farce. But I took the number, and, with Ahmad's permission, I took it to another meeting with Mike.

"We ran that telephone number you gave us," Mike told
me later. "It's not even real. It hasn't been used in a year. Your
buddy is just playing you."

The Wall

I PULLED ON my running shoes and headed outside. I went through the heavy bulletproof door of the compound and down the long cement chute, a gauntlet of blast walls with a checkpoint at the far end. I ran south about fifty yards and swung around the coils of razor wire, jumped from the cement wall into the dirt. Three stray dogs who had befriended me recently were there to greet me. Their leader was Prancer, or so we called him, because of the way he sprang around, overjoyed at our presence but afraid to be touched; a second mutt was Nadim; and the third dog we hadn't bothered to name. With the three dogs following, I ran across the junk-strewn field, pausing again to step carefully over another coil of razor wire. The dogs snaked through the wire on their own, noses down, and then wandered off. I ran a little more and then climbed up onto a patch of pavement that lay between Abu Nawas and the banks of the Tigris. A group of Iraqis who manned a guard post were sitting around; they looked over at me and said nothing. They'd been there for several months. They didn't have uniforms, though I figured someone must have been paying them. On the wall of their little white shed they kept a small photo of a shouting Muqtada. I put my half-liter bottle of water down on the pavement and headed north.

Running wasn't so easy anymore. My route had shrunk to a fraction of its old self: about three-quarters of a mile between two posts of armed Iraqis. My old path along the banks of the Tigris, the one I'd used since 2003, was finally rendered impassable by several new coils of razor wire. Still, a second stretch of pavement ran closer to Abu Nawas—I could use that. If I ran between the two checkpoints six or seven times, I could make five miles.

The guys in the first checkpoint, the one with the photo of Muqtada, were friendly but not overly so. In the summer we told the Iraqis who maintained the bureau to carry water out to them. They didn't say much but I knew they drank it. In the winter, the guards hacked branches from the few trees that remained in the park and burned them for warmth. Once, when I wasn't around, the fire burned out of control, scorching what was left of the dead grass the Americans had planted the previous year. Everything was like that in Iraq: anything anyone ever tried burned to black. At night, during the World Cup, the guards had dragged a television out there, which they ran off of our electricity. That made me feel good, the idea that they might need us, even in a small way. A female colleague ran with me occasionally, and the guards used to ask about her when she was gone.

Things happened I didn't fully understand. Like the day the guards in the white shed beat up one of the guards who worked for us. Really pummeled him; he was crying and ran home. I couldn't get a straight answer from anyone on that, why they'd done it. But the incident struck me as odd, since our guards far outnumbered the guards in the white shed. Sometimes when I'd get back from a lap, my water bottle would be missing. I'd put it on the pavement and run off and come back and it would be gone. I'd look over at the guards and their faces would be blank.

The northern checkpoint was more official—these guys had uniforms—but it was scarier, especially after dark. The wall, about five feet high, ran from the Tigris all the way to Abu Nawas; there was no getting past it. As I approached on foot, I'd often see their heads peeking over the top of the wall. They had a searchlight, which sometimes they turned on when they saw me coming. But usually they left it off, and that was worse. I didn't want to surprise them in the dark. I didn't want them to mistake me for an insurgent trying to overrun their post. I'd run right up to the wall and touch it, even in the dark—I needed the distance for my run—and often I could run all the way up to the wall and not one of them would say a word. Often I wouldn't say anything either. I'd run all the way to the wall, and at the last second I would catch sight of one of them, his face level with mine, staring at me in the dark. It would scare the hell out of me. Probably them, too.

Often, though, it was the dogs that saved me. The wild dogs who lived in the reeds down by the river had multiplied. Without anyone culling their ranks, the colony had grown so large that some of the dogs had migrated into the park itself. There were dozens of them now, living in the folds of dirt, using the last of the eucalyptus trees to shade them from the sun. And at night, as I ran past them, I'd set them into a frenzy of howling and barking. The dogs would come up into the road, dozens of them, maybe a hundred. I hated the things— they were so aggressive—but their yipping and yapping often alerted the guards to my approach, and they'd switch on their searchlight and see me coming.

Running at night: it was madness. I was courting death, or at least a kidnapping. The capital was a free-for-all; it was a state of nature. There was no law anymore, no courts, nothing— there was nothing at all. They kidnapped children now, they killed them and dumped them in the street. The kidnapping gangs bought and sold people; it was like its own terrible ecosystem. One of the kidnapping gangs could have driven up in a car and beat me and gagged me and I could have screamed like a crazy person, but I doubt anyone would have done any- thing. Not even the guards. They weren't bad people, the guards, but who in Baghdad was going to step in the middle of a kidnapping? The kidnappers had more power than anyone.

I had been in Iraq too long. Going on four years. I'd lived through everything, shootings and bomb blasts and death, and I'd never gotten so much as a scratch. I guess I was numb. I guess I felt invincible. The danger seemed notional to me now, not entirely real, something I wrote about, something that killed other people. The mechanism I used to calculate risk, the one I had relied on since 2003, had been fueled by an acute sense of self-preservation, of sensitivity to danger. And now I couldn't force myself to care all that much; I figured I'd always get away. I always had before.

The one thing left I wasn't numb to was the running itself.

Running out there on the Tigris, with the dogs, in the dark, in the dying city, was one of the few things that I could still feel. In Baghdad, the most hopeless of cities, for a few blissful minutes, my heart would race.

I approached the second checkpoint. The birds rustled in the eucalyptus trees. The dogs began to yip and howl, but tonight they kept their places. The sky was clear, the streets blissfully still. An orange moon was rising above the city. Just above the wall was the silhouette of a soldier's head. He was looking, too. "Good, good!" he said from behind the wall.

CHAPTER 18

Fuck Us

IN THE MORNINGS, you could stand on the rooftop of the government center in downtown Ramadi and watch the Iraqis trickle into the streets far away. The cityscape was obliterated for a mile in each direction. Total ruin, like Grozny or Dresden. The marines had given names to the blown-up buildings: Swiss Cheese, Battleship Gray. The human activity unfolded beyond that, at the outer edges of the destruction. From the top of the government center, the Iraqis seemed like tiny figures in a greater landscape, trudging to some end they did not know. By noon, the landscape would be empty again.

It was a joke among the marines posted there, "the government center," since there wasn't much of either. The center of the city was obliterated and the government had ceased to exist. There was a governor, a half-crazed man named Mamoon Sami Rashid, but most everyone else in the government was dead or in hiding. A few months before, Rashid's secretary had been beheaded. Rashid lived a weird, cloistered life, driving with the marines, flying with the marines, surrounded by the marines in the rubble of his hometown.

There were two worlds at the government center, the rooftop and the interior. Unless you were going out to fight, fully loaded, the outside was off-limits. The moment you stepped out of the building you had to run. You had to run everywhere, even to your Humvee. No standing. It was the snipers. The toilets were broken, naturally, since there was no water, but you couldn't go outside for that, either. There were no port-a-lets because the snipers would have gotten them. You had to do your business indoors, into a small green sack called a Wag Bag, named for the flammable chemicals it carried in its lining. When you were done you'd tie up the Wag Bag and toss it into a regular trash bag, and one of the grunts would take it out at night and set it on fire.

The snipers were good. In Iraq, the insurgents might have been raggedy-assed guys who scored by rigging blasting caps to rusty artillery shells, but a number of them were former soldiers, and some of them were snipers. They carried Russian Dragonoff rifles with huge scopes and long barrels. They aimed for the neck, in the soft spot between your helmet and flak jacket.

The marines, all from Kilo Company, lived inside, about seventy-five at a time. The place reeked, of course, of stale piss and old clothes and so many bodies pressed too close together. There weren't any showers; you showered after you came out. The urinals didn't really work but they used them anyway; sometimes the piss would drain through the pipe and sometimes it would leak out on the floors and go stale. The guys slept eight to a room, stacked together like kids in a dorm. The rooms had windows, but most of them had been shot out and boarded up.

The tours at the government center lasted two weeks, long enough to make anyone crazy. One marine, David, lived by himself in a tiny crawl space on the second floor opposite the stairwell that took you up to the roof. He was from Tampa. His job was to keep the rest of the marines supplied with water and food, which wasn't much of a job, a kind of make-work thing. He was sort of a Boo Radley character, friendly but a little slower than the others. Most of the time David stayed inside the cubbyhole, playing violent video games. Whenever I walked past his room I could hear the explosions. "I've never been on the roof," David said, gesturing toward the sunlight in the stairwell. "Ain't never going up there." And nobody was forcing him to.

The marines were young and they made the most of their

circumstances. They kept a weight room on the first floor, dark and sandy, and they played Metallica and pumped iron till they fell asleep. Banging music and banging weights. They slept more than you would think. Generators kept the AC going and the boarded-up windows made the rooms dark, and most of the guys would sleep right through the gun battles on the roof.

The heat outside was astounding, but the guys still went out most days, loaded with gear and guns. Into the night, into the rubble. Looking to waste people. Sometimes when they ran, they tossed canisters that threw up green smoke. I never heard them talk about hearts and minds.

"We go out and kill these people," Captain Andrew Del Gaudio said. He was in charge.

There was a primal simplicity to being in Ramadi that made it refreshing, even in the stink of it. There were no politics to complicate things, like there were back in Baghdad. People were fighting to the death.

I asked Del Gaudio how his men were doing.

"Let's see, Lance Corporal Tussey, shot in the thigh.

"Lance Corporal Zimmerman, shot in the leg.

"Lance Corporal Sardinas, shrapnel, hit in the face.

"Corporal Wilson, shrapnel in the throat.

"That's all I can think of right now," the captain said.

Del Gaudio was thirty, an Italian from Parkchester in the Bronx. Sitting there glowering in his T-shirt, he reminded me of one of those tough guys from a 1950s movie. Brando without the charm. I guess he had a right to be angry, trapped in this desert shithole and charged with killing people. I asked Del Gaudio to take me out on one of the night patrols and he told me to forget it. "You'd probably step on something and blow us all the fuck up."

I left his office and closed the door behind me. There were some guys standing around a sign-up sheet. A clipboard and a pen. They were talking about Lara Logan, the sexy CBS correspondent who had visited a couple of weeks before. The sign-up sheet was recording suggestions for the logo on Kilo Company's T-shirt. The boys were going home soon.

"Kilo Company," one of the marines had written. "Killed More People Than Cancer."

"Kilo Company: Fuck Iraq."
"Kilo Company: Fuck Ramadi."
"Kilo Company: Fuck Lara Logan!"
"Kilo Company: Fuck Us."

IT WAS QUIET and dark on the roof when Lance Corporal Joseph Hamlin began to talk about his life.

"I'm nineteen; I'll be twenty in September," he said. I couldn't see him; it was like listening to a disembodied voice in the night. "I'm from western Georgia, on the Alabama line. LaGrange. They say it's the biggest little city in Georgia. It means 'the farm' in French. Lafayette was there."

Hamlin was standing at Post 1, overlooking Ramadi from the northwest corner of the government center. The post was a concrete-block hut covered in sandbags. There was just enough room for the two of us.

"This is my first time ever," he said. "I joined in May '05. Right after I graduated high school. Graduated high school on Friday, showed up for boot camp on Monday. Didn't take any time off."

He laughed. The streets below were mostly invisible in the dark. Even at 11 p.m., the temperature hovered at well over 100 degrees. Every few minutes or so, Corporal Hamlin picked up his night-vision scope and peered down the alley that jutted directly north from his post.

A volley of shots rang out in the distance.

"Over yonder there," he said, pointing with a slow roll of his hand.

"Jeff Foxworthy, he bought some land in LaGrange," Corporal Hamlin said. "You know him, they call him a country comedian. 'You must be a redneck,' stuff like that. He bought some land down there to hunt on. It's good hunting."

He peered into the scope of his rifle.

"I'm a decent shot. Pretty good," he said. "Not like the snipers."

Another shot echoed in the distance.

"What do I hunt? Whatever is in season: deer, squirrel, turkey, dove. I love to hunt. If I could have a job where money didn't matter, I'd be a hunter."

Corporal Hamlin had laid out four weapons: an M-240 belt-fed machine gun, an M-16 rifle, an M-79 grenade launcher and a rifle called a Sam-R that he especially liked.

"It's like my .308 Remington—it's got a free-floating barrel, too," he said. "That's my favorite.

"I joined the marines. I'm hoping to go to college. When I'm in, I'll do what I can for my country. Do something to help this country."

Cradling the Sam-R, Hamlin looked into the blackness.

"Here it's more difficult," he said. "It's not like all you have to do is be quiet and still and just shoot whatever comes by. Like a duck blind. These guys will play. A turkey don't play. A turkey don't shoot back. He just turns around and runs. They shoot back."

The night wore on. Because of the lack of electricity, Ramadi was dark. What light there was came from the stars, arrayed in their particular way from horizon to horizon.

"I wish they had some police out here," Corporal Hamlin said. "You know, the gangs. We have gangs in places like New York City. They wouldn't stand a chance here. They would have their heads cut off. These are the real gangs here.

"People say this is the worst place in the world. But it isn't bad. They need to fight for themselves," he said. "Everybody has a civil war. We had ours. We got stronger. Maybe they need to have theirs and get it over with."

Midnight neared. Corporal Hamlin turned back to his favorite subject.

"Oh yeah, they got pigs down there. They like to play. You shoot one of them with a .357 right in the head and they keep running. My dad got gored by one of them once. That's some cool hunting.

"I want to kill some bear. I want to go with a bow. A long bow. Not even a compound bow," he said. "You know the difference? A compound bow has the pulleys. Long bow is just the bow. I want to go with a long bow. Kill a big-ass bear.

"My dad lived in China," Corporal Hamlin said. "He ran the Duracell plant there. I lived there. I learned martial arts. Aikido, which is Japanese. Tae kwon do, which is Korean. I'm a second-degree black belt.

"If I had a choice between this, martial arts and hunting, I'd take hunting easy. No alcohol, women or anything like that, like some guys."

Three nights before, the government center had come under attack by about twenty guerrillas. The firefight lasted two hours. The marines had fired hundreds of rounds of ammunition, dropped bombs and artillery. Corporal Hamlin had been asleep in his bunk.

"I shot a couple of guys," he said. "When you're young, seeing movies and everything, you're brought up to think killing is wrong. That's what people do in gangs. Weird. You just shoot. They attack you. Either you are going to shoot and go back to your family or they are going to kill you and keep on killing everyone else. I don't really know what to think of it."

"If I shoot, I get to go back to my family, my girl," he said.

He scanned the streets through his rifle scope.

"I'm a Christian. East Vernon Baptist Church."

Corporal Hamlin was silent for a time. The streets, too, were quiet.

"I asked other people before what it was like to kill somebody. I wasn't sure I could kill somebody. I didn't know what it would be like. Now, I don't know if I feel that much.

"I did have a girlfriend until two days ago. We were together for five years," he said. It happened on the telephone. "She doesn't handle my being gone. She says it's hard. I think whatever I'm going through here is harder. Whatever problems she's having at the house, she doesn't have RPGs being shot at her."

The telephone conversation with his girlfriend, Hamlin said, left him feeling blue. The couple had planned to marry. "Yes, I was wanting to. We were going to get an apartment."

He considered the possibility that she had gotten another boyfriend back in LaGrange.

"Absolutely. She probably does. She might be lying.

"She is a full-blooded Indian. Mohawk. I'm just a pale-skinned white boy.

"I'll get with her when I get back, talk to her," he said. "See if I can work things out. It'll be okay."

Another young voice entered from outside Post 1. It was Corporal Hamlin's relief. He'd been six hours on post. It was midnight, time for bed.

"Good talking to you," he said.

The corporal picked up his rifle and walked downstairs.

THE HUMVEE CRAWLED forward, down a street strewn with trash. The marines sat inside, searching the road with their eyes. Saying nothing. The Humvee advanced. Stones cracked beneath its wheels. At headquarters a map of the city was marked with small white flags wherever the marines had discovered a bomb. There were dozens of them; some of the streets were crammed with tiny white flags.

The Humvee inched up the street. An Iraqi man stood at the gates of his house, his hand cupped over his eyes. The Humvee moved some more. A kid waved.

"Toss him a soccer ball," Gunnery Sergeant John Scroggins said.

A ball bounced from the Humvee's turret.

The street was littered in debris. Look for wires, the marines had said, but the wires were everywhere, snaking out of garbage piles and old electric motors. We rolled past the skeleton of a goat, bleached white and splayed. Behind our goggles our eyes were straining to see. At the base someone had tacked up a photo of a marine after a blast. His face was shredded like hamburger but he'd worn his goggles and his eyes were beaming bright and wide.

Some Iraqis stood on a corner, eating slices of watermelon.

"Look at that, right there," Scroggins said.

The Humvee stopped. There, the gunnery sergeant said, pointing. We rolled along the side of it. On the left, down.

Two green wires, thin, the kind used in a transistor radio, curled out from a piece of a pipe and into the ground. The pipe was three inches across and two feet long. The dirt, which covered the bomb itself, had been patted down with such care that the dig marks were invisible. The wires ran up and out of the ground and into the pipe and then to the trigger, which would have detonated had we run over the pipe. A pressure switch. Crush the pipe and you die.

A toy merry-go-round lay in the street a foot away, tipped over.

"Okay, let's go," the gunnery sergeant said, and our Humvee began to crawl forward again.

The Iraqis on the corner were gone.

THROUGH NIGHT-VISION GOGGLES, the elementary school shimmered in pale green. The Humvee pulled up next to it and stopped.

"Anything?" a marine said.

"Nothing," a second one said.

The Humvee lurched forward. I pulled my goggles down for a second and saw nothing. Only darkness. I put them back on and the pale green returned.

The days were so hot in July that the marines had been scaling back their daytime patrols in favor of night. They still went out during the day, but not on foot. Not anymore. Too many guys were collapsing. The insurgents had stopped coming out in the daylight, too. They attacked the tiny Marine base in downtown Ramadi every day, but they waited for the sun to go down.

The Humvee drove through the darkness. It was a little cooler now, maybe 100 degrees. We peered into our goggles. A greenish shadow flitted across my line of sight. It was a car, passing through an intersection, here and gone.

"Probably a spotter," the marine said.

"Maybe a car bomb," his buddy next to him said.

The Humvee stopped in front of a warehouse. We got out and walked inside. Through the goggles it seemed a lighted cave, glowing and cavernous. There was nothing. No one.

"Let's get out of here," one of the marines said.

We climbed back inside and circled back toward the school. Same street as before, ten minutes later. A backtrack. The Humvee lurched to a halt.

"I'll be damned," the driver said.

Two metal cans, ten gallons each, standing next to each other, sat in the road. A wire ran between them. In the goggles, the cans were pale green.

"Incendiary," the driver said.

"Yeah," said his buddy.

We backed up and took a different street.

ONE MORNING the marines were preparing to escort the Anbar governor through downtown. I asked to go along.

"No problem," Corporal Jonathan Nelson said. He was twenty-one, from Brooklyn.

It was an ordinary drive in an ordinary Humvee. Nelson and the others delivered the governor to the Ramadi government center, and I got out. They drove away.

A few minutes later I heard an explosion.

"IED," someone said.

Half an hour later, Nelson stepped into the building. The bomb had struck the Humvee and ruined its front end. Everyone was okay. Nelson looked fine. He even looked exhilarated.

"Best feeling in the world," he said, eyes bright. "To get hit with an IED and live. It's like bungee jumping."

You serious? I asked.

"Yeah," Nelson said. "You get these vibrations all over your body like somebody pounded the hell out of you."

Right. What about the gash on your head?

"I hit the window," he said.

How many times is that?

"This is my fifth," he said. "The first time we were going to Abu Ghraib, the prison, and it hit our Humvee. Wounded one of the guys. Really weird, you know, your first time."

Right, I said.

"Second time was Garma, June '05," he said. "I was looking at it when it went off. I thought I was dead. I couldn't feel my body. I couldn't move. I thought I had died."

His Humvee mate, Lance Corporal Trent Frazor, was listening over his shoulder. Frazor was from Pickens, South Carolina. He was also twenty-one.

"Dude, you bring your bad luck into the truck," Frazor said.

They laughed. Nelson went on.

"So there was this other time, when I saw the thing, it was

two .155 shells stacked and a Motorola cell phone," he said. "I walked up on it. It didn't go off."

Nelson and Frazor laughed again.

"It will happen one day," Frazor said, not laughing anymore.

Nelson was looking at him.

"You'll be in a convoy one day, and all of a sudden it will happen," Frazor said. "It will happen when it's going to happen."

Nelson shrugged.

Later on, at a cafeteria in a base across town, two marines, possibly from the same Humvee, were carrying their trays to a table.

"So, you saw the IED in the middle of the street, and you kept on driving?" one marine asked the other, moving toward the table. "What the fuck were you thinking?"

LANCE CORPORAL Sean Patton wheeled the Humvee down the street and the children cried out to him.

"Football! Football!" they squealed, and his men tossed a ball from the turret. It bounced in the street and the children ran after it.

Patton guided his Humvee around the corner, down a narrow street. I was in the back seat behind him, and he was wearing a helmet and flak jacket, so I couldn't see much of him. He wheeled the Humvee with poise; he had a sense of where he was.

"This is not the safest neighborhood in the world," Patton said, cranking the wheel around. "But the people are friendly."

Patton waved out the window. Most people just looked at him. A few waved back.

"The people are in the middle," Patton said. "Between us and the insurgents. Whoever is friendly, they will help."

Patton turned right, moving toward an intersection with a kebab stand and a pharmacy. It was late in the afternoon and the people were coming out as the sun cooled. Some of the kids were kicking a soccer ball.

Then the Iraqis started moving. Walking away. The intersection was suddenly empty. The Iraqis were gone. Patton stopped in the middle of the intersection.

"They're going to hit us," he said, scanning the streets. He kept the truck in the middle of the intersection.

We sat for what seemed like an age. The marine next to me was standing up through the turret with his hands on the MK-19 grenade launcher. His legs were banging my shoulders. He'd left a copy of *Surfing* magazine on his seat.

"We're going to get hit," another marine said, in the seat next to Patton.

I picked up *Surfing* and started leafing through it to distract myself, stopping at an article about the waves in Nicaragua.

Patton pulled out. He crept through the intersection and drove two blocks and turned right. As the Humvee swung round, I looked back and saw the Iraqis walking back into the intersection.

Patton drove some more and wheeled the Humvee around. The people were filling the intersection again. The soccer game had resumed.

We rolled into the intersection, the same spot as before.

The Iraqis started moving again. No panic on their faces. Just walking away.

"We're going to get hit," Patton said, gripping the steering wheel.

I picked up the magazine again.

"They're going to hit us," the other marine said.

The attack never came.

CHAPTER 19

The Boss

MAMOON SAMI RASHID, the governor of Anbar Province, spun the wheel of his armored Toyota and pointed toward the wreckage on the side of the road.

"You see, over there, that is where the suicide bomber tried to kill me," Rashid said with a smile.

Across the road, where he was pointing, lay the charred shells of half a dozen automobiles.

"Over here," he said after a time, pointing, "this is where they tried to shoot me."

Car bomb, suicide bomb, mortar, gun; in his car, in his house, in a mosque: insurgents had tried to kill Rashid so many times and in so many different ways that a man less mad would have lost count. Twenty-nine times, he reckoned, on the morning I drove with him to work.

"They want to kill me," Rashid said, spinning the wheel, "because I will not let them have power."

With a confident scowl impressed on his face, Rashid drove through the rubble of downtown Ramadi: shattered buildings, shot-up storefronts, rutted, invisible streets. He swung into the parking lot of the government center, whereupon, like everyone else, he ran inside.

I followed him into his office. He was a curiosity, Governor Rashid: the man who was the government. The government himself. The only moving part. Was he mad? Was he a strange breed of war profiteer; an opportunist in a ruined city owned by foreigners? Or was he, against all odds, a courageous man?

It was hard to tell by looking at him. Rashid was a hulking figure, resembling a professional wrestler. His round head, thick neck and sloping mustache—and hands the size of catcher's mitts—gave him an even more imposing aura. He wore a pale green tunic that wrapped around him like a tent.

The Americans followed close behind him. Major General Richard Zilmer, the commander of thirty thousand marines in Anbar, and Colonel Sean MacFarland, who oversaw Ramadi, hovered about Rashid as if he was their only friend in the world. Which, at the moment, he was.

"The governor is a powerful symbol of progress," General Zilmer said, delicately. I felt bad for Zilmer: He was in charge of an annihilated city. His men were dying at a rate of thirty a month.

Rashid sat behind his desk, Zilmer and me on the couch, MacFarland across the room. The governor was already working, moving papers, signing things, ordering a row of subordinates who hung by the door.

"Go ahead," Zilmer said. "Ask your question."

I started with the obvious, which is to say I went right for the jugular. Governor Rashid, I said, your immediate predecessor, Raja Nawaf, was kidnapped and murdered. Your deputy, Talib al-Dulaimi, was shot to death. Three months ago, the chairman of the provincial council was killed. Just last month, your personal secretary was beheaded. What makes you think you'll survive?

"I am the lawful authority here," Rashid said, offering a non sequitur. "I am the governor."

I was already starting to like him. Anyone who gave me a straightforward answer wouldn't have taken the job.

"I am from Ramadi," Rashid said. "I've been an engineer for twenty-eight years. The people know me and respect me—I am related to many of them. It is the criminals who don't like me."

They've tried to kill you twenty-nine times, I reminded him.

"I am a Dulaim," Rashid said, referring to the dominant tribe in Anbar Province. "We don't kill each other. They are all my relatives. I know them all the way to the border."

Rashid was a restless man, squirming in his chair, answering but not looking at me. I won't have him for very long, I thought.

Who is trying to kill you then?

"The terrorists, people like Zarqawi, I told you," he said, glancing at his watch. "They are not mujahideen, they are Ali Baba."

He laughed at his own joke. Ali Baba was a famous thief in Arabic literature.

My time was running short. General Zilmer, next to me, was starting to sigh.

Okay, Governor, I asked, Anbar Province is 98 percent Sunni Arab. The overthrow of Saddam Hussein put a new government in Baghdad that is dominated by Shiites. Isn't Anbar doomed to the status of a rump state? Aren't you doomed, too?

He was squirming again.

"Everyone thinks that Anbar Province was a pro-Saddam place," he said. "But Saddam wanted to have the only say here, he wanted to have his personal rule. A lot of the tribes, they didn't agree with him. He dealt with the tribes brutally. He did not respect laws, did not respect traditions—only himself.

"Since 2003, there has been no law here in Ramadi, no order—only chaos," Rashid said. "The tribal leaders are looking for a way to protect themselves. The law cannot protect them. That is all. It is a confusing time, a time in flux.

"So that is the challenge," Rashid said, pushing himself up from the desk. "People are trying to choose between the old and the new, between anarchy and the constitution."

It was the summer of 2006, more than three years after the Americans arrived. I'd given up hope long ago that anyone in the American military knew any better than I did. Outside, Anbar seemed hopeless. Ramadi lay in ruins. But there seemed something authentic in Rashid, something lacking in the exiles who lived their cloistered lives in Baghdad.

I didn't know Rashid from the next sheikh. Until I came to

Ramadi I had never heard of him. In Anbar, everyone claimed to be a Dulaim; everyone *was* a Dulaim. But, sitting behind his desk—driving through the rubble to work—Rashid seemed as tough and as ruthless as any of the people who were trying to kill him. He didn't live in the Green Zone; he lived in his own house, with his two wives and seven children, in a city that looked like Dresden. He drove to work in his own car. He carried his own gun. He didn't care what I thought; he didn't care what anyone thought. It wasn't difficult to see why the Americans had latched on to him, whoever he was.

A pair of soldiers walked into the room. They were carrying a life-size cutout of John Wayne, the American movie icon. It was one of those giant cutouts you stand next to at theme parks and get your picture taken. No matter where you went in the Middle East, no matter what people thought of America, everyone loved American movies. In Iraq, they loved macho guys—Stallone and Schwarzenegger. The Duke was wearing a ten-gallon hat and a white kerchief round his neck and a gunbelt low round his waist. He was grinning like he'd just shot a bunch of cattle rustlers.

General Zilmer and Colonel MacFarland stood up. They were smiling at each other; it was their little surprise. The governor remained behind his desk, standing, looking bewildered, like a confused wrestler. The soldiers propped the John Wayne photo on the floor and stepped out of the way.

General Zilmer cleared his throat.

"Colonel MacFarland has told me that you, like me, are a fan of John Wayne," he said to the governor. "He was, as you know, a tough guy like you are, a sheriff in a bad neighborhood, and he gave the bad guys nightmares."

Someone translated for Rashid. It took a minute or so. The governor listened, thought for a second and finally got the joke. He walked around his desk. The three real warriors gathered round the fake one, smiled together and posed for a picture.

COLONEL FRANK CORTE looked around the room and took stock: six of thirty-nine ministers of the Anbar provincial government had showed up for the meeting. Marines outnumbered Iraqis. Corte took a deep breath and turned to Governor Rashid.

"I'm very glad to see your directors general here today," said Colonel Corte, putting the best face on things. "They are very brave men."

The first topic was a series of school renovation projects in the neighborhoods of Tamim and Qaldiyah. The work on several of the jobs had stopped.

"Our workers are being intimidated," one of the Iraqi ministers said.

Rashid twisted his head. "I'm surprised," he said.

The minister shrugged. Another marine broke in.

"We tracked down the contractor in Baghdad, and he says he's going to do the work," the marine said.

"Why is he not getting the job done?" Rashid asked.

The discussion moved to another series of school renovation projects in the towns of Hit, Ramadi and Haditha. The work on several of them had stopped.

"On the school in Haditha, we have had to put that on hold," one of the marines said.

"Why aren't these schools being rebuilt?" Rashid asked, looking at the Americans, at the Iraqis.

"Somebody is threatening the contractors," the marine said.

Rashid glowered. The schools had to be ready when the school year started in two months, he said. "We need to put pressure on the contractors."

The ministers looked at each other.

"There is a tremendous amount of fear and intimidation," Corte told the governor. "We need to be able to say, Your family won't be killed, your workers won't be killed. We can't really say that."

"Isn't it possible to protect these people?" Rashid asked.

"We're working on that," Corte said. "Sometimes it's like plowing water in the sand."

They moved to the next topic: the bank robbery. "Yesterday, about 10 billion Iraqi dinars disappeared from the Rafidain Bank in downtown Ramadi," one of the marines said. "That's about $7 million."

"It's most of the bank's deposits," Rashid said.

"How did they do that?" Colonel MacFarland asked. "There is an American overwatch post right next door. You'd need several trunks to carry out that much money. Did anyone see anything?"

"Apparently no one saw anything," Governor Rashid said.

"There were more than 150 people in the bank that day," Colonel Corte said. "That doesn't sound right to me, Governor."

The governor agreed.

"It is hard to believe that with this much military presence next door, they could do this," Rashid said. "It must have been an inside job."

MacFarland weighed in again. "People's life savings were in there," he said. "Were the deposits insured?"

The governor allowed himself a small smile.

"In Iraq, we don't have that," he said.

After an hour, the meeting ended. We stood up and gathered near the front door.

A marine gave the usual warning.

"Sniper area—run!" he shouted, and everyone leaving the meeting ran.

THE MARINES GATHERED at battalion headquarters to hear the plan. The reporters were sworn to secrecy. Inside the briefing room stood a large map of Saddam Hospital in Ramadi.

"Five hundred rooms and a whole shitload of people," one of the officers said.

He turned to the map.

"We think there are terrorists in there," he said. "Torture chambers in the basement."

Before dawn, the Americans assembled, more than three hundred marines and soldiers. Under the night sky they climbed into their Bradleys and into the backs of the seven-ton trucks, smeared mud on their faces and checked their rifles a final time. Special Forces teams moved first to take out the snipers. A ripple passed through the company. This might be big, they were saying.

One of the officers mentioned that some Iraqi army soldiers would be coming along, twenty-seven of them, but I didn't see them at the briefing. As we climbed into the trucks, there was still no sign of them.

"I think they're totally worthless, but that's just my personal opinion," Major Thomas Hobbs, the Third Battalion's executive officer, said.

At 3 a.m., the marines swarmed into the hospital. They surrounded the complex and rushed inside for maximum surprise. They broke the locks on all the doors, to the supply rooms, the operating rooms, the patient wards. The marines ran to the top of the building and fanned out across all nine of its floors. They set up machine-gun posts at each end of each floor to isolate the violence in case things got out of control.

They didn't find much. A garbage bag full of bomb triggers and cell phones had been hidden behind a ceiling panel. The marines made a big deal out of that. There were no torture chambers in the basement. No terrorists. The marines corralled the hundred-odd Iraqi patients, mostly befuddled old people. They shuffled down to the first-floor lobby, where they sat on the floor and waited, none saying a word. A few of the patients couldn't make the trip, like Ahmed Sala, a sixteen-year-old who'd been shot in the gut. He said he'd been hit by an American sniper, which made sense, but there was no way to know.

"I was going to my dad's shop," he said. "I was walking through the cemetery." The cemetery was a big insurgent hangout. His stomach was bloated and his skin was hard and shiny. He was sweating.

"He's septic," one of the doctors said.

About an hour later, after they'd let the reporters in and the hospital was mostly secure, I saw the Iraqi soldiers. I was on the first floor when they came sauntering in. The Americans told me later the Iraqis had gone in with them. They looked good: nice uniforms, well trained. The Iraqi soldiers fanned out and began searching the rooms the Americans had left for them. I tagged along with them for a while. With the Americans looking on, the Iraqi soldiers kicked open each ward door with great precision and swung their rifles inside and stormed in, to find only emptiness.

After about an hour of this I wandered over to one of the

empty wards on the seventh floor. Some of the Iraqi soldiers were already sleeping there. It was after 4 a.m. I leaned up against the wall and slid down. I stretched out my legs and closed my eyes. Before long, I noticed that a couple more Iraqi soldiers had joined me, about a half dozen in all. We had a good nap. The marines didn't say a word.

That morning, the Americans sent out a press release. I didn't see it until much later, after I got back to Baghdad.

"Early this morning Iraqi Security Forces, with support from Coalition forces, began searching a hospital in northern Ramadi, which was being used as a center for insurgent activity," the release said. "This Iraqi Army–led operation will deny the insurgents use of the Saddam Hospital."

CHAPTER 20

The Turning

FOR ALL THE ANARCHY of the place, it was sometimes easy to miss the changes. A new checkpoint went up on Sadoon Street, Al-Qaeda crept into Adamiyah: those were easy. The deeper changes were more difficult to spot: the shifts in the culture, the turnings inside people's brains. The confusion lay in the violence. After witnessing a car bomb, or wading through a bloody emergency room, I sometimes forgot that the violence in Iraq had a shape; that it had direction, that the violence had purpose. So much violence and so many purposes, all of them competing and crashing into one another, reshaping the country in their own distinctive ways. In the madness, it was sometimes hard to see.

And so it was one afternoon in late 2005 when I drove to the Um al-Qura Mosque to see Harith al-Dhari, the head cleric there. The Um al-Qura, just off the airport road in western Baghdad, stood as the unofficial headquarters of the Sunni insurgency; Dhari, an austere, humorless figure, was its voice. On the surface, the Um al-Qura maintained no connection to the young men with guns, but the mosque served as the closest thing the movement had to a political headquarters. Dhari and his like-minded imams regularly called press conferences to denounce the Americans and demand that Iraqi prisoners be released. Iraqis came from miles around to demonstrate in the mosque's parking lot. The Um al-Qura itself was a sprawling, ornate complex, constructed during

Saddam's time; its minarets were built to resemble the Scud missiles the dictator had fired into Israel during the first Gulf War. American soldiers regularly raided the Um al-Qura and detained its clerics, including Dhari. The back-and-forth, between occupier and occupied, seemed to go on with no end in sight.

Then one winter day while waiting to see Dhari I noticed a crowd of Iraqi women gathered around an office next to the mosque. I moved in a little closer. Their faces hung slack and gray. They were holding little photos, and when they saw me they surged.

"The police took my son and he is gone!" a woman shouted, her eyes bulging red.

"Do you know anyone who can release one of my sons?" another moaned.

A woman held three fingers in the air.

"They took my three sons!" she said.

The cries rose and multiplied until they became a collective hysteria. The women were shouting: at me, at no one, at everyone, waving their photos. My son! In the tumult there was nothing to do, not even listen, and I left the grieving mothers in the office by the mosque.

But their message was clear, and I would go back to the little office again and again. The civil war was under way. It had taken months to get going and even more months to spot. After the elections in January 2005, the Shiite hard-liners who had taken power stuffed the ministries with their own gunmen, gave them uniforms and identification cards, and turned them loose. It was only then, in the cold of the Baghdad winter, in an office next to a Sunni mosque, that the evidence at last began to reveal itself, in the form of wailing mothers.

And hollow-eyed fathers. One of them was Ahmed al-Jabouri, whose son, Ali, had been taken away a few weeks before the father came to see me. There was open warfare now inside the Sunni neighborhoods, making them more or less off-limits. I sent Iraqis I worked with into the neighborhoods, where they could travel more safely, to bring people like Jabouri to me. It was safe inside our compound, comfort-

able and a little strange. It's not often that you listen to a crying father tell you the story of his disappeared son while sipping tea on an expensive couch.

"They came at 5 a.m.," Jabouri said as we sat together. He
was missing teeth and his face had a pinkish cast. "They had
three cars with dark windows. They were wearing uniforms.
One of them was wearing a mask. They kicked open our gate
and they began kicking the door, and that's when I answered
it. I asked them if they had come to loot my home, and they
said, No, we are from the Ministry of Interior.

"They threw me onto the floor, and one of them put a boot
to my head. And four of them went immediately for my son; it
was as if they knew where his bedroom was. He was in his
underwear. I was hoping they would allow his wife to look
decent first but they did not wait. He was recently married."

The *Times'* cook, Alan, entered the room with a tray of tea
and biscuits. Without looking, Jabouri took a cup.

"The man with the mask came in and pointed at my son
and said, 'Yes, this is the guy,'" Jabouri said. The police
roughed him up for a while, Jabouri continued, and then they
took him away.

"There were Ministry of Interior insignias on the doors of
the cars," he said.

"My son was not a member of the resistance—he was a
guard for a British company," Jabouri said. He spoke listlessly
now, as if he knew that it did not matter.

"The next day," Jabouri went on, "someone called and told
me to come to the morgue. That I would find my son there."

When he got there, Jabouri recalled, the bodies were piled
high, bodies fresh and bodies old. He looked at the faces and
also at their right arms, where his Ali wore a tattoo. It was a
good thing, the tattoo, because the faces, Jabouri said, had
been burned. "They were mutilated so that you could not recognize them," he said. His son was not among them.

A few weeks later, Jabouri said, his telephone rang again.
This time it was the police.

"'Your son is with us,' a voice said. 'We want $40,000. If
you talk to anyone, we will cut your son into pieces and throw
him at your front door.'"

Then, Jabouri said, the kidnappers played a tape of Ali's voice over the phone.

"Mother and father," Jabouri recalled the voice saying. "It is Ali."

Jabouri's face was still pink as he told his story, and, remarkably, his eyes still dry. I thought perhaps he had told the story many times already.

"And so I sold my house," he said. "For $20,000. It was not enough but I begged them."

After many phone calls and much negotiation, Jabouri drove to an intersection in a Shiite neighborhood, where he met a group of men he did not recognize. They were not wearing uniforms. In the car next to them was a young man.

"It was not my son," Jabouri said, and he had finally begun to tear. "I collapsed right there."

Not long after I spoke with Ahmed al-Jabouri, I drove to the offices of the Iraqi Islamic Party, the big Sunni political party. The party's compound was in Yarmouk, a mixed neighborhood that then was still relatively safe. There, in a small office on the second floor, I met Omar al-Jabouri.

Omar wasn't related to Ahmed, but he wore a troubled look just the same. At the door of his office stood a line of grieving parents not unlike the ones I'd encountered at the Um al-Qura mosque.

We talked for a while, then Omar rose from his desk and walked to a cabinet. He returned with a large book. It was a photo album. The first page was a tableau of photographs, of corpses with shriveled skin.

"These people were burned with acid," Omar said, pointing with his index finger.

Omar flipped the page. Another terrible photograph.

"This man, they used an electric drill," he said.

Another page.

"Can you see this?" Omar said, turning the book so I could see. "They drove nails into his head."

Finally, Omar sighed.

"They have invented new methods," he said.

. . .

ELECTRIC DRILLS were a Shiite obsession. When you found a guy with drill marks in his legs, he was almost certainly a Sunni, and he was almost certainly killed by a Shiite. The Sunnis preferred to behead, or to kill themselves while killing others. By and large, the Shiites didn't behead, didn't blow themselves up. The derangements were mutually exclusive.

With all that brutality, you might conclude that the sectarian war that swept the mixed cities of Iraq was a collective fever, a psychosis of ancient hatreds. It certainly became that. But in the beginning, the sectarian violence and the ethnic cleansing were almost entirely calculated. They were planned and mapped like a military campaign. The ethnic cleansing, for instance, was initiated by the Sunnis, who started expelling Shiites from their homes in the countryside around Baghdad. Then they moved in closer, into the mixed neighborhoods on the fringes of the capital.

The theory advanced by the Shiites in the government was that the Sunni insurgents were cleansing the mixed villages so they could operate more freely. A Sunni city cleansed of Shiites would be free of informers. "Intelligence-free zones," one Iraqi official called them.

To test the theory, I drove to a camp in the northern Baghdad neighborhood of Shoala, where Shiite families had fled from outside the capital. Only a few months before, the camp had been a vacant lot. The day I arrived it contained about six hundred people, all of them living in tents.

One of the newly arrived was Kharmut Hanoon, a forty-year-old farmer from Abu Ghraib, the Sunni city west of Baghdad known for its prison. Hanoon had abandoned his home and wheat fields after masked gunmen, driving Opel sedans, started killing Shiites in the neighborhood. "You cannot see their faces," Hanoon said to me, "just their eyes."

Hanoon was sharing a pair of tents with fourteen of his family members, including three grandchildren. Degradation was new to Hanoon, a proud and prosperous man. So was humiliation. Even in his tattered circumstances, he offered me a cup of tea. "Can you imagine that anyone would ever leave his home, for any reason?" Hanoon said, waving a cigarette as he spoke. "Only bad people and gypsies live in tents. What can you say about women having to live here? What can you say about the food?"

Whatever the motives of the people who expelled Hanoon, the effect on his own views seemed lasting and deep. His brain was turning. As he packed his belongings and prepared to leave his ancestral home, Hanoon said, not a single one of his Sunni neighbors stopped by to say goodbye.

"It's in their genes," Hanoon said. "It's a disease. They hate the Shiites. I don't think things will ever go back to normal between Shiites and Sunnis."

Once it got going, the sectarian war in Iraq developed its own vocabulary, its own rituals. Often, for instance, the cleansing of a neighborhood began with notes slipped under people's doors. Many of the refugees inside the camp in Shoala had been expelled this way. Ismail Shalash, for instance, was telling me his story when he reached into a folder and produced a note. Shalash was a father of three from Dora, a violent neighborhood on the edge of Baghdad that the insurgents had taken over.

"To the family of Abu Faisal," the note said, using Shalash's nickname. "You have to leave our neighborhood in forty-eight hours. This is your final warning." The note was signed: "The Islamic Army in Iraq." When he fled his neighborhood, Shalash had carried with him his most valuable belongings: his diploma, the family gold—and the little slip of paper that drove him away.

At the same time, a new bit of Arabic began slipping into the chatter of ordinary Iraqis: "allas." Literally, "one who chews." The word had come to denote an Iraqi who led a group of killers to their victim, a denouncer of sorts. Typically, the allas pointed out the Shiites living in a predominantly Sunni neighborhood for the gunmen who were hunting them.

"The allas is from the neighborhood, and he had a mask on," Haider Mohammed, a Shiite from Abu Ghraib, told me. "He pointed to my uncle." So the gunmen chased his uncle, Hussein Khalil, who had been driving in his Daewoo sedan. The gunmen ran Khalil off the road and shot him twice in the back of the head. Mohammed found his uncle facedown in a garbage dump.

Allas came into use during the summer of 2005, at the same time that Iraq's leaders were gathering in the Green Zone to write the country's new constitution. The constitution, of course, was all about words: "Islam," "federalism," "nation." Words that empowered nobody, restrained no one. All the while, outside the Green Zone, men with masks were busy pointing, creating whole new vocabularies of their own.

ONE DAY IN the spring of 2006, as I drove to the compound of Abdul Aziz Hakim, a small but startling change caught my eye. Hakim was the fish-eyed, Marlboro-smoking chief of the Supreme Council for the Islamic Revolution in Iraq, SCIRI, one of the big Shiite parties. Whenever I'd gone to his compound before, I had to allow myself to be searched by Hakim's guards, members of the Badr Brigade, SCIRI's Iranian-trained militia. It wasn't difficult to tell that the Badr gunmen were professional: when they were just standing around, for instance, they kept their index fingers locked straight above the triggers. Their camouflage uniforms were clean and pressed.

Now, the same guards were standing around out front. They carried the same Kalashnikovs, and they wore the same camouflage uniforms. Their fingers were over their triggers. The only difference was that patches had been sewn onto the shoulders of their tunics. "Ministry of Interior," they said.

"Self-incorporated." That was the phrase an American official used when I told him what I saw. Two thousand Badr gunmen, once employed by the Supreme Council, had just donned police uniforms. Or sewn patches onto the uniforms they already had. "The chain of command is basically intact," the American official said. "They answer to SCIRI."

That's how the civil war worked: the death squads became official. The Badr Brigade and the Mahdi Army, the two big Shiite militias, just joined the police forces of the Shiite-led government. It was like a revolving door, always spinning. One woman told me that her son had been taken away by the Iraqi police, and then, the next day, she'd received a phone call from a man claiming he was with the Mahdi Army. He said he had her son. He wanted ransom. She never got him back.

Another Iraqi woman recalled the night she watched from her window as a group of eight men wearing Iraqi army uniforms pulled up and parked their two cars, a black sport utility vehicle and a white sedan. From the back of the SUV, the woman said, the men in army uniforms hauled out a blindfolded passenger, who appeared to be alive, and moved him to the trunk of the sedan. Then the men shed their army uniforms, tossed them into the vehicles and drove away. "It's such a terrible situation," she said.

That the Shiites had turned the tables was not exactly lost on the Sunnis. One afternoon that same summer, word spread that a battalion of Shiite police were on their way to the Sunni neighborhood of Adamiyah. So the locals went for their guns. They dragged fallen date palms into some of the streets and piled bricks across others.

When the Shiite commandos finally came, wearing government uniforms, the men of Adamiyah were waiting for them. An all-night gun battle erupted, with dead on both sides. The commandos finally retreated. I couldn't go to Adamiyah anymore, so I had one of our drivers bring some of the Adamiyah locals to me.

"For us, as Sunni people, we know that if the police take you, they will interrogate you and shoot you," Mohammed Jaffar told me. He was twenty-four, educated and well-groomed.

It seemed straightforward enough: they just didn't want to die. And then, without prompting, the young Jaffar plunged into conspiracy theory. "The Shiites have a secret fifty-year plan to turn Iraq into an Islamic state like Iran. There will be very few Sunnis left in Iraq, and they will not be able to resist."

"Are you sure?" I asked him.

"Oh, yes," Jaffar said. "We know this from the Sunnis who live in Iran."

It wasn't just the Shiites frothing with revenge. The Sunnis had their own death squads, even the Sunnis in the government. The Iraqi government had given each of its twenty-seven ministries its own "facilities protection forces," 145,000 gunmen in all. Some of them were Shiite, some were Sunni.

One such group, the 16th Brigade, was charged with guarding the oil pipeline that ran into the refinery at Dora. The 16th Brigade was mostly Sunni, and it started carrying out assassinations of local Shiites. When their commander, Colonel Mohsin Najdi, tried to stop them, they killed him, too.

Among those who gathered in the Green Zone to write the constitution were Shiites, Kurds, current and former militia commanders, sheikhs in white robes and sayyids in black turbans, and even a representative of a tiny group that was said to worship angels. And, remarkably enough, there was a group of Sunni Arabs, too. One of them was Fakhri al-Qaisi.

Qaisi had an ear-to-ear beard, and he was a dentist with an easy laugh. The first time I met him, he was seated at a white plastic table in a café inside the Green Zone during a break from constitution drafting. Among the Sunnis, Qaisi was something of an anomaly: he was an adherent to the ultraconservative Salafist wing of Islam and he maintained links to the insurgents. But, unlike many of his Sunni cohorts, Qaisi was willing to deal with the Americans if he thought he could speed their departure from the country.

"Everyone is trying to kill me!" Qaisi said, shaking his head and laughing. "The Americans, the Shia, the Sunnis—everyone!"

It seemed probable enough. Qaisi being a Sunni fundamentalist with links to the insurgency, the Americans thoroughly mistrusted him. Seventeen times, Qaisi told me, the Americans had raided his office and homes. "The Americans even drove a tank into my dental office," he said, laughing again.

And Qaisi was being targeted by Shiite death squads. Only a week before, his brother had been gunned down in Baghdad. Qaisi suspected the Badr Brigade, the militia controlled by SCIRI. "I know for a fact that it was Badr," Qaisi told me.

As a Sunni cooperating with the Americans, Qaisi was being hunted by Sunni insurgents, too. The same week I met him, two of his Sunni colleagues on the constitution-drafting committee had been shot dead in the street.

Indeed, it was amazing how Qaisi survived at all. He lived in the western Baghdad neighborhood of Gazaliya, one of the city's most dangerous, without armed guards. To save himself, Qaisi had begun sleeping in his car, a white Toyota with a front seat that reclined. He had four wives, all of them in separate houses, and he typically dropped in on one of them during his drives around the capital.

"I keep my enemies guessing," he said, brightening again.

As Qaisi and I talked, a group of four Iraqi men sat down at a plastic table next to ours. One of them I recognized immediately: Hadi al-Amari, the head of the Badr Brigade, the very militia Qaisi believed had murdered his brother.

Suddenly I felt an animal electricity in the air. Qaisi and Amari were eyeing each other.

Qaisi stood up; so did Amari. I wondered if they were armed.

"My friend," Qaisi said, "it is so good to see you."

"Yes, it has been a long time," Amari said.

The two men embraced and kissed each other on their bearded cheeks.

"We really must get together," Amari said.

"Yes, really, wc must," Qaisi said.

THAT SAME SUMMER, I rode into the area of the Green Zone known as Little Venice. The neighborhood, once home to Saddam's senior officials, was so called for the canals and bridges that crisscrossed its streets. It was now the place where Iraq's new leaders lived, including Barham Salih, the deputy prime minister. Salih, an Iraqi Kurd, was one of the straightest, hardest-working civil servants in all of Iraq. As the nation around him imploded, Salih, through savvy and will, was still able to make the government work. I was going to see Salih about the latest rumors of corruption that were racing around town, of Iraqi leaders spiriting hundreds of millions of dollars out of the country.

I walked into the courtyard of Salih's home, which was carpeted in bright, cropped grass, defying the summer heat. He was standing in the walkway, talking into his phone. He looked up and waved, as if to say, Not now.

"Yes, of course I understand, madam," Salih said into the phone. "We will do whatever we can."

He listened to the voice at the other end. Then he put his hand over the phone and spoke to one of his aides, Taha al-Hashemi.

"Take $5,000 out of the contingency budget," he said. "Cash."

Hashemi nodded and made a phone call, and Salih put the phone back to his ear.

"I am very sorry, madam," he said. "We will do whatever we can."

Then he hung up.

"It's a woman; her son's been kidnapped," Salih said to me. "He's thirteen. They're going to kill him today unless she pays them $5,000."

The woman, crazed with grief, had gone to a local mosque, where she'd spotted an Iraqi reporter for a Baghdad radio station. She begged and pleaded, and the reporter had given her Salih's number.

Salih laughed bitterly.

"I am the deputy prime minister of Iraq," he said, "and this is how I spend my days, paying ransom for mothers whose children have been kidnapped. You would be amazed how much time I spend on things like this."

In places like Dora, Gazaliya and Sadiya, the insurgents had taken to killing the garbagemen. It seemed strange at first that they would do that, kill a man who collected the trash. Then they started killing the bakers. In those places, naturally enough, the garbage piled up in the streets, heaps of it, mountains of it, and there wasn't any bread. Then they started killing the teachers, and the teachers stopped going to the schools. And the children stopped going, of course. So: no bread and no schools and mountains of trash. Ingenious, I guess, if you wanted to stop the functioning of a neighborhood.

Not long after, I talked about these things with Yusra al-Hakeem, one of the Iraqi interpreters I worked with. Yusra was one of my best Iraqi friends. She was bright, funny and loud, one of those Iraqis who had taken immediately to the new freedoms. And yet in the past year life had changed dramatically for Yusra, and Yusra had changed herself. A Shiite and a liberal, Yusra had begun wearing a long black abaya, which she loathed but which was necessary, she believed, to protect her from the militias in her neighborhood. Yusra usually tore it from her head the second she walked inside the *Times* compound. "Stupid thing," she'd say, hurling it onto the couch.

And now Yusra had decided to leave the country. At first she joked in her usual way. "After 1,400 years, the Shiites have had their chance, and look at the mess they made. The Shiites, they cannot govern Iraq—bring back the Sunnis!" And then a laugh. Yusra didn't mean it—she loathed Saddam. But the danger was different now, debilitating in a way it had not been during the years of Saddam.

"I am so tired," Yusra said. "In Saddam's time, I knew that if I kept my mouth shut, if I did not say anything against him, I would be safe. But now it is different. There are so many reasons why someone would want to kill me now: because I am Shiite, because I have a Sunni son, because I work for the Americans, because I drive, because I am a woman with a job, because"—she picked up her abaya—"I don't wear my stupid hejab."

She took my notebook and flipped it to a blank page. This was Yusra's way of explaining her situation and, sensing the limitations of language, she would sometimes seize a reporter's notebook and diagram her predicament. She drew a large circle in the middle.

"This was Saddam," she said. "He is here. Big. During Saddam's time, all you had to do was stay away from this giant thing. That was not pleasant, but not so hard."

She flipped to another blank page. She drew a dozen circles, some of them touching, some overlapping. A small galaxy. She put her pen in the middle and made a dot.

"The dot in the middle, that is me—that is every Iraqi," she said. "From everywhere you can be killed, from here, from here, from here, from here." She was stabbing her pen into the notepad.

"We Iraqis," she said. "We are all sentenced to death and we do not know by whom."

And so she would leave Iraq. For Jordan, for Syria—and then, if she was lucky, for America. All she was waiting for, she said, was for her son to graduate from university. He had one semester to go.

"And then," Yusra said, "my responsibility as a mother will be complete."

And we laughed.

CHAPTER 21

The Departed

NIGHTTIME in Anbar. No lights. A group of men and women gathered round a shed next to a landing strip. The sand muffled the sound of their steps. Most of the soldiers had just finished dinner; they'd left their guns and packs in their bunks. In a few minutes they would be in bed.

The doors swung open. Six soldiers stepped out. They carried a long black bag, zippered at the top. In the darkness, the bag was barely visible. A line of blue chemical lights marked the way to the landing strip.

The soldiers carrying the bag stepped into the sand; their feet made no sound. As they passed, the men and women saluted, even a wounded man on a stretcher. No one said a word.

A young man named Terry Lisk was in the bag. He was twenty-six, from a troubled home in Fox Lake, Illinois. That morning, Lisk had been standing in an intersection when a mortar shell landed about thirty paces away. A shard of metal had pierced the soft spot under his right arm, in the narrow strip between the armor plates.

"What's his name?" Colonel Sean MacFarland, his commander, had said then. "What's his name?"

Lisk was already on his way to the field hospital. A few minutes later he died. His friends said he'd had a sense of humor.

The pallbearers lifted the bag into the back of an ambulance, a green truck marked by a large red cross. Then they fell in with the others. The ambulance began creeping silently across the sand, and everyone gathered behind it and walked. The blue lights showed the way.

From a distance came the sound of a helicopter. Without lights, it shimmered gray in the moonlight. How quiet helicopters could be in the desert at night; a whisper in the wind. With its engines still whirring, it landed, then it lowered its back door.

The six soldiers walked out to the chopper and lifted the bag into it. The door went back up. The helicopter flew away.

The soldiers saluted a final time.

In the darkness, as the sound of the helicopter faded, Colonel MacFarland walked to the front of the group.

"I don't know if this war is worth the life of Terry Lisk, or 10 soldiers, or 2,500 soldiers like him," the colonel said. "What I do know is that he did not die alone.

"A Greek philosopher said that only the dead have seen the end of war," Colonel MacFarland said. "Only Terry Lisk has seen the end of this war."

The soldiers turned and walked back to their barracks in the darkness. No one said a word.

THE SHAMOON FAMILY gathered in the parking lot of their apartment complex. An orange and white GMC sport utility vehicle was waiting with its back door open. It was half filled already with provisions. Basil, the father, wearing a purple Izod shirt, lifted a fifty-pound sack of rice and shoved it in. Iman, the mother, swung a clear plastic suitcase up and inside. Inside the apartment, two of the children, Brian and Bright, sat in states of half sleep on the couch, while the younger ones, Ban and Yusuf, lay asleep on the tile floor. It was dawn, before the heat. Basil's mother, Miriam, was already outside, standing in her nightgown, muttering to herself in Syriac, the language of the Chaldean Christians. The driver, hired to take the family through the desert, leaned against his GMC and watched as the Shamoons prepared to leave.

"Make sure you don't forget the blankets," Miriam said.

The day before, I sat with the Shamoons while they told me their story. We're leaving in the morning, they'd said. I was feeling a weird sense of urgency; people were leaving the capital in such numbers and so quickly that I felt it might be empty soon.

The Shamoons lived in Zayouna, Christians in a Shiite neighborhood in eastern Baghdad. When I got there, the garbage was piled in heaps in the courtyard of the complex, called the Zayouna Flats, and dozens of wires crisscrossed their way to a gasoline-powered generator. The electricity had recently improved, the Shamoons said: nine families had left for Syria in the past month, which had freed up some of the generator's capacity. Three children in the neighborhood had been kidnapped as well; two of them had been released, one of them killed.

"It's not an easy thing for me to leave my country," Basil said. He sat on a couch in his Izod shirt. Iman sat at the other end in her blue jeans and T-shirt. Her hair fell around her shoulders. Bright and Ban sat between them.

"But even Jesus said that if you are not safe in your country, then find another one to live in."

The Shamoons recited a now familiar story. There was Majida, Basil's sister, whose family ran a beauty salon in Dora until she started getting threats from the fundamentalists. She'd fled to Syria. There was Nabil, Iman's brother, who ran a wine shop in Karada until it was bombed. There were the two nephews, Sami and Rami, ages six and three, who died in a mortar attack near the Sadeer Hotel. And so on and so forth, a death here and a kidnapping there, until a note was slipped under their own door a few weeks before. "You're next," it said, "either you or your boy."

"We don't know which insurgent group," Basil said, and he and Iman looked at each other for a second.

I asked Basil why. Why would they do that?

He looked down at the tile floor. Iman looked into the distance. One of the children squirmed on the couch, and Basil looked up.

"I don't care about myself," he said. "Only my children."

I had a feeling there was something they weren't telling me, but there didn't seem much point in pressing them. And so at dawn the next morning I was there to watch as they stuffed the GMC and prepared to go to Damascus. Basil's brother, Tariq, had come over, and he'd brought his wife and children, and the men loaded the truck: with carpets, a gas stove, a family-size box of corn flakes. Basil's mother and his father stood in their nightclothes, too old to offer their labor.

Iman went inside to get the children. In a few minutes she came out, and she and Basil placed them in the small pockets that remained in the overstuffed GMC. They had not yet found a place for Ban.

"We will lose our relationship outside of Iraq," Iman said to Miriam, her mother-in-law. "It will crumble."

"No, no, my love," Miriam said, and they embraced and cried.

Miriam looked on as the Shamoon family climbed in and the driver started the engine. Her eyes seemed to be searching the GMC, as if she was counting the number of children.

"They tried several times to leave, and I told them not to go—this is our country," Miriam said, her eyes still searching the truck. "How can you leave it?"

Then she began to mumble to herself again in Syriac, her eyes still wet.

As the driver revved his engine, the neighbors came out into the courtyard. Others gathered on their balconies on the second and third floors. They waved.

Carpets were jutting out the back of the GMC; the side windows were blocked by boxes. Basil climbed into the front passenger seat; he put Ban on his lap.

"Take care of Father," Basil said to Tariq.

The GMC began to roll forward, and Miriam and Tariq's wife stepped forward with pitchers of water, which they used to splash the back of the GMC. It was a Middle Eastern tradition: Come back safely, it meant. The GMC rolled forward slowly, and the two women followed it into the parking lot in their bare feet, emptying the last of their pitchers.

"We will pray for you," Miriam said, before slipping into Syriac again.

AT THE END of a long week, I went searching for her tomb. I spoke first to the priest at the Armenian Orthodox Church, who pointed me to a cemetery down the road. I went there, and a toothless, old, blue-eyed lady pointed me to the next one. Then, in the quiet of a compound off clamorous Tehran Square, I found her.

Gertrude Margaret Lowthian Bell—or Miss Bell, as the Iraqis still called her—lay in the Anglican church's cemetery in a raised tomb. She had been decisive in the creation of the modern Iraqi state, imagining it in the ruins of the Ottoman Empire, and she'd allowed herself to be buried here when she died. I kept a few books on Miss Bell, and she seemed, in those grayish photographs, a mythic figure, drawing borders, conjuring nations.

"I feel at times like the Creator about the middle of the week," Miss Bell said. "He must have wondered what it was going to be like, as I do."

Mansour Ali, the grave keeper, walked me across the rocky cemetery ground to the foot of Miss Bell's tomb. It was summer, and her tomb was dried and crumbling in the Iraqi sun. The British delegations that had arrived to pay homage in the months after the invasion had stopped coming recently because of the danger. A ring of jasmine trees and date palms planted the year before by Ahmad Chalabi's daughter, Tamara, "in recognition of Gertrude Bell's historic contribution to Iraq," were mostly dead.

"The soil is too salty," Ali said. He jabbed a finger into the earth.

Then I drove north, into the Waziriya neighborhood of northern Baghdad. There, the British war cemetery sat in a fenced-in field across the road from the Turkish Embassy. In the hour before sunset, the gates were high and locked, so I rattled and banged. After a few minutes, a man named Jasim Koli appeared, and he let me in.

A thousand graves stretched out in rows. The tombstones stood three feet high, with the chiseled faces of some too worn to read. Some were toppled and crumbling. In some places the grass reached to my chest.

I walked among them, stopping here and there. The story of each man was reduced to fit on the face of a headstone, but it was still large enough to suggest its own epic:

George Percy Wilder
Middlesex Regiment
11th July 1918 Age 38
In ever loving memory
of my only child
From his sorrowing
Widowed mother

Most of those buried in the cemetery were younger than Wilder by twenty years. About a dozen were unidentified: "Here Lies a Soldier of the Great War," the headstones read. "Known unto God."

At 6 p.m., when the sun had cooled, a crew of Iraqis filed inside. They held scythes, and they began to hack the tall grass. Every couple of weeks, the Iraqis said, a man showed up to pay them. When an American died in this war, he was flown home in a black bag, zippered at the top; the British, killed long ago, were buried across the old realm from here to Trincomalee. There hadn't been any refrigeration then, and the ships had been too slow. The British were buried where they fell.

I walked past a metal sign, dated November 20, 1997, announcing a renovation. It was pockmarked with bullet holes. I stopped at the northeast corner before an inscription, cut into a large stone, which explained the presence of about two hundred more graves.

These here have been recovered
And interred
The bodies of
British officers and men
Who after the fall of Kut
Being prisoners
In the hands of the Turks
Perished during the march
From Kut
Or in the prison camps
Of Anatolia
These are they who came
Out of great tribulation

I walked over to the northwest corner, toward a stone pagoda. It had been built for Stanley Maude, the commander of the Mesopotamia Expeditionary Force. Maude had lost thirty thousand men, the inscription said. He died of cholera, a year before the war ended.

A gunshot rang out. Then another. Koli waved, and I started back to the car, pausing once more before I was gone.

Private J. Bleakley
Royal Army Ordnance Corps
6th July 1918 Age 21
He Died for Us

Laika

IN CAMBRIDGE, I go running at night, when the city is quiet. It's quiet during the day; at night more so. After 10 p.m. I run down the residential streets, passing the homes, and listen to the padding of my own shoes. There are hardly any cars. The people of Cambridge have built quiet lives for themselves here; built homes that keep out the sound. Their yards are trimmed and carefully demarcated.

One night, running down a street near the Harvard campus, I encountered a skunk. It was standing in front of someone's house. I had never seen a skunk outside of a picture book. Its hair was soft and black, like a cat's, with the bold white stripe. I stopped to look at it for a while, braving its foul spray, and the skunk allowed me to do this for several minutes before slinking into some bushes.

Sometime after that, in the afternoon, a hawk began appearing on the Harvard campus, landing on the larger buildings and monuments like Memorial Hall. It was a large red-tailed hawk, with wide wings, and it announced its presence with a shriek. I often heard it while walking out of Widener Library at lunchtime. I was usually the only person who seemed to notice. The hawk's cry was plaintive but edgy; I thought that perhaps he had lost his way and was expressing confusion at this world without trees. One day, when Widener was closed, the hawk followed me a half mile to the law school. The hawk soared past me a few times and landed on a rooftop and a steeple and gave out a cry. By the end of summer he was gone.

In the library, the chairs are soft and full, a café serves French pastries, and at the front door a machine dispenses plastic bags to cover your umbrella when you come in from the rain. Across the street sits Memorial Hall, a Gothic structure whose walls are adorned by plaques with the names of 136 Harvard students killed during the American Civil War. One of them was Robert Gould Shaw, who led one of the first regiments of freed slaves. I saw the names, engraved in marble, when I first arrived at Harvard and took the guided tour. I went back several times after that, but each time I found the building closed.

One day, Ashley, the Australian photographer and my friend from Falluja, called on the phone. He asked me what I did in Cambridge and when I told him there was a silence on the line. Ash took the train up from New York, and we went into Widener Library together and he took a photo of me at one of the long wooden tables, among my notebooks. We got drunk that night and Ash slept on my couch. He left the next day.

I tried to stay in touch with my Iraqi friends, even some of the Afghans and Pakistanis. Waleed, who drove me all over Iraq and saved me from the mob that day, sent his family to live in Syria. He stayed in Baghdad, moving from house to house, trying to stay safe. I always forgot Waleed was a Sunni; he made me forget he was a Sunni. Being a Sunni in Baghdad was not a good thing to be.

Many of my Iraqi friends are out. Warzer Jaff, my Clint Eastwood interpreter, survivor of Falluja and Najaf and the wars against Saddam, lives in an apartment on Central Park West in Manhattan. It was a long story; he married an American woman, one of the *Times'* reporters. He kept going back to Iraq. One day, walking through Central Park, I ran into him quite unexpectedly. He was sitting on a bench, holding a new puppy—a King Charles Spaniel, he said.

Zaineb Obeid, one of the *Times* interpreters, ended up in Hamilton, Ontario; I am not sure how she got there. She wrote to say she was applying for a scholarship at McMaster

University and that she'd fallen on the ice and broken her ankle. "Just got out from the hospital after they have put in plates and screws, imagine!!!!" she said.

Abdul Razzaq al-Saiedi, whose brother was hanged by Saddam, came to Harvard to study for a graduate degree. Razzaq walked more upright at Harvard than he ever did in Iraq, and on some days I did not recognize him. Sometimes, when we'd get into conversations in Cambridge, he would interrupt me, something he never did before. That gave me a little thrill. The war in Iraq was not popular at Harvard, and more than a few times when a well-meaning student proclaimed the American invasion a moral disaster, and Islam peaceful in its heart, Razzaq rose to instruct them. He wore a dark Calvin Klein jacket to protect him from the cold, one his American girlfriend had picked out for him in an outlet mall in the suburbs.

Yusra al-Hakeem, who drew the diagrams to explain her life with Saddam and without, sent word that she'd won a scholarship to study in the United States. I had written her a recommendation. "I believe you added much of your flavor but I am happy although it is more than what I was," she said. After she won, Yusra sent me a photo of herself from a lunch with the American ambassador and the other Fulbright Scholars. She was wearing more makeup than I had ever seen her wear before. Her hair was uncovered and styled, and she was smiling broadly.

Khawar Mehdi, a Pakistani interpreter with whom I was arrested in 2002, and who was subsequently expelled from his country, took a job at a 7-Eleven in Washington, D.C. He spent most of his time on the phone talking to his friends back in Pakistan. Khawar called me whenever he learned something interesting. He didn't think he would ever be able to go back, no matter who became prime minister.

Majeed Babar, another Pakistani I'd hired after the Afghan war in 2002, somehow made his way to the United States, too. I'd heard the government in Pakistan had gone after him, and that there was some fear he would be killed. I'd fallen out of touch with him, and then one day while I was eating lunch in *The New York Times* cafeteria in Manhattan, he tapped me on the shoulder. "It's me!" he said with the same smile as before, and for a moment I thought I was in Tora Bora. He had a job sorting mail.

For months after my return I searched for Farid Yusufzai, the young Afghan doctor who told me about the Arabs in Kabul back in the summer of 2000. We'd been arrested by the Taliban; I'd been expelled and he had been imprisoned and beaten horrendously in front of my eyes on a street in downtown Kabul. And then, a few months later—I was already back in the United States—Farid escaped. I'd helped him flee to America. The last time I had spoken to him was in September 2001, shortly after the attacks, and he told me he'd moved to a small town in West Virginia to marry a woman with blond hair that ran down her back. Then I lost touch.

Seven years later, after coming home from Iraq, I'd searched everywhere for Farid, scanning databases and property records and driver's licenses. I'd plundered the memories of Afghan exile leaders from Washington to Los Angeles. No luck. And then one day Farid found me. We had a long talk on the phone. He had just completed medical school in Atlanta and was beginning his residency in a local hospital. The marriage to the West Virginia gal was going strong; he had a five-year-old daughter named Swelina. "Yes, I am amazed at how well it's all worked out," Farid said.

Then there was Khalid Hassan, a Palestinian Iraqi who worked for the *Times* in Baghdad. One summer day on his way to work he was shot and killed by a group of gunmen who pulled alongside his car. Khalid lived in Saidiya, a Sunni-Shiite neighborhood that was being contested by insurgents on both sides.

Khalid was loud, fat, twenty-three and fearless, and he had taken to America and its gadgets and its liberties like no other son of the Muslim world I had ever met. He was a night owl, and so was I, and on many nights I would wander into the *Times'* Baghdad newsroom at one or two in the morning, and I'd find him sitting there, looking like an American teenager lost in his own world. He'd be surfing the web and talking on his cell phone and sending a text message and maybe eating a bowl of popcorn with melted butter. The two television sets in the newsroom, which were supposed to be tuned to news channels like Al Arabia or Al Jazeera, would inevitably have been switched to the Movie Channel and MTV. If I asked Khalid to do something for me he'd put his phone down and look at me like I was a burdensome parent. And I'd shake my head and say, "Khalid, if you moved to America, your life would not change." And we'd laugh. It was our little joke. There was no other Iraqi I ever said that to.

Once, as I was preparing to leave Baghdad for New York, Khalid asked me to mail a package for him to a woman in the United States. She lived in Pensacola, Florida. What was inside, I asked him? "Iraqi gifts for my sweetheart," he replied. It turned out he had met an American woman on an Internet dating site and spent a romantic weekend in Amman, Jordan: the dream of every Arab male. She was big, too, like Khalid, and married to an American soldier in Iraq at the time.

Then Khalid asked me about the TV series *Sex and the City*. I told him I'd never managed to see an episode. Khalid gave me a funny look. "I've seen every episode two or three times." He said he was quite envious that I was going to New York, with all its beautiful people and easy ways. And I told Khalid, "America is not like that. That's just a TV show." And he looked at me and said with the authority of a pop-culture maven: "Oh yes it is!"

When I was in Iraq, I might as well have been circling the earth from a space capsule, circling in farthest orbit. Like Laika in Sputnik. A dog in space. Sending signals back to base, unmoored and weightless and no longer keeping time. Home was far away, a distant place that gobbled up whatever I sent back, ignorant and happy but touchingly hungry to know. And then I was back, back in the world with everyone else, looking back on the ship myself though not returning all the way, still floating like Laika, through the regular people in the regular world.

Back in the world, people were serious, about the fillings in their sandwiches, about the winner of last night's ballgame. I couldn't blame them, of course. For me, the war sort of flattened things out, flattened things out here and flattened them out there, too. Toward the end, when I was still there, so many bombs had gone off so many times that they no longer shocked or even roused; the people screamed in silence and in slow motion. And then I got back to the world, and the weddings and the picnics were the same as everything had been in Iraq, silent and slow and heavy and dead. Your dreams come alive, though, when you come home. Your days may die but your dreams explode. Not with any specific recollections; they were more the by-products of the raw material I carried back. Rarely anything I ever actually saw.

People asked me about the war, of course. They asked me whether it was as bad as people said. "Oh, definitely," I told them, and then, usually, I stopped. In the beginning I'd go on a little longer, tell them a story or two, and I could see their eyes go after a couple of sentences. We drew closer to each other, the hacks and the vets and the diplomats, anyone who'd been over there. My friend George, an American reporter I'd gotten to know in Iraq, told me he couldn't have a conversation with anyone about Iraq who hadn't been there. I told him I couldn't have a conversation with anyone who hadn't been there about anything at all.

After I got back I called the mother of a marine I'd gotten to know over there, a nineteen-year-old from a small town in Georgia, and when I told her who I was she told me she'd framed the story I had written about her son in Iraq and hung it on the wall.

After he'd come home, for about six weeks or so, she had him sleep in bed with her, on account of his nightmares. He'd turn in his sleep and sweat and moan, and sometimes scream, and she'd hold him and look at him and try to help him ride out the terrible storms. She seemed kind of embarrassed for telling me that, but I didn't mind.

The soldiers and their wives and the moms and the dads: they wanted to talk. Maybe nobody else did but they did. Back in the world, there was a kind of underground conversation about Iraq and Afghanistan. Underground and underclass. The rest of the country didn't much care. In Pearland and Osawatomie and LaGrange, Iraq and Afghanistan lived on, and people wanted to talk. I think they liked talking to me because I wasn't one of them; I came from Cambridge, not

Osawatomie. They were tired of talking to each other. I was tired of talking to myself.

They were always happy when I called. And they wrote letters. Some of the notes had a pleading quality, like the ones from John Knospler, father of Jake, who lost his jaw and part of his brain. "Would you, could you, can you, and will you publish my Son's predicament so he can finally receive the treatment needed to get back the quality of life he deserves to have!" Yeah.

Most of the grunts I knew left the military as soon as they could, so they didn't have to go back to Iraq. Most of them, the ones I talked to, seemed about the same as I was, floating Laika-like among the normals. Ralph Logan, the corporal who'd refused to throw some Iraqis into the Tigris, robbed that hotel lobby in Ohio at knifepoint. I couldn't blame him for that. Scott Nolin, one of the marines, became a cop in New York City, which sounded like a good fit to me. A year or so later I called him and he told me he was driving down to his old base, Camp Lejeune, to see his buddies, and I could hear it in his voice. Are you going back in? I asked him. "Ah, hell, I'm thinking about it," he said.

I visited Billy Miller one last time. I flew to Little Rock and rented a car and drove north to Greenbrier, in the foothills of the Ozarks. Susie and Lewis, his parents, met me there. The Millers were officially still living in Pearland, where Billy's sister, Sabrina, lived, and where his name was emblazoned on a plaque in town. But since Billy was here, in the family cemetery, they'd taken to renting an apartment nearby. When I steered my Chevrolet Cobalt into the June Beene apartments, Susie walked out into the parking lot to greet me. She was wearing a bright red T-shirt with a Marine Corps insignia and Billy's name sewn into it.

The Millers joked and smiled, they talked of Billy and his life, almost as if he were still there. Their cheerfulness was relentless. They did not flinch. I told them I thought about Billy every day, about how he had taken a bullet for me and Ash. Stepped in front of us so we could get a photograph. "He was just doing his job," Susie said. "He died doing what he wanted to do." She was ready for that one. I gathered the cheerfulness was a front, a Potemkin thing, and one whose construction had come at no small effort. Still, it made me sad, even a little frustrated.

We drove out to the cemetery and walked out to Billy's grave. There was a tombstone made of rose granite, adorned by an American flag and a bouquet of plastic flowers. Onto the face of the granite the Millers had emblazoned a pair of photos of Billy—one solemn, the other smiling—which were protected by sliding metal covers the shape of teardrops. The cemetery dated back to the middle of the nineteenth century, and there were many former soldiers there; even, in the back, in unmarked tombs, a handful of family slaves. We ate catfish at a local restaurant. The Millers gave me a couple of magnetic stickers they'd made up after Billy's death, an American flag and a ribbon and a photo of Billy. "For your refrigerator or car or whatever," Lewis said. I hugged Susie and promised her I'd come back, Ashley and I both. Lewis led me through Conway in his truck and out to the interstate. I pulled over right before I got onto the freeway to shake hands, and I looked back and waved one more time as I merged with the passing cars.

ACKNOWLEDGMENTS

WRITING ANY BOOK IS A JOURNEY, and this one more than most, and if I acknowledged the kindness of every person I enjoyed in my nine years in the Middle East and South Asia, I would have to write another. Of all the pleasures I experienced in the world between Delhi and Suez, the one I treasure most is its extraordinary tradition of hospitality, which I enjoyed, almost without exception, whether stranger, friend or foe. In at least one way, I'll never go home again.

I am grateful to my bosses at *The New York Times*—Arthur Sulzberger, Jr., Bill Keller, Jill Abramson and Susan Chira—who gave me the time to write this book, and, more important, who help make the *Times* the extraordinary institution that it is. In this era of American war, no newspaper or television network has dedicated more resources to covering the conflicts, thought harder to understand them or given its reporters greater support. Thanks, too, to Gerry Marzorati and Scott Malcomson at the Sunday magazine, who sprang me for the big pieces and edited them with care.

The people at Alfred A. Knopf believed in this book, and in me, from the very beginning, and all the way until it hit the shelves. Jonathan Segal helped shape my unwieldy ideas and an even more unwieldy manuscript with a skill that seems to have otherwise vanished from the world. My agent, Amanda Urban, never wavered in her enthusiasm and support from the moment I met her.

I would have had very little to write at all had it not been for the help of the Iraqis, Afghans and Pakistanis who risked their lives so that I might understand the countries where they lived. They are comrades and friends. In Afghanistan, thanks to Abdul Waheed Wafa, Sultan Monadi and Ahmad Fahim Qasimi; and in Pakistan, Majeed Babar, Salman Massood, Khawar Mehdi and Rahimullah Yousafzai. Also, a warm embrace for Ashraf Ali, who miraculously calmed a gun-wielding Talib by gently stroking his beard.

In Baghdad, *The New York Times* bureau is a journalistic and logistical wonder, and I must tip my hat to the extraordinary Iraqis who risk their lives to make it work. They guided me, instructed me, protected me and humbled me. In particular, I want to thank Khalid al-Ansary, Thaier al-Daami, Mohammed Ezzat, Yusra al-Hakeem, Ali Adeeb Abdul Kader, Mona Mahmood, Qais Mizer, Omar al-Neami, Sahar Nageeb, Zaineb Obeid and Falih "Abu Malik" Hussein Wahieb. Thanks, too, to the sisters Alber: Marie, Eman and Rita.

I must single out the three Iraqis with whom I worked the most. Waleed al-Hadithi navigated Iraq's streets with aplomb and, at great risk to his own life, pulled me from certain death that day at the ICRC. Warzer Jaff led me through danger and complexity with shrewdness and charm. Abdul Razzaq al-Saiedi taught me more about Iraq—and its darkness—than anyone else.

To Fakher Haider and Khalid Hassan, my murdered colleagues, I promise never to forget you.

In Amman, I want to thank Ranya Kadri, for always coming through, and Nadia Huraimi, who spent a grueling tour in Iraq when the insurgency was finding its legs.

I benefited greatly from my *Times* colleagues in Baghdad, who have done such remarkable work in such horrendous conditions. Thanks, in particular, to Ian Fisher, Jim Glanz, Richard Oppel, Alissa Rubin, Kirk Semple, Sabrina Tavernise, Ed Wong and Bobby Worth. Above all, I want to thank John Burns, my colleague, mentor and friend, who imagined, created and presided over that miraculous enterprise. Without John, this book would not have been possible, and without John, I would probably not have survived. Thanks, too, to Jane Scott Long, who, in Kabul and Baghdad, did the hard work of setting up the bureaus and making them work.

In Afghanistan, thanks to David Rohde and Barry Bearak, and to Barnett Rubin of New York University for sharing his incomparable knowledge of the country.

At the *Los Angeles Times*, Simon Li, then the foreign editor, took a chance and sent me abroad. The late Anthony Day, then the editor of the editorial page, took an even bigger leap and gave me my start.

I am grateful to the many photographers with whom I have worked and for the fine company they made in hard places: Lynsey Addario, Christoph Bangert, Tyler Hicks, Michael Kamber, Chang Lee, Robert Sanchez, Johan Spanner, Joao Silva, and Stephanie Sinclair. James Hill was a companion in the invasions of both Iraq and Afghanistan, and until then I never knew what great friends war could make. To Ashley Gilbertson, with whom I endured the assault on Falluja, I am joined forever, in friendship and gratitude and sorrow.

In the three and a half years that I spent in Iraq, I met regularly with the nation's leaders, who always made time for me despite the more pressing work of trying to govern their country. Reporters are supposed to keep their distance, but in the inferno through which we passed the barriers fell away. Thanks to Ahmad Chalabi, Faisal Istrabadi, Raja al-Khuzai, Adel Abdul Mahdi, Mahmood Othman, Adnan Pachachi, Mowaffak al-Rubaie, Barham Salih and Fareed Yasseen.

I spent many weeks accompanying units of the marines and army, and I am grateful to the enlisted men and officers who told me their stories, shared their knowledge and kept me alive. Not least among these was Captain Read Omohundro, the commander of Bravo Company of the 1/8 battalion, which led the way in the Falluja assault. A cooler man under fire, and a cooler guy in real life, I have never known.

I relied on the SITE Intel Group for their incomparable efforts to comb the Internet for jihadi documents and translate them into English. Thanks, in particular, to Rita Katz and Adam Raisman.

Many thanks to AC/DC for allowing me to reprint lyrics from their song, "Hells Bells."

Dan Kaufman, Charles Wilson and especially Jillian Dunham helped make this book more accurate; and their keen eyes and good judgment saved me from many errors. Alain Delaqueriere of *The New York Times* library lent me his eagle-like skills of research.

Bob Giles, the curator of the Nieman Foundation at Harvard University, gave me a place to retreat after the furies of Baghdad. Sarah Sewall, the director of Harvard's Carr Center for Human Rights, provided me with an office and support to finish this book. In Cambridge, Wallada al-Sarraf and Kanan Makiya had me to their home again and again, making me feel, with their warmth and hospitality, that I'd never left Iraq.

My good friends shared my obsession, read my book and helped it on its way. Thanks to Bo Boulenger, Susan Chira (again!), Roger Cohen, Jeffrey Goldberg, Eliza Griswold, Sarah Lyall, Ana Menendez, George Packer, David Remnick, Robert Sanchez (again!), Alan Scharf and Michael Shapiro. Thanks, too, to my mother, father and step-mother.

Fotini Christia read every word I wrote with care, and brought me back to life after I left Baghdad. Without her love and heart, and her laser-like intelligence, I could neither have written the book nor become human again.

I fared better than many of the people I wrote about in this book; yet even so, over the course of the events depicted here, I lost the person I cared for most. The war didn't get her; it got me.

NOTES

A Note on Sources

EXCEPT WHERE OTHERWISE NOTED, this book comes entirely from my own experiences and my own reporting.

In the nine years I spent in the Middle East and South Asia, I spoke to hundreds of people about their lives and work. I also spent many weeks accompanying American soldiers, sailors and marines. The interviews with these people, along with the events that I witnessed, form the basis of this book. I filled 561 notebooks. I have gone back to some of the principal characters to gain additional detail or to fortify or correct my recollections. In some cases the additional interviews were conducted by members of *The New York Times'* Iraqi staff. Given the security situation there, it was not always possible to locate people again. Some of them are dead.

I first went to Afghanistan as a correspondent for the *Los Angeles Times* in April 1998, and I continued reporting from that country until the summer of 2000, when I was arrested and expelled by the Taliban.

On September 11, 2001, I went to Ground Zero as a reporter for *The New York Times*. I returned to Afghanistan shortly after the attacks and reported from there through much of 2002.

In March 2003, I went into Iraq at the start of the American invasion and continued working there, as a correspondent in *The New York Times'* Baghdad bureau, until August 2006. I returned to Iraq for a reporting assignment in 2007.

Much of the material in this book appeared in different form in both newspapers.

I benefited greatly from the reporting—and from the memories—of my colleagues at *The New York Times*. Also, in trying to reconstruct the past, I drew upon the visual record of the photographers with whom I worked. I depended on the *Times'* local staffs in Baghdad, Kabul and Islamabad for their reporting and translation.

As the notes below indicate, I also relied on the SITE Intelligence Group, of Bethesda, Maryland, for translations of jihadi documents posted on the Internet.

Chapter 1: Only This

13 Come sit with us: I witnessed the execution and amputation, and met with several Taliban officials, with a group of Western journalists in September 1998.

15 "O ye who believe": The announcer at the execution ceremony appeared to be reading a passage from the Koran: "O ye who believe!

Retaliation is prescribed for you in the matter of the murdered; the freeman for the freeman, and the slave for the slave, and the female for the
female. And for him who is forgiven somewhat by his (injured) brother,
prosecution according to usage and payment unto him in kindness. This
is an alleviation and a mercy from your Lord. He who transgresseth
after this will have a painful doom. And there is life for you in retaliation, O men of understanding, that ye may ward off (evil)." Sura, "The
Cow," lines 178–179 (Mohammad) Marmaduke Pickthall, *The Meaning
of the Glorious Koran* (New York: Knopf, 1930), p. 46. In the ceremony,
my translator used the word "revenge," not "retaliation."

17 If I raised a hand: I am indebted to Ana Menendez for her recollections
of some of the events depicted in this chapter. We went to Afghanistan
in 1998 together and witnessed most of the same events and talked to
most of the same people. Inevitably, some of the quotations that appear
are identical to those which appeared in the stories she wrote at the
time. She wrote about them in "Afghanistan: Peace at the Cost of Freedom?" *Organica* (Summer 2000): 7, and other publications.

18 I've got the boys' picture on a bookcase: I interviewed Abdul Wahdood
with Christopher Kremer, a reporter for the *Sydney Morning Herald*. His
account of the trip is contained in his book, *The Carpet Wars: A Journey
Across the Islamic Heartland* (New York: HarperCollins, 2002).

30 "Omar just got hold of his eye": In his contemporary history of
Afghanistan, Steve Coll writes, "Taliban legend holds that Omar cut his
own eye out of the socket with a knife. More prosaic versions report his
treatment at a Red Cross hospital in Pakistan where his eye was surgi-
cally removed." *Ghost Wars: The Secret History of the CIA, Afghanistan and
Bin Laden, from the Soviet Invasion to September 10, 2001* (New York:
Penguin, 2004), p. 288.

35 "I was a teacher of Persian": Witnessed by Ana Menendez, who traveled
with me to Afghanistan in September 1998.

35 "there will be no whiskey and no music": Quoted by John. F. Burns,
"Afghan Fights Islamic Tide: As a Savior or a Conqueror," *The New York
Times*, Oct. 14, 1996.

Chapter 3: Jang

56 He said he was taking him to the hospital: Abdul Hadid interviewed by
my colleagues James Hill and Chris Chivers in Kunduz, and appeared in
a story written by Filkins and Chivers for *The New York Times*, "A
Deathly Peace Settles on Kunduz's Streets," Nov. 27, 2001.

60 Dostum was chatting: This scene with Dostum at Qala Jangi prison was
witnessed by my colleague James Hill, Nov. 29, 2001.

63 More than anything, Nasir said: After the interview, I passed Nasir's
name and that of several other prisoners to the International Committee for the Red Cross in Mazar-i-Sharif. A staff member there told me
some months later that the ICRC never found Nasir or the others. In all
likelihood, they were killed.

65 Then it reached the Americans: My colleague John F. Burns returned to
Khan-i-Merajuddin seven months after I was there. He confirmed my

initial report and filed a more detailed account of bin Laden's presence in the village in November–December 2001. See "10-Month Afghan Mystery: Is Bin Laden Dead or Alive?" *The New York Times*, Sept. 30, 2002.

Chapter 4: Land of Hope and Sorrow

76 "He dressed me in the morning": Abdul Razzaq al-Saiedi spoke to my colleague Roger Cohen and me about his family in February 2005. I talked to him many times after that. Cohen wrote about Saiedi in "Despite the Folly of It, Iraq Was the Right War," *The International Herald Tribune*, Feb. 23, 2005.

Chapter 5: I Love You

92 The hole was there still: For his actions that day, Corpsman Smith later received the Bronze Star, at http://www.news.navy.mil/search/display .asp?story_id=13430.

94 I lay in the road: I didn't see the dead dog until I woke up the next morning.

Chapter 6: Gone Forever

106 Saddam had climbed onto: A video purportedly showing Saddam Hussein in the area on April 9, 2003—the day his regime fell—surfaced on Abu Dhabi Television. The video shows Saddam surrounded by adoring crowds, at http://youtube.com/watch?v=TUX6U547yog.

The Kiss

111 I felt I was living the scene: For three and a half years I continued to run in Baghdad, only slightly modifying my routes, often at night. I never encountered the slightest hostility from Iraqis.

Chapter 7: A Hand in the Air

119 As was often the case in Falluja: Throughout the book, I use the term "insurgent" to encompass the array of armed groups operating in Iraq. Their goals varied and so did their means: some were fighting to expel the Americans while others also attacked Iraqi officials and police, while still others, like the terrorists of Al-Qaeda, specialized in murdering civilians. "Insurgent" is a necessary but imprecise term.

120 Bassem had an assistant: Ahmad is not his real name. I've changed it here to protect him.

Chapter 8: A Disease

138 "I don't like seeing this at all": George Packer of *The New Yorker* witnessed this scene with me, and the two of us interviewed the Iraqi doctors together. He wrote about it in his book, *The Assassins' Gate*, pp. 198–200, and in *The New Yorker*, "War After the War," Nov. 24, 2003.

144 "Six months of work": From Christine Hauser, "Iraqi Uprising Spreads; Rumsfeld Sees It as 'Test of Will,'" *The New York Times*, April 8, 2004.

Chapter 10: Kill Yourself

168 In the first five years: Mohammed Hafez of the University of Missouri at Kansas City and the author of *Suicide Bombers in Iraq* (Washington, D.C.: United States Institute of Peace, 2007), counted 928 suicide bombings between 2003 and April 2008. These numbers do not include car bombings in which there was no suicide; there were hundreds of those. The tally also does not include stationary bombs—improvised explosive devices (IEDs)—of which there were thousands.

169 "Never say that you do not do suicide work": "This Is the Road to Iraq; For Those Who Want to Get Through to the Land of the Mujahedeen in the Land of Two Rivers," posted and translated by SITE in June 2005.

171 It was a slick production: For the most part, Al-Qaeda in Iraq, or, as it was also called, Al-Qaeda in Mesopotamia, appeared to act independently of the main Al-Qaeda group, whose leaders were believed to be hiding along the border of Pakistan and Afghanistan. In that way, Al-Qaeda in Iraq resembled a franchise.

171 First came portraits: "Baghdad Badr Attack," a Video from Al-Qaeda in Iraq of the Suicide Bombings at the Palestine and Sheraton Hotels in Baghdad. SITE Institute, Bethesda, Md., Nov. 28, 2005.

173 It exploded: The anecdote about the donkey bomber came from my colleague Sabrina Tavernise, who was embedded with American forces in Ramadi in 2005.

174 Sometimes, all of them before breakfast: In 2005 alone, there were 908 suicide and car bomb attacks. In that same period, there were 14,375 IEDs, though many of those were unexploded. Source: Multi-national Corps-Iraq, Baghdad.

174 After a while, everything started to sound like a bomb: Wendell Steavenson, another reporter in Iraq, felt much the same thing. "Iraq, 2004," *The New Yorker*, June 12, 2006.

174 They always said that when the bomb went off: "Top Ten Attacks Against U.S. Forces in Iraq," a video by the Islamic Media Front, Aug. 11, 2005. Translated by SITE, Washington, D.C.

Communiqués (1)

234 The mujahideen stayed in the area: "Ansar al-Sunnah Announces the Capture of an American Marine and the Murder of Eight Others in

Haditha," Internet posting by Ansar al-Sunnah, Aug. 3, 2005. Translation provided by SITE Institute, Washington, D.C.

235 Insurgent groups claiming responsibility: I compiled this list over a five-month period in the summer and fall of 2005. I drew on several of the websites that served as clearing houses for jihadi groups operating in Iraq. The major ones were Ansar al-Jihad, http://ansar-aljehad.blogspot.com; Al-Jaish al-Islami (The Islamic Army), http://www.iaisite.org; Al-Hesba, http://www.alhesbah.org/v/forumdisplay.php?f=30; Baath Party, http://b3th.jeeran.com; Akhbal al-Mujahideen (Mujahideen News), http://www.albayanat.blogspot.com. I also drew on SITE.

In many cases, the postings claiming responsibility for an attack disappeared from a website after a few hours or a few days. In some cases, the websites could no longer be accessed. Thus some of the translations that were seen at the time on the common jihadi sites are listed here by their SITE reference.

Many of the groups listed here appear to be affiliated with larger groups like Al-Qaeda and Ansar al-Sunnah. Al-Bara'a bin Malik Suicide Brigade, for instance, claims to be affiliated with Al-Qaeda. The Thi al-Nooraine Brigade claims to be affiliated with Ansar al-Sunnah.

238 The growing number of mujahideen: Leaflet found by my colleague Sabrina Tavernise in Ramadi in 2005.

Chapter 13: Just Talking

243 Her neighbors shuffled past her: The first three scenes in this chapter are from January 2005; the fourth one is from December the same year.

Chapter 14: The Mahdi

245 May God make his son triumphant: The "his" in the first three chants refers to the Mahdi—Shia Islam's messiah—and the last three lines establish a momentous link between him and Muqtada al-Sadr.

Communiqués (2)

269 There is no doubt . . . between us and the infidels: The full text of Zarqawi's letter is available at http://www.state.gov/p/nea/rls/31694.htm.

270 We the group of Al-Sahaba Soldiers: "Jama'at Jund al-Sahaba Claims Responsibility for Bombing of a Shia Temple in Sal-Sayedia," posted on the Internet, May 20, 2005. Translation provided by SITE.

270 A Tahwid lion: "A Statement from the Mujahideen Shura Council Claims the Destruction by a Suicide Operation on the Interior Police in Al-Nasariya," Jan. 31, 2006. Translation provided by SITE.

270 The lions of the Al-Bara'a bin Malik Suicidal Brigade: "The Mujahideen Council Announces a New Attack on a National Guard Center in Al-Moshahada," Jan. 18, 2006. Translation provided by SITE.

Chapter 16: The Revolution Devours Its Own

272 he agreed to make the drive: My colleague Sabrina Tavernise and I met
     twice with this group of insurgents. It was impossible to independently
     verify their tale, but the plausibility of their stories and the wealth of
     detail they provided convinced us both that they were authentic. At the
     time we did the interviews—early 2006—reports of fighting between
     the more nationalist-minded insurgents and the more Islamist-minded
     groups like Al-Qaeda were scattered. But in the following months, the
     split widened and was exploited by the Americans. "Al-Sahwa," or "The
     Awakening," became the name of the uprising of Iraq's Sunni Arab pop-
     ulation against Al-Qaeda and other jihadi groups. In retrospect, Tav-
     ernise and I were obviously seeing the beginnings of it.

Chapter 17: The Labyrinth

281 "Sir, Jill is being held": Ahmad is not his real name; I have changed it
     here to protect him.
288 Then the Americans took Abu Marwa away: I was able to confirm that
     Abu Marwa was taken to the Iraqi prison at Abu Ghraib.
291 He thanked us and called us: Ahmad's claim that he paid $35,000, and
     that he was therefore owed more than we gave him was not resolved.
291 One day, though, Ahmad called: Akbar is not his real name; I've
     changed it to protect him.
291 My dealings with Ahmad: Jill Carroll was freed by her kidnappers on
     March 30, 2006, nearly three months after her abduction.

Chapter 20: The Turning

323 "Everyone is trying to kill me!": Fakhri al-Qaisi not only survived, he
     returned to Baghdad. I called him in the summer of 2006, when I heard
     he was back in town, and we had a long negotiation about where it
     would be safe to meet. I invited him to come over to the *Times* com-
     pound, and he declined, saying that, as a Sunni, it was too dangerous for
     him to travel to the eastern bank of the Tigris River, which ran through
     the middle of Baghdad. Qaisi's statement was a measure of how far
     along the civil war was. We ended up meeting in the Mansour Hotel, on
     the western side of the Tigris. Qaisi still had two bullets in him then;
     otherwise he seemed fine. He finally left Baghdad altogether and moved
     to Tikrit.
325 "You would be amazed": After Taha delivered the $5,000, the woman
     did not call him back. Taha said later that he assumed that the son was
     returned safely to his mother.
326 She took my notebook: Yusra first showed my colleague Kirk Semple
     the diagram of her past and present lives, and Semple wrote about it for
     The New York Times, disguising Yusra's identity because of the danger.
     "Correspondence: City of Dread; Where the Collateral Damage Is in
     the Mind," *The New York Times*, July 30, 2006.

Chapter 21: The Departed

330 I had a feeling there was something: More than a year later, when I tried to track down the Shamoons in Syria, a family member told one of the *Times'* Iraqi employees that they had fled Iraq after one of their children was kidnapped and murdered.

INDEX

Wasit Province, Iraq, 141–4
Waziriya (Baghdad neighborhood), 332–4
weapons of mass destruction (WMDs), 254, 261
Wells, Lonny, 8, 199, 206
Widener Library (Harvard University), 335–7
Wilde, Wade, 87–8
Williams, Sam, 209, 211
Wilson, Jerry, 129, 130
women, Afghan, 17, 19, 22, 26, 28–9, 31, 34–5, 36, 43, 59
women, Iraqi, 210, 242, 243–4, 279, 316, 320, 321–2, 325–7, 337
  insurgents use of as shields, 90–1, 187–8

kidnapping of, 98
  as offered to jihadis for marriage, 169
  rights of, in new Iraqi state, 259–60
  U.S. detainment of, 158–9

Yarmouk (Baghdad neighborhood), 173, 243, 318
Yusufiya, Iraq, 275, 287
Yusufzai, Farid, 42, 338

Zarqawi, Abu Musab al-, 175, 269, 309, 351n
Zaydon, Iraq, 127–8
Zilmer, Richard, 308, 309, 310

ILLUSTRATION CREDITS

A NOTE ABOUT THE AUTHOR

Dexter Filkins is a foreign correspondent for *The New York Times*. Since 2001 he has covered the wars in Iraq and Afghanistan, and before that was the New Delhi bureau chief for the *Los Angeles Times*. His reporting from Iraq won a George Polk award and two Overseas Press Club awards. In 2002, he was a finalist for a Pulitzer Prize for his work from Afghanistan, and, with a group of *New York Times* reporters, from Iraq in 2008. He lives in Cambridge, Massachusetts.

A NOTE ON THE TYPE

This book was set in Janson, a typeface long thought to have been made by the Dutchman Anton Janson, who was a practicing typefounder in Leipzig during the years 1668–1687. However, it has been conclusively demonstrated that these types are actually the work of Nicholas Kis (1650–1702), a Hungarian who most probably learned his trade from the master Dutch typefounder Dirk Voskens. The type is an excellent example of the influential and sturdy Dutch types that prevailed in England up to the time William Caslon (1692–1766) developed his own incomparable designs from them.

Composed by North Market Street Graphics,
Lancaster, Pennsylvania
Printed and bound by Berryville Graphics,
Berryville, Virginia
Designed by Virginia Tan